D1168613

Palm Beach State College
Library Learning Resource Center
1977 College Drive
Belle Glade, FL 33430

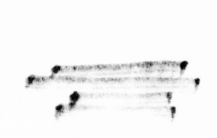

SCREW
— *the* —
VALLEY

SCREW
the
VALLEY

A COAST-TO-COAST TOUR OF AMERICA'S
NEW TECH STARTUP CULTURE:
NEW YORK, BOULDER, AUSTIN, RALEIGH,
DETROIT, LAS VEGAS, KANSAS CITY

TIMOTHY SPRINKLE

BenBella Books, Inc.
Dallas, Texas

Copyright © 2015 by Timothy Sprinkle

All rights reserved. No part of this book may be used or reproduced in any manner whatsoever without written permission except in the case of brief quotations embodied in critical articles or reviews.

BenBella Books, Inc.
10300 N. Central Expressway
Suite #530
Dallas, TX 75231
www.benbellabooks.com

Send feedback to feedback@benbellabooks.com

Printed in the United States of America

10 9 8 7 6 5 4 3 2 1

Library of Congress Cataloging-in-Publication Data
Sprinkle, Timothy.
    Screw the valley : a coast-to-coast tour of America's new tech startup culture : New York, Boulder, Austin, Raleigh, Detroit, La s Vegas, Kansas City / by Timothy Sprinkle.
        pages cm
    Includes bibliographical references and index.
    ISBN 978-1-940363-30-1 (hardback) — ISBN 978-1-940363-54-7 (electronic)
1. High technology industries—United States.   2. New business enterprises—United States.   3. Computer industry—United States.   4. Entrepreneurship—United States.   I. Title.
    HC110.H53.S69 2015
    338'.040973—dc23
                                                                2014028394

Editing by Erin Kelley
Copyediting by Vy Tran
Proofreading by Michael Fedison and
    Rainbow Graphics
Indexing by JigSaw Indexing Services
Cover art and design by Pete Garceau

Jacket design by Sarah Dombrowsky
Text design and composition by
    Publishers' Design and Production
    Services, Inc.
Printed by Lake Book Manufacturing

Distributed by Perseus Distribution
www.perseusdistribution.com

To place orders through Perseus Distribution:
Tel: (800) 343-4499
Fax: (800) 351-5073
E-mail: orderentry@perseusbooks.com

Significant discounts for bulk sales are available. Please contact Glenn Yeffeth at glenn@benbellabooks.com or (214) 750-3628.

To Kristin, for making this happen,
and Harold, for convincing me it was
worth doing in the first place.

Contents

7

Raleigh-Durham   185

8

Boulder   219

Introduction

"Entrepreneurs embody the promise of America. The idea that if you have a good idea and are willing to work hard and see it through, you can succeed in this country. And in fulfilling this promise, entrepreneurs also play a critical role in expanding our economy and creating jobs."

—*President Barack Obama, January 2011*

S HORTLY BEFORE his scheduled State of the Union address in January 2011, President Barack Obama, Treasury Secretary Timothy Geithner, and a group of leaders from the private industry set off on a road trip through the hard-hit upper Midwest—the so-called "Rust Belt." The trip was part of the kickoff for the administration's new small business development program, Startup America. The idea was to focus attention on high-growth, high-potential startup companies in areas like information technology, clean energy, and software by publicizing a series of new Small Business Administration–backed loans that were being offered to startup founders to help get their companies off the ground.

It was an auspicious way to kick off this new initiative, but the White House had a lot on the line at the time. With the wounds from the 2008–09 recession still raw, job growth and economic development were critical issues for the administration heading into an election year, and the Obama team was prepared to go all in on the promise of America's entrepreneurs.

"This mission to promote entrepreneurship is a core component of President Obama's national innovation strategy for achieving sustainable growth and quality jobs," the White House wrote on its blog at the time. "Not only do startups bring a wealth of transformative innovations to market, they also play a critical role in job creation across the United States. Those entrepreneurs who are intent on growing their businesses create the lion's share of these new jobs, in every part of the country and in every industry. Moreover, it is entrepreneurs in clean energy, medicine, advanced manufacturing, information technology, and other fields who will build the new industries of the twenty-first century and solve some of our toughest global challenges."

Northeast Ohio was a particularly effective place to kick off this new push. The manufacturing sector has been a key part of the Cleveland-area economy for generations—thanks to local companies like Procter & Gamble, Sherwin-Williams, Hoover, the NCR Corporation, and others—and was particularly hard hit by the downturn, leaving many in the region out of work. What's worse, these former manufacturing workers often found themselves underskilled and unable to compete in the new, technology-based economy. The numbers don't lie. According to the Bureau of Labor Statistics, there were nearly 15 million people working in manufacturing in the United States as of 2003. By 2013, that number had tumbled to less than 12 million.

Clearly, manufacturing centers like those in Ohio needed new jobs in new industries, and they needed them fast. High-growth tech startups were viewed then, as they are now, as a large part of the solution to this shortfall.

"Because the new businesses created by entrepreneurs are responsible for most of the new jobs in our country, helping them succeed is essential to helping our economy grow," Obama said in 2012, when announcing November as National Entrepreneurship Month. "That is why my administration has fought tirelessly to invest in entrepreneurs and small businesses so they can do what they do best—take risks, develop new ideas, grow businesses, and create new jobs."

The effort was far-reaching. Since 2010, the Obama administration has signed into law eighteen tax cuts for small businesses, partnered with the private industry to launch the Startup America Partnership, which made more than $1 billion worth of business services available to the nation's entrepreneurs, worked with federal agencies to streamline the public-private partnership process for new businesses, and launched an online portal called BusinessUSA to better enable all businesses to leverage the federal resources they need.

"As long as America's daring entrepreneurs are taking risks and putting themselves behind new ideas and innovations, the federal government will serve as a partner to support their endeavors and catalyze their success," Obama said. "This month, and during Global Entrepreneurship Week, let us renew the spirit of innovation that has fueled more than two centuries of American progress and promises to drive us in the years to come."

AOL founder Steve Case, a key private industry supporter of the "startups are our future" effort and the first chairman of the Startup America Partnership, agrees, citing the fact that the US economy has been forged in large part by entrepreneurs throughout history, from the nation's earliest days as a global power to the recovery from the Great Depression that took place in the 1940s and 1950s. "Our nation once again looks to these creative risk-takers to unleash the next wave of American innovation," Case said when he was appointed as chairman, "and I am pleased that President Obama has made supporting and celebrating entrepreneurs a major priority of his economic strategy."

It's about innovation, it's about investment, and it's about jobs.

The fact is, the 2008 recession did more to kick-start the entrepreneurial revolution than anything, forcing people to think about work in new ways and open their minds to the opportunity of heading out on their own. And it's not the first time this has happened.

"America's greatest companies, after all, have rarely conformed to the rules of economic or political crises," wrote the Ewing Marion Kauffman Foundation in its 2012 report "The Startup Uprising," on the state of US entrepreneurship. "General Electric was founded by Thomas Edison in 1890, toward the end of an economic boom and shortly before the Panic of 1893 plunged America into a profound four-year depression. Hewlett-Packard was established on the eve of the Second World War. Microsoft sprang to life in 1975, in the midst of a recession and oil crisis, and Google grew up in the wreckage of the post-dot-com era. Apple and Starbucks were once scrappy little companies trying to make payroll, and they have survived booms and busts. Great startups adhere to the schedules and ambitions of their founders rather than the vagaries of government debt, inflation targets, and employment data."

But the 2011 Startup America road show, like the effort behind it, highlighted another employment trend that was just emerging at that point: tech startups as a national option for both entrepreneurs and workers. Although the San Francisco Bay Area remains the most important and most vibrant American technology center, innovation is no longer relegated to Silicon Valley. Cities large and small across the country are starting to get in on the act.

Cleveland, for example, wasn't just the site of America's manufacturing collapse and the staggering job loss that accompanied it; it was also home to a number of small, two- and three-person tech startups when President Obama came to town. This slice of the local economy was just getting started when the president visited, but it has since blossomed. According to a report released in July 2013 by Cleveland State University, small tech businesses like these were contributing some $200 million to the Cleveland economy annually by 2012, with the 127 startups surveyed for the report generating about 1,650 new jobs in Northeast Ohio and 2,100 jobs statewide.

"These are all startups and they are having an impact," Ziona Austrian, a coauthor of the report, told the Cleveland *Plain Dealer*. "We all have to remember, startups take time. Many of them are high-tech companies and they are growing."

The numbers are still small, to be sure, especially when compared to the millions of manufacturing jobs that have been lost. But it's a start.

And that's really what this book is all about. Silicon Valley remains a vital force in the US economy and will likely hold on to its place as the center of the tech world for the foreseeable future. But entrepreneurship, tech entrepreneurship most of all, is blossoming in American cities and towns from coast to coast. In the last several years, technology has emerged as a major player in the New York City economy, helped reshape the long-term outlook for Detroit, changed how the core of Downtown Las Vegas views its prospects, and taken root everywhere from college towns to small cities to the off-the-beaten-path regions that many overlook.

And the entrepreneurs in these new tech hubs are starting to get some well-deserved attention.

"America's always been a nation of doers," President Obama said back in 2011. "We build things, we take risks, and we believe that if you have a good idea and are willing to work hard enough, you can turn that idea into a successful business. Today, entrepreneurs are everywhere. In labs and garages all across America, they're working on new sources of clean energy, cures for life-threatening diseases, and innovations that will transform the ways we see the world.

"At a time when companies can set up shop anywhere there's an Internet connection, we need to make sure that the next generation of mentors and innovators can thrive right here in America.

So let's celebrate these new ideas. Let's help them grow. Let's make sure America continues to be home to the best minds and most innovative businesses on Earth."

They're out there. You just have to go looking for them.

1

Startup America

"Silicon Valley is not a place, but a state of mind."

—*John Doerr, venture capitalist,*
Kleiner Perkins Caulfield & Byers

B LAME THE $4 TOAST.
And the corporate shuttle buses.

And the sky-high office rents.

And the borderline-insane local housing market.

Most importantly, blame the seemingly never-ending hustle to find, train, and retain top development talent, which forces technology company founders to go so far as to take out ads on the sides of city buses and all but throw money at Stanford's engineering department in hopes of landing the top candidates they need. All in a kill-or-be-killed competitive environment that, for many small-time tech startups, can make it nearly impossible to get noticed, let alone funded.

For some tech entrepreneurs, it has all gotten to be a little too much.

This is life in California's Silicon Valley, situated at the south end of the San Francisco Bay. It has long been the center of America's innovation culture, considered the ideal breeding ground for tech startups. And for good reason. The area is overflowing with engineering and software development talent, thanks to nearby Stanford University and the University of California, in Berkeley; it is home to pretty much every major venture capital firm in the country, thanks to the long-established culture of tech funding and investing in the area; and it is an idea-rich environment that brings like-minded people together, creating more opportunities for outside-the-box thinking. In short, it's where smart people go to do big things.

But the Bay Area is not perfect. And locating a new business in Silicon Valley is not always the answer for every tech entrepreneur. It's crowded, it's hypercompetitive, and it's becoming staggeringly expensive. The city's consumer price index—which measures how much everyday purchases cost—is now rising at a rate of 2.5 percent per year on average, and the rent for a one-bedroom apartment in San Francisco was up to an astonishing $2,800 a month as of 2013, according to Priceonomics. The city's median rent, $3,250 per month, and median home price, $900,000, are both the highest in the country, and only 14 percent of homes in the city are considered affordable to the middle class.

"Every day in every way, from rising rents to rising prices at restaurants to its private buses, the tech world is becoming an object of scorn," wrote former mayor Willie Brown in a November 2013 op-ed in the *San Francisco Chronicle*. "It's only a matter of time before the techies' youthful luster fades, and they're seen as just another extension of Wall Street."

This growing scorn is not entirely without cause, since the area has also lately developed something of a reputation for arrogance. "As the tech industry has shaken off the memories of the last dot-com bust, its luminaries have become increasingly confident about their capacity to shape the future. And now they seem to have lost all humility about their place in the world," wrote former *Wall Street Journal* reporter Farhad Manjoo in a November

2013 story about the Bay Area tech scene's growing superiority complex.

The examples are numerous. Stanford professor Balaji Srinivasan, the cofounder of genetic-testing company Counsyl, has suggested that Silicon Valley secede from the United States. PayPal cofounder Peter Thiel has floated plans to build a *Waterworld*-style artificial island off the coast of California where tech-minded residents can live outside the jurisdiction of US laws. And then, of course, there is former AngelHack CEO Greg Gopman, who created a controversy in late 2013 when he posted on Facebook that San Francisco's homeless residents were "trash" who have no place in the nicer parts of town.

"It is becoming excruciatingly, obviously clear to everyone else that where value is created is no longer in New York. It's no longer in Washington; it's no longer in LA. It's in San Francisco and the Bay Area," venture capitalist Chamath Palihapitiya said on the tech industry podcast *This Week In Startups* in October 2013. "We [the tech industry] are becoming the eminent [vehicle] for change and influence, and capital structures that matter. If companies shut down, the stock market would collapse. If the government shuts down, nothing happens and we all move on, because it just doesn't matter. Stasis in the government is actually good for all of us."

Attitudes like these notwithstanding, the real issue for entrepreneurs these days is that Silicon Valley is simply getting very crowded. There are so many startups at work in the Bay Area that it can be hard for a small team to get attention and, by extension, get funded. Even if they do manage to get funding, it's equally challenging to find technical talent to help get that product off the ground. It's a big pond, and it is overflowing with both big and small fish. The odds are stacked against many of the new small-time founders trying to break into business in the Bay Area.

But the fact is, the tech landscape isn't just about California anymore. Entrepreneurs have plenty of other options these days, such as Austin, Texas; Raleigh-Durham; Las Vegas; Kansas City; and even New York. All of these cities, and more, have emerged as tech startup hubs in recent years, offering founders access to tight-knit entrepreneurial communities, solid engineering talent, and even some investment capital to get their ventures off the ground, all without the high pressure and added challenges that can come with a Silicon Valley address.

"There certainly are several jurisdictions that have been working hard to develop venture capital environments lately," Mark Heesen, president of the National Venture Capital Association (NVCA), told me in late 2012. "It's very long-term play, but it has been effective in certain areas."

It's true. In New York City, former mayor Michael Bloomberg put a new focus on entrepreneurship in the city during his term in office (his namesake company even created its own $75 million early-stage venture fund, Bloomberg Beta, in 2013) by rallying investors and supporting local entrepreneurs via a range of city-backed initiatives. Austin has been a destination for tech startups since the early days of Dell, bolstered by the nearby University of Texas. Chicago has shown that one company, in its case Groupon, can have a major impact on shaping the startup ecosystem in an entire metropolitan area.

"Cities are starting to realize that the real engine of job growth is entrepreneurial companies, not big, established companies," Heesen said.

With this trend in mind, AOL founder and Startup America Partnership chairman Steve Case started a $200-million fund dedicated almost exclusively to investing in companies outside of the Bay Area in 2013. The fund, called Revolution Ventures, complements Case's more traditional venture fund, the $450 million Revolution Growth that he started in 2011, by casting a wider net in hopes of snagging promising companies that other venture capitalists aren't seeing.

"This isn't negative on Silicon Valley. We think Silicon Valley is awesome," Case said at the launch. "But there are also a lot of great entrepreneurs in other parts of the country, and there is not as much capital focused on them. Not all great companies are in Silicon Valley, so we'd like to shine a spotlight on some people and ideas and companies in some off-the-beaten-path places."

Of course, there are limitations to this approach. These emerging startup ecosystems are often much smaller than what exists in Silicon Valley, limiting the number of opportunities that they can offer, and can be difficult places to find significant local funding. And that's not to mention the challenges of finding talent outside of the Bay Area or generating publicity for your new app when you don't have a large core of nearby users to test-market your product. The challenges are different, but they're challenges nonetheless.

This is all to say that, in terms of new tech companies, the Bay Area is far from fading away. In fact, it's still growing. According to the MoneyTree™ Report, produced quarterly by PricewaterhouseCoopers and the National Venture Capital Association (NVCA), Silicon Valley accounted for nearly 46 percent of all venture capital deals in the third quarter of 2013, with 305 deals accounting for more than $2.6 billion in funding, which is on pace for a five-year annual high. Since 2012, the region has accounted for 52 percent of all the largest startup exits via initial public offering (IPO) or acquisition, while New York, Massachusetts, Southern California, and Illinois combined accounted for just 28 percent of such exits in the same time period. The region has seen some $31.5 billion in venture capital investments across more than 3,000 deals since 2009.

And that's not all. The city of San Francisco is now growing at a faster rate than New York, up 1.5 percent from 2011–2012, while Gotham's population remained roughly flat during that time. Technology companies, both in San Francisco and in the Valley, are clearly driving this growth. According to the 2013 *Silicon Valley Index* report, about 46 percent of the 92,000 new jobs added in the Bay Area in 2012 were in Silicon Valley, where "innovation and specialized services" was the fastest-growing segment with 8.7 percent job growth for the year. Software employment in the area increased by 9.8 percent in that time.

"It's pretty actively moving, I would say," explains San Francisco–based entrepreneur and startup mentor Tristan Kromer, of the Bay Area startup scene since 2013. "There are a lot of early-stage startups and there's a tremendous amount of incubators. And, as you can imagine, pretty much everybody from every other ecosystem kind of tries to migrate here to get their Series A. So yeah, even if there wasn't anything happening locally there would still be everybody else from the rest of the world—Estonian, Ukrainian, Mexican startups are coming over. It's pretty crazy right now."

It's active, he explains, but the day-to-day of startup life in the Bay Area is still roughly the same as it was before the dot-com bust. There are still plenty of dreamers. There are still those people wandering between meetups, trying to get a developer to build their product for them. There is still a shortage of technical cofounders. There are still plenty of hackathons, people exchanging ideas, and talented employees jumping from one startup to another in hopes of landing on their golden ticket. But, according to Kromer, it's getting more realistic than it was in the nineties.

"There is a lot less focus on promoting the big dream on a piece of paper and getting $20 million for it. It's so saturated with startups now that people sort of expect results from their $50,000 investment, so if you can't show something for that, you don't get much further."

It's a numbers game now, Kromer says. Sure, you'll still find apps that can tell you which pair of jeans make your butt look best or if a couch will fit up the stairs to your apartment, but the fact that there is so much happening in the local startup space these days simply means that there is a little of everything.

"I don't think it's fundamentally different than what I've seen in other cities," Kromer says. "In many ways it seems to be more amplified. I've gone to accelerators in the Ukraine; Helsinki, Finland; Lincoln, Nebraska; New York; Boston; and all of those places are really very, very similar. You have people who are, you know, saying 'maybe in a few years we'll go to Hollywood.' That's very much what Silicon Valley represents for a lot of people. Their long-term goal is to move to Silicon Valley from wherever they are now. And there are very valid reasons to do that, but there are also very valid reasons to stay where they are."

The truth is, there's an ecosystem in place in Silicon Valley that's all but impossible to replicate anywhere else. Stanford University, one of the best engineering schools in the world, provides the local ecosystem with a steady stream of young development talent. The local venture capital community, founded when the primary products coming out of Silicon Valley were actual silicon-based processing chips, is well versed in the technology space and has the deep pockets needed to backstop and nurture high-risk, high-reward Web 2.0 startups like Twitter, Dropbox, and Facebook. And with more than fifty years of exits in its win column to date, the region is also home to many of the tech world's most successful entrepreneurs—founders who have made fortunes in software and services and are available to help the next generation of CEOs find their way in the industry. It's a like-minded community with a nonstop stream of technical events—including meetups focused on everything from Python programming, to data trend analysis, to Android app development, and to literally dozens of other topics, every night of the week—and a culture of innovation that supports and rewards risk-taking. For technology, it is still the center of it all.

"You know, I've been around in Silicon Valley for more than twenty-five years," says Darius Dunlap, longtime Bay Area entrepreneur and member of the board of advisors at the Silicon Valley Innovation Institute, "and I think the biggest thing about the area now is that a lot of people are more convinced than ever that they can do it. You know? There's that attitude of 'I can start a startup.'

"The downside of that, I think, is you have a lot of people with really half-baked ideas who are just sort of going on the romance. They really have no idea what they're in for or how they're going to do it. It's just this sort of 'let's do it, we'll get rich' thing, sort of a forty-niner kind of trend. There were a lot of serious miners that came to California for the Gold Rush, but there were also a lot of people who had fantasies of getting rich quickly as well. And I think there's a bit of that, particularly in Silicon Valley. You see a lot of people coming to Silicon Valley because that's where it is, that's where things are happening, but with very little idea as to what they're going to do when they get here."

But, he admits, that probably isn't going to change anytime soon. According to Dunlap, out-of-town tech companies are increasingly sending their executives to the Bay Area to take advantage of what the Valley has to offer—the events, the conferences, the access, the kind of tech community that they may not have back home. It's Valley mystique by osmosis, and it allows entrepreneurs to stay in touch with the industry at large even if they don't live there. The simple fact that this is happening, Dunlap explains, is proof that the Bay Area remains at the center of gravity for the entire high-tech industry.

"It's kind of like, take the music industry or the acting profession," he says. "It's always been that if you wanted to be an actor you have to go to New York or LA. Yeah, there's a lot of work for actors elsewhere, but that's where the whole thing is."

It's an apt metaphor, because the general vibe these days nationwide is that Silicon Valley is becoming a sort of new Hollywood for tech workers. It's where the money is; it's where "the dream" happens.

"People want to be Mark Zuckerberg like they used to want to be Michael Jordan," Kromer says. "So it's like some people don't even care passionately about the project that they're working on; they just want to be famous. It's like, this is the best way to be famous nowadays, to have a hot startup."

And that attitude—all too common in the Bay Area, Kromer admits—is a problem for some founders.

"I've been doing this for twenty years in both Texas and California," says John Price, CEO of Austin, Texas–based consumer products search engine, Vast.com, and former executive with legendary Austin enterprise software firm Trilogy. "So I've been living the comparison."

Price graduated from the University of Texas at Austin (UT) in 1982 and immediately moved to the Bay Area to start his career in electrical engineering. His first experience with entrepreneurship came at Neuron Data, an artificial intelligence firm that he cofounded with a group of French scientists. He joined Trilogy in 1992 alongside "a bunch of Stanford kids," where he spent more than a decade managing sales and business development. At its peak, Trilogy employed some 1,200 people and generated more than $250 million in annual revenue. Its training program for new employees—Trilogy University—was the subject of a 2001 feature in the *Harvard Business Review,* and its recruitment program, which managed to attract more than 1,000 high-level engineering grads from MIT, Stanford, Caltech, and other top programs to Austin, landed it in a 1998 issue of *Rolling Stone* under the headline "Wooing the Geeks." The company effectively imploded after the dot-com crash and went through multiple rounds of layoffs before emerging as a shell of its former self.

But, in the mid to late nineties, Trilogy was the big time; a multimillion-dollar software success story, even though it was running into problems in the Bay Area.

As Price told *Forbes* in 2012 about those early years, "We already could see the signs of how difficult it was going to be to build a startup in the Silicon Valley where the competition for talent [was so fierce]." So he and the company's founders decided to move the bulk of the Trilogy operation from California to Austin, Texas, to take advantage of the state's business-friendly regulatory environment and its rich talent base, courtesy of UT. It was a radical move at the time—tech in Austin was all but unheard of at that point—but in hindsight, the relocation plan looks amazingly prescient.

Now, the Texas capital has a reputation as a tech-friendly small city, complete with plentiful office space, diverse housing options, and plenty of after-work entertainment. (Austin's official motto is the "Live Music Capital of the World," and more than 100 local venues host live acts every night of the week.) The cost of living is reasonable, the tax structure is extremely pro-business, and the city's well-known "laid-back cool factor," courtesy of events like the annual Austin City Limits music festival and the South by Southwest music/film/interactive conference held every March, make it easy to recruit from out of town. To hear the locals talk about it, everyone wants to move to Austin. It's what the Bay Area's tech scene would look like if it was purely urban, Price says, rather than stuck out in the San Jose suburbs. ("The lights go out at nine o'clock in Silicon Valley," he says with a laugh.)

"So here in Austin we skipped the Silicon Valley stage and now we're just like San Francisco. Austin has tipped as an urban city. Five years ago downtown was where you partied, not where you lived. Now there are condos, lofts, literally people are moving out of the suburbs and moving downtown. It just tipped. And there are all these techies hanging around downtown and running startups."

Price is not alone in this realization.

Jay Gierak and Nathan Labenz learned that there is tech life outside of California in 2012 when they relocated Stik, their social-based recommendation app, from San Francisco to their hometown of Detroit, Michigan.

"It was really an easy decision for us to make," Gierak says from the company's new office near the Detroit Lions' home at Ford Field. "The fact is, it kind of sucks to be in Silicon Valley if you're not well funded. It's difficult to retain talent in that environment, and it can be really difficult to stand out from the crowd. It's the best place in the world to be if you have $50 million in the bank, but for the rest of us it can be really tough."

Detroit, it turned out, was the answer for them. The area is home to a surprising community of engineering and scientific talent, thanks to the thousands of workers who moved to the area over the years to work in the auto industry, and the University of Michigan and Michigan State University are nearby for more software-specific workers. The cost of living is shockingly low, so founders don't need to pay their developers as much as they would in the Bay Area, and given the lack of overall competition in the area, staffing a startup is generally an easy prospect in Michigan. The tech community isn't as deep as other cities, but local entrepreneurs say there is enough talent to go around and poaching generally is not a problem.

Stik operates out of the Madison building, a venture-backed coworking space located a few blocks from the Detroit River in the center of downtown, where the founders and their employees can work surrounded by more than a dozen like-minded tech companies. Urban, loftlike living is available right around the corner.

"We found that we could attract and retain better talent here than we could in Silicon Valley," Gierak says, citing the nearby research universities and the low cost of living in what is, believe it or not, becoming a pretty nice place to live.

It is also an opportunity to be a part of something bigger than just the next hot app or the next Facebook clone.

"Downtown Detroit is developing something special around its burgeoning tech community, and we want to be part of it,"

Labenz said in a statement at the time of the move. "We are excited to collaborate with other Detroit-based companies that are making a positive impact, and we are eager to grow our business with some of the best tech talent in the country."

The fact is, bright ideas are not geographically limited, and innovation is happening every day in cities all over the country and around the world. What's more, it is now cheaper than ever to start a technology company, thanks to plug-and-play platforms like Amazon Web Services that all but eliminate the need for expensive hardware and infrastructure. It's becoming less risky, too, as more and more founders are following the popular lean startup model that encourages quick deployments, bare-bones testing, and "failing quickly" when an idea doesn't find a profitable market.

The primary hurdle at this point is coming up with a good idea and finding a way to monetize it. And Silicon Valley doesn't have a monopoly on that.

"People's perceptions of places like the Valley are colored by the notion that they have some sort of advantage," explains Thom Ruhe, vice president of entrepreneurship at the Ewing Marion Kauffman Foundation in Kansas City, Missouri. The Kauffman Foundation is a nonprofit dedicated to advancing entrepreneurship, among other things, and is a strong supporter of coast-to-coast startup ecosystems. "What they really have going for them [in the Bay Area] is population density, so startup [founders] feel that they have to go there to be successful. It's like an actor going to LA to be successful. But there's no rule that ideas are limited to the coasts. It's not about having the ideas; it's about having the support system around to take the ideation phase to a commercial operation."

That's where startup ecosystems outside of the Bay Area typically fall short. They may have access to great minds and all sorts of new ideas, but without a true support network in place—including engineers to build the product, MBAs to sell it, and venture capitalists to fund it all—it can be difficult for new entrepreneurs to get too far beyond the "thinking about it" phase to create a viable business. These are significant limitations, and the solutions aren't yet obvious.

"In places like here in Kansas City, for example, it's the polite Midwest," Ruhe says. "And part of that culture is holding us back. It's very nuanced, but it's hugely significant. If you're in Menlo Park and you bump into someone at a party, the first thing they'll probably ask is what you do. Out there, if you've worked at four different companies in three years, that doesn't matter, they don't care. Your identity is what you do. I'm a CFO, or I'm an engineer. Come to Kansas City, Omaha, Minneapolis, and take the same scenario, but the question isn't 'what do you do?' It's 'who do you work for?' Your identity here is around who you create value for. It's a slight difference, but the implications for our economy are significant."

It's a mind-set, he explains. In some areas, you have workers saying, "I can function in various companies and organizations." In others, it's more along the lines of, "I'm a cog in a wheel."

"That's not where job growth is happening in this economy; it's not helping us," Ruhe says.

The good news, according to Ruhe, is that these attitudes are now changing as Silicon Valley–type support networks have begun spreading across the country as VCs, angel networks, and other investors expand their search for the next big thing in tech. Smart investors know that good ideas and low valuations are easier to find in out-of-the-way places like Miami, Portland, and Raleigh, among others, so it's a way for them to get in on the ground floor before it enters the mainstream.

"I think that with increased social awareness and by educating people about the importance of entrepreneurship, the climate for startups nationwide is getting better," Ruhe says. "In Kansas City, we have things like *Silicon Prairie News* that's starting to increase awareness, and more and more community building is happening around this. At the risk of sounding cliché, it doesn't take a village but it takes a region to do this. You need a continuum; you need people with ideas and vision; and you then need to have the activists, the change agents, who might not be creating the ideas but have the gumption to act on them and do something about it."

Consider Boulder, Colorado, for example. In the last ten years, the city has emerged as one of the hotter technology cities in the country, becoming home to a blossoming startup community centered on the now-national accelerator program TechStars and venture capital firms including The Foundry Group. As of 2013, about 23 percent of Boulder's workforce was employed in the technology sector, which includes startups, larger companies, government agencies, and the nearby University of Colorado Boulder. Not too shabby for a borderline ski town that until recently was probably better known outside the city limits for the 1970s sitcom *Mork and Mindy*, the murder of Jon Benét Ramsey, and the annual, open-air marijuana festival on the university campus.

What brought tech entrepreneurs to a city like Boulder? Lower costs, for sure, but there are cultural elements at work as well. Boulder has a reputation as one of the "nicer" cities in tech, which isn't something you often hear about Palo Alto or Menlo Park. There's a real community feel in the town, where give-before-you-get is the prevailing attitude, and founders feel safe to step up and help each other out, competition be damned. It's a small community—reputations are important. And what Boulder might lack in resources it makes up for with quality of life, which makes it easier to attract talented, out-of-town workers and keep them there over the long term.

It's not just Boulder. In Austin, you get all the resources of the University of Texas system with heavy helpings of Texas hospitality, acres of inexpensive office space, and a beautiful, easygoing quality of life. Ditto for Raleigh, where the Research Triangle Park serves as the anchor, along with Duke University, the University of North Carolina at Chapel Hill, and North Carolina State University. In Detroit, there isn't a strong local university (unless you count the University of Michigan, thirty minutes up the road in Ann Arbor), but there is a core group of dedicated investors working to create a viable tech ecosystem as part of the city's overall revival. And the examples go on and on.

In short, there are ways to do business in these new hubs that may not be possible in Northern California. Not necessarily better, not necessarily more effective, but different. As a result, there are now ways to stand out from the crowd and make a splash in technology without swimming in the same Bay Area pool as thousands of other entrepreneurs. And, the fact is, in this data-driven age, startups don't really need to be in the Valley anymore. With a high-speed line, talent can be effectively located anywhere.

The investment numbers are starting to catch up to this new reality. According to the National Venture Capital Association (NVCA), New England, primarily Boston, accounted for about $3.2 billion in VC funding in 2012, followed by $2.7 billion in the New York metro area, and $2 billion in greater Los Angeles. A decade ago, all three of these areas accounted for just $5.6 billion in funding combined. Texas is on the rise at $1.9 billion as of 2012, followed by the combined Midwest region encompassing Kansas City, Minneapolis, and Chicago at $1.4 billion, and the Southeast region at $1.1 billion. Denver/Boulder saw $683 million in venture investment in 2011, while the Washington, DC, area generated $979 million.

Some of these regions are also becoming known for specific technologies. Orange County, California, has an emerging reputation for ophthalmology startups, for example, while Minneapolis–St. Paul is known for its medical device companies. Raleigh has a strong base of biotech startups, while New York City has zeroed in on technologies to support financial services companies. As with any economic development effort, developing a specialty is about leveraging established local industries and building on a city's past successes.

This kind of "clustering" is good news for everyone involved, explains NVCA president Mark Heesen. Venture capitalists who are interested in investing in medical device startups, for example, know that eastern Minnesota is a good place to look for opportunities due to the cluster of device startups that are located there. And it has a snowball effect. Money gets invested into the Twin Cities ecosystem, supporting the companies that are there and leading to the development of more similarly minded firms nearby. These startups, in turn, attract even more outside investment, and the cycle continues. For developers, salespeople, and the other employees of these startups, local competition like this is a good thing; there's always another place to send your resume if your current shop goes belly-up, which is a characteristic of a healthy ecosystem.

Still, Heesen says, even the best-known startup hubs face an uphill battle:

> It's difficult to see another version of Silicon Valley springing up in the next thirty to forty years. Israel has tried to replicate it, China has tried to replicate it, even Russia has been trying to replicate it, but it's a very difficult thing to do. The colleges in the Valley were an integral part, but we also saw several incredibly successful companies take off and, most importantly, stay in the area. Everything else grew from there. It was a perfect storm that we probably won't see again in our lifetimes.

But it won't be for a lack of trying. Improving the odds of startup success outside of the Bay Area was the idea behind the Startup America Partnership (SUAP), a national organization dedicated to creating strong startup ecosystems from coast to coast. Launched in 2011 alongside the Obama administration's startup initiative, and now part of an organization called UP Global with

Startup Weekend, the group is backed by the Kauffman Foundation and the Case Foundation, along with a collection of corporate sponsors like American Airlines, American Express, Dell, Intuit, and Microsoft.

"We highlight the importance of startups as innovators and job creators," the organization writes on its Web site. "We give startups access to the relationships, opportunities, and knowledge they need to succeed. We celebrate entrepreneurship as a core American value. We aspire to make creating or joining an American startup the most desirable job in the world."

What started out as an effort to deliver free and low-cost support and services to entrepreneurs (via SUAP's network of corporate partners) has evolved into a regional network of startup ecosystems, connecting founders, investors, workers, and, eventually, potential customers. So far, in addition to gathering more than $1.2 billion worth of service offers that have benefited some 3,000 young companies, the group has worked to develop a collection of mentors in these far-flung cities and towns, tapping local entrepreneurs, investors, and others in hopes of growing and sustaining these ecosystems.

"The job of SUAP . . . is not to offer more of the fine words and sugar highs that abound in the world of entrepreneurship, but to redraw the landscape of America's economy so that more people felt confident enough to start their own businesses," the organization wrote in its 2012 report on the state of US entrepreneurship. "There would be cheerleading, of course. But there also would be hard work in the many areas that affect entrepreneurship. That hard work would include drawing attention to, and encouraging the study of, legal and policy barriers faced by entrepreneurs. Among the issues that have arisen are tax incentives that could help both startups and the broader economy; changes to the immigration laws to enable more talented people to stay and work in the United States; new models of venture financing, such as crowdfunding; helping to lower the burden of student loan

repayments; and providing more free resources to help entrepreneurs spend less to get started."

In the words of SUAP chairman Steve Case: "What you are
doing as entrepreneurs isn't merely about providing that product and supporting your family. The collective effort is what
makes this nation great. What's your part in the tapestry of
entrepreneurship?"

This regionalism isn't one size fits all, though. Tech ecosystems do
share many similar qualities, but the range of needs and unique
challenges between cities can be significant. Florida has a large
community of high-net-worth individuals and plenty of available
capital, but its investors are not familiar with the tech market
and as a result are less likely to put their money to work in local
startups. Iowa has an established community of IT, software, and
biosciences companies, but is having a hard time getting them all
to think outside of their silos and work together as an ecosystem.
Texas is very capital-rich, but, like Florida, that money isn't finding
its way to startup founders, while Connecticut has money but no
functional startup community to invest in. Massachusetts has a
wealth of resources of all types available, but they're all centered
in Boston instead of being spread across the state, while states like
Nebraska, Vermont, and Maryland are having trouble attracting
and retaining talent in the first place.

"The most frequent problem in the regions is that ideas aren't
big enough or innovative enough," says Donna Harris, managing
director of the Startup Regions at SUAP. "Once they grasp that
they don't need our permission to act, the creativity starts to flow.
You don't need man-on-the-moon ideas, just very simple, new
ways of thinking about old problems."

Entrepreneurs themselves are fully aware of the pros and cons
of starting a business in one of these new tech cities. For example,
Rich Winley, the cofounder of independent restaurant discovery
app No Chains, has written widely on the distinctions between the

startup ecosystem in the Bay Area versus the rest of the country. He started his company in his hometown of Greenville, South Carolina, before eventually moving the operation to Houston.

"I've heard the founders of some of the iconic companies in the Valley say things like, if you want to be a politician go to DC, if you want to be in fashion go to NYC, if you want to be an actor you go to Hollywood, and if you want to be in tech you need to be in the Valley," Winley wrote on his blog in late 2013. "Now, this statement has a great deal of validation, of course, and I'm not arguing that your chances of succeeding are probably a bit higher if you live there. My problem with the statement is that it can make an aspiring tech entrepreneur feel like he or she can't make it anywhere but the Valley. So, in my humble opinion, I think statements like that hinder the creativity that we [tech entrepreneurs) are infamously known for in this world. Don't get me wrong, I know we have small bubbles of tech in other areas of the country, but what do you think really drives a successful tech community? I think it's based on who's been there, done that, and exited."

The real issue, he argues, is that Silicon Valley has a long history of innovation and success backing it up, with dozens of successful companies and founders that have exited and reinvested their capital back into the local community. So when a founder sets up shop in that area, they have access to all of that expertise, funding, and mentorship. And when they eventually exit, they'll often give back to the community themselves. In short, the Bay Area has an ecosystem that has been refreshed and reinforced over and over again through the years by early players like Hewlett-Packard and Intel to more recent success stories like Facebook, Google, and Twitter.

"So all of these VCs and angels on Sand Hill Road came from being early in a company or exiting out of a company in the Valley ecosystem," Winley writes. "What makes it work is that they invest back into that community. So with all that being said, it's hard to build a community like the Valley unless you have some major wins."

Having that community matters, especially for startup founders, because by definition they are getting started in a business that doesn't come with a game plan. There's no template for creating a successful startup; it's a different kind of business than most, and part of the startup experience is figuring out a way to find success without a map.

"If you're going to start a real estate brokerage, there's a template," explains Darius Dunlap. "It's very much known, it's very controlled by laws, and there's a way you go about it. And, other than the subtleties of it being a relationship-based thing, other than actually running the business and making it successful, you know what business you're in and you know what the value proposition surrounding it is. You know what you're going to sell. With a startup, by definition, at least some of those things are unknown, and you've got to figure them out as you go, so a community can be really helpful."

The flipside, of course, is that entrepreneurs need to give back to their community once they find success of their own in order to keep the ecosystem going. That's the grease that keeps the system running year after year, everywhere from Silicon Valley to Muncie, Indiana: that culture of reinvestment and giving back to the city and community that helped you get where you are. It enables future founders to get a foothold in the market and, over the years, keeps the ecosystem together, that spirit of "give before you get."

That's the driving force behind Boulder, Colorado–based venture capitalist Brad Feld's 2012 book *Startup Communities: Building an Entrepreneurial Ecosystem in Your City* and his general approach to ecosystem development overall. There are cultural elements at play in every startup city, he argues, many of which are unique to that area, but the importance of community and inclusion are universal.

"Startup communities need both leaders and feeders," Feld wrote. "The problem comes when the feeders try to lead or when there is an absence of leaders. If the startup community has a culture of inclusiveness, it will constantly have entrepreneurs step up into leadership positions. . . . The entrepreneurial leaders also need to be inclusive of any feeders who want to participate."

According to Feld, the startup community needs to be a big tent, open to anyone and everyone who wants to participate. But it also needs to have enough structure and leadership in place to ensure that it survives over many years. Investors need to be at the table alongside serial entrepreneurs, job-seeking developers, business mentors, and wannabe founders. The primary rule? The entrepreneurs themselves need to be the leaders of the ecosystem and the ones to decide where the scene is going.

"Today, we are in the midst of a massive shift from the hierarchical society that has dominated the industrial era to a network society that has been emergent throughout the information era," he wrote. "The Internet is ushering in a postinformation era, one in which the machines have already taken over and are waiting patiently for us to catch up with them. This postinformation era is one in which man and machine are interwoven.

"In this world, the network dominates in both the online and the physical world. Throughout the network are nodes, each of which began as a startup. Nodes are continually emerging, and a rigid, top-down hierarchy no longer dominates. The energy, activity, and innovation in society is diffused across the network and concentrated in unexpected places that often didn't exist before."

"How important is high-tech employment growth for the US labor market? As it turns out, the dynamism of the US high-tech companies matters not just to scientists, software engineers, and stock holders, but to the community at large," wrote economics professor Enrico Moretti, author of *The New Geography of Jobs*, in the Bay Area Council Economic Institute's 2012 tech industry employment report. "While the average worker may never be employed by Google or a high-tech startup, our jobs are increasingly supported by the wealth created by innovators. The reason is that high-tech companies generate a growing number of jobs outside high tech in the communities where they are located. My research shows that attracting a scientist or a software engineer to a city triggers a multiplier effect, increasing employment and salaries for those who provide local services."

This is why I see entrepreneurship as the key to fixing America's stalled economy. It takes creativity to uncover new markets and create demand for new products, but that's what we're going to need to drive economic growth down the road as legacy industries like manufacturing, brick-and-mortar retail, and financial services shrink over the next several decades. This is where growth will be happening in the near-term.

"There's an oversupply of innovation in America and an undersupply of rare, truly gifted entrepreneurs," Moretti writes. "To fix this, we need to make identifying entrepreneurs as intentional as we do finding kids with genius IQs or recruiting the next football, basketball, and baseball stars."

It sounds flippant, but this stuff matters in the big picture of the US economy, as evidenced by the fact that President Obama addressed the growing importance of the startup economy in his 2012 State of the Union address.

"You see, an economy built to last is one where we encourage the talent and ingenuity of every person in this country," Obama said. "That means women should earn equal pay for equal work. It means we should support everyone who's willing to work and every risk-taker and entrepreneur who aspires to become the next Steve Jobs. After all, innovation is what America has always been about. Most new jobs are created in startups and small businesses. So let's pass an agenda that helps them succeed. Tear down regulations that prevent aspiring entrepreneurs from getting the financing to grow. Expand tax relief to small businesses that are raising wages and creating good jobs. Both parties agree on these ideas. So put them in a bill, and get it on my desk this year."

According to the US Bureau of Labor Statistics (BLS), there were about 6 million Americans working in high-tech jobs as of 2012, up 3.3 percent compared to 2011, and that number is expected to grow by 16.2 percent by 2020. For computer and information technology occupations in particular, the market is expected grow by 22 percent by 2020, adding more than 750,000 jobs, while the market for computer systems design and related professionals is expected to increase by 47 percent in that time.

None of this is anything new, of course. According to the Bay Area Council Economic Institute, since 2004, employment growth in the tech sector has outpaced growth in the private sector as a whole by a ratio of 3:1, and this trend is on track to continue until at least the end of the decade. All this while employment for the country overall is expected to grow by just 13.3 percent. What's more, the average tech industry worker earns between 17 and 27 percent more than a comparable worker in another field, meaning tech jobs are more valuable to the economy than those in other industries.

"A strong and vibrant technology industry is critical to supporting an economic recovery, and while the tech industry has weathered the downturn better than most, we can't take its strength for granted," says former TechAmerica Foundation president Jennifer Kerber in response to the BLS job growth numbers. "Global economic and market forces continue to put the technology industry in a position of intense competition—a competition for innovation, where labor and intellectual property provide the foundation for growth. America can only realize the full promise of an innovation economy with smarter public policies focused on developing and attracting the best talent, investing in research and development, and growing and securing our information infrastructure."

Despite the title, this book is not intended to be an indictment of Silicon Valley culture or success. Nor is it intended to question or otherwise shed doubt on the economic forces that have been working quite effectively in the Bay Area for the better part of a half century. The fact is, the Silicon Valley region is home to the most vibrant and effective technology ecosystem in the world, bar none. There's no taking away from that achievement or the innovations that still come out of the Bay Area on a daily basis.

Rather, the idea here is to shine a light on all of the interesting things that are happening everywhere else—away from the spotlight, away from the big money, and away from the unique cultural advantages that have made the Valley what it is. It's one thing to build a multimillion-dollar company in Mountain View, but it's another thing entirely to do that in a place like Downtown Detroit, or Central Texas, or off the Las Vegas Strip. These are cities without the built-in advantages that come with a Bay Area address, and, as a result, exiting in one of these off-the-beaten-path markets is a lot more difficult.

Those that are able to pull it off say it's a get-your-name-in-the-paper, your-photo-on-the-news, cement-your-position-as-a-pillar-of-the-local-startup-ecosystem kind of a big deal, and with good reason. Sure, the exits are usually (but not always) smaller than the eye-popping deals that happen in Silicon Valley, and they happen less often, but the economic impact on these cities is very real. A $100 million startup in Durham, North Carolina, that employs fifty people? That's an important part of the local economy, not to mention a pretty important part of the lives of those fifty employees.

This isn't happening everywhere yet, though that is likely coming sooner rather than later, but a number of US cities have emerged as startup hubs in recent years, each with their own unique challenges and advantages. Over a period of about ten months in 2013, I visited seven of them—Boulder, Colorado; Kansas City, Missouri; Detroit, Michigan; Las Vegas, Nevada; Raleigh, North Carolina; New York, New York; and Austin, Texas—talking with entrepreneurs, meeting with investors, touring incubators and accelerators, and generally getting a hands-on feel for what being a startup founder or employee in each city was really like. This book is the result of what I found to be a universal truth among all of these startup ecosystems: Sometimes it's about money, sometimes it's about community, sometimes it's about individual leaders, but the driving force behind every startup ecosystem comes down to one thing—a city's culture.

2

Detroit

"Detroit still has assets that appeal to investors. The resources in terms of the people, the businesses, the history, and the culture are all here to have a great city in the future."

—*Warren Buffett, November 2013*

MARCH ROLLS IN COLD in southeastern Michigan. And breezy. It isn't necessarily a snowy time of year, though that depends on how tight the Midwestern deep freeze holds on through the winter, but what snow there is tends to linger, piling up in parking lots, along highways, and tucked into out-of-the-way places. The sky is steel gray and overcast.

But when I arrive at the monthly Grow Detroit meetup inside Mango Languages in Farmington Hills, Detroit, in March 2013, the scene is anything but chilly. The open-floor plan of the office is packed with at least 100 of the region's most promising entrepreneurs and technology boosters, mingling over pizza and "fancy" beers in the home of one of metro Detroit's more notable recent tech success stories.

Up the elevator and through the glass entry doors, we may as well be stepping out of the Midwest "spring" and into Startup-land, USA. Overhead, the exposed gray ductwork is interwoven with random ceiling tiles, open space, and orange accents, with a touch-screen panel wall on one side of the room and a slick kitchen and workspace, complete with bar and bistro seating, on the other. About two dozen low-walled workstations, arranged into pod-like units, are scattered around the rest of the space.

Ignore the view out the window and it would be easy to mistake the scene for an office park in San Jose or Sunnyvale. But the fact is, this office is just twenty minutes outside of Downtown Detroit in a modern, two-story office building off of a frontage road that could be located in just about any suburb in America.

But that's where the similarities end.

"Things are really happening in Detroit," says Mango co-founder and COO Mike Goulas, his eyes wide like an evangelist preacher, before regaling me with details about the ins and outs of Michigan's startup culture and how things are improving for entrepreneurs in and around the city (the same city that declared bankruptcy in July 2013). The company itself, which creates and manages a library of Web- and mobile-based language learning software programs, has been around since 2007, and when I visit is in the process of outgrowing its suburban workspace. The solution, according to Goulas, may in fact be a move to Downtown Detroit.

That's right, Detroit. The city that's called America's forgotten city and is generally considered one of the most dangerous cities in the country. "There's just so much going on down there now," Goulas says, "even more now than just a year ago. And downtown is just so much more exciting; the spaces are amazing."

The attraction now, he explains, is the large number of technology startups that are moving into what the locals call Detroit's urban core—the downtown area bordered by I-75 to the north and the Detroit River to the south, near the General Motors headquarters and the Detroit Tigers' Comerica Park. Essentially, this is the area's new "innovation district." Money is flowing, companies are opening, and the market for technology talent in the Motor City has never been hotter.

Again, this is Detroit we're talking about.

"It's an old city," says Jason Teshuba, Mango's cofounder and CEO, "but now Detroit is itself a startup, and I love being part of a startup. You know New York, if you look at it in terms of companies, New York is a stable blue chip. Chicago, same thing. Atlanta is probably a medium-sized company that's kind of had its growth spurt. But I see Detroit, especially the 'new' Detroit if you will, as really this amazing startup story in terms of the city. I think we'd like to be part of that."

For Mango Languages, a move downtown would make perfect sense. The forty-six-employee company—which is self-funded and self-sustaining—has reached the point where it can benefit from proximity to other companies in the software space. Although similar-minded operations are spread out in Farmington Hills— the rest of the Mango building is filled with law offices, bankers, and private medical practices—Downtown Detroit is where the real action is at this point. With a space along Woodward Avenue, for example, Teshuba would have convenient access to neighbors like Quicken Loans, app developer Detroit Labs, and startup training center Grand Circus, with whom they could swap ideas, talk shop, and just generally help contribute to the area's new tech ecosystem, not to mention the boost that this proximity would offer in terms of hiring and recruitment.

"So in this building here, for example, there are a lot of law firms," Teshuba says, "and they just opened up a gynecologist's office on the first floor. So culturally speaking, if we were to go to Detroit, every other company that would be in a building with us would be a tech company. Maybe we'll be in a building with other app developers. We might be in a building with, you know, some other creative technology companies. So for us it would be a better fit. Plus a lot of the talent that we're trying to attract on the design and programming side, they have a natural affinity to that area of Detroit."

In short, it's where they as a company need to be. It's where they want to be. And they aren't alone.

There are literally dozens of new technology startups currently up and running in the city of Detroit and the surrounding suburbs, mostly focused on software and business-to-business services, that are reinventing what the economy of southeastern Michigan can look like. It's a recent trend, one that's really only been happening since about 2010, when billionaire financier Dan Gilbert moved his company, Quicken Loans, into new offices downtown. It is evolving and changing on a weekly basis as new companies get started, new buildings come online, and new neighbors move in.

It's part of a deliberate effort to overhaul the state's "muscle economy" that for generations has been focused on manufacturing and the auto industry. In fact, the Big Three American automakers (GM, Ford, and Chrysler) were such a dominant part of the Michigan economy for so long—from roughly the 1890s to the late 1980s—that little else had sprung up in the area to employ the citizens or support the local economy after the industry collapsed in the 1990s. The choice for much of the city's modern history was either to go and work for the Big Three or move.

Now that's changing, and many in the area feel that software startups can be part of the solution, offering a high-growth, high-potential new alternative that could one day emerge as an anchor for the city's economy.

"It's about speed in which growth can happen," says Jared Stasik, an associate with local venture capital firm Detroit Venture Partners (DVP), the largest software-focused VC firm in Michigan, with $50 million under management as of 2013. "A technology startup is so capital efficient that we can make a $500,000 investment that will last the company a year and create a few jobs. But it has high growth potential. If they find the right product that is the right fit for the market then, boom, whatever it might be could actually become a big employer. When we first invest in these companies, the number of jobs is not huge. But the idea is that they are extremely high-growth, high-potential jobs."

And for the down-and-out Detroit job market, this is nothing but good news.

Tech entrepreneurship might seem like a new thing for Detroit, but, in fact, technology has been part of this city's DNA since the very beginning. First, the region's abundant natural resources made Detroit a leader in the horse-drawn-carriage industry in the mid- to late-nineteenth century. Then, Henry Ford arrived on the scene and those same carriage makers become some of the first to build bodies for automobiles. That, of course, grew into one of the great success stories of American business, but we all know how that story ended.

At its peak, the automotive industry formed the foundation of the Detroit economy, helping make the city the fifth-largest in the US and a key player in the country's postwar economic boom. Fast-forward half a century and things in and around Detroit have changed dramatically. The city's population has shrunk from its 1950 peak of about 1,850,000 to just 701,000 as of 2013, with about 25 percent of residents having moved out of the city in the last decade. Prior to declaring bankruptcy, Detroit was some $18.5 billion in debt, with $3.5 billion of that tied up in pension obligations.

But that's the bad news. Since declaring bankruptcy and working to restructure its debt obligations, the city is now going all in on Internet technology in hopes that it could make up at least some of the economic slack from the long-struggling automakers. Optimism is high.

"The idea is that generally for these online software companies, their audiences can be anywhere in the world," explains Ted

Serbinski, vice president of Detroit Venture Partners (DVP), at his office in the Madison Building. "You go way back to 500 AD, if you wanted to bake bread you had to live next to a river to grind the flour. With the invention of electricity, now I can plug my KitchenAid into the wall, and I can make bread in here with my little toaster oven. The same thing is happening with the Internet. I can plug into Amazon Web Services, and now I can have a startup that serves millions of customers around the world. And now I don't need to be in New York or Silicon Valley anymore. I can actually do it in Detroit."

For fans of the Midwestern way of life, this has been a very significant development. Now they don't have to choose between the work they want to do—software development—and the lifestyle that they want to live. And make no mistake: There are worse places to live than southeastern Michigan, despite all of the negative press that Detroit attracts. The cost of living is low, the lake districts are beautiful ("Traverse City: Pure Michigan"), and the state's midcontinent location makes both the East and West Coasts a reasonably short flight away.

The business side of startup life in Detroit comes with a distinctive Midwestern bent as well. The focus here isn't on the latest and greatest app or attracting the most users or page views. Conversations among Michigan entrepreneurs often turn on topics like "sensible growth" and "capital efficiency." It's a little old-fashioned, it's a little conservative, but it's exactly what many people would expect out of the Rust Belt. And, for some founders, it's a good fit.

"I moved here from California," says Serbinski, "and one thing we're seeing is people that are kind of looking to start a family, so they'd like to buy a house and have a backyard. That's kind of what my wife and I were looking for when we moved here. You have the Great Lakes and you have Traverse City, which is just this undiscovered gem up north. You can have a really nice life here with great schools and great values."

It's also proving to be surprisingly profitable for some entrepreneurs.

Mango Languages is a self-funded startup—"No thanks, we're good," says CEO Jason Teshuba about his interactions with potential investors—but in fact it is just one of several non-VC-funded businesses that I found in Detroit. Billhighway, which offers a cloud accounting solution for "shared bills" like those among roommates or membership organizations, is also funding its own growth, as is app maker Detroit Labs. It's a little surprising at first—after all, venture backing is a fact of life for many technology entrepreneurs on the coasts (and a badge of honor for some)—but this more conservative approach just comes with the territory in Michigan. Rather than rely on money from outside the area, and the limitations that often come with it, many of these startups truly want to go it alone, and they structure their businesses to be revenue-positive and growth-oriented from the start.

As a result, they're also taking their time as they grow.

"You've got to give yourself the time to succeed," says Mango's CMO Ryan Whalen. "You're going to fail, but what you don't want is to build a cost structure that will hit you if you don't grow as fast as you expected. Focus. Find your niche. There's power in focus."

It's about reasonable, organic growth. It's about playing your own game. "Don't worry about where other people are," Whalen says, "just worry about where you are. There are enough pieces of the pie to go around for everybody." And, most importantly of all, staying in the black. Entrepreneurs don't come to Detroit (or stay there) to swing wildly at pie-in-the-sky ideas. The point in this town is to create revenue, create jobs, and help contribute to the rebirth of the city.

It might be quaint, but there's no denying that this attitude is making gains. The Detroit area's startup scene has grown dramatically in recent years, taking the city from a tech backwater to a bona fide player on the national map.

According to Automation Alley, more than 201,000 people were working in technology jobs in Detroit as of 2013. The area was named the fastest-growing region for tech employment in 2011, according to job search site Dice.com, up an amazing 101 percent since 2010. Things have only expanded since then. Rents are up in the downtown core, condos and other residential options have begun to spring up, and street life is returning to central Detroit for the first time in at least a generation.

At the center of this effort is Detroit-born billionaire Dan Gilbert, the founder of Quicken Loans and majority owner of the Cleveland Cavaliers. Since moving his company's headquarters from the suburbs to downtown in 2010, the Michigan native has made it his personal mission to transform the core of Downtown Detroit back into the vibrant, successful, functional place that it once was. The first step was overhauling his company's workspaces, which are scattered across half a dozen downtown properties and feature bright, colorful offices and hip, worker-friendly amenities. Now, he's trying to bring the rest of the city up to these modern standards.

And he's doing it the old-fashioned way: by buying up empty or otherwise available properties throughout downtown, rehabbing them, and then renting them out to new tenants. The idea is to attract the kind of high-growth, high-potential companies to Downtown Detroit that would otherwise be working out of office space in the suburbs by reinventing what life in Downtown Detroit is really like.

Needless to say, this is no small undertaking. If he hopes to be successful, there needs to be capital to fund new businesses, jobs to attract high-tech workers, and workspaces and housing to support them as they grow. So Gilbert and company decided to start the process by creating a tech accelerator program in January 2012. The resulting nonprofit organization, Bizdom, is housed in the Madison, a historic theatre that Gilbert gutted and renovated, creating the downtown area's first startup coworking space and one of Michigan's leading tech incubators.

But Bizdom is not alone. The Madison is also home to DVP, Gilbert's for-profit venture capital firm, and a number of its portfolio companies, including Detroit Labs, design firm Skidmore Studios, and more than a dozen in-progress new startups.

It is, to put it mildly, a very busy, very unique place.

As for the five-story structure itself, it at one time housed offices for the long-ago demolished Madison Theatre, which was razed to make room for a parking lot in 2000. Now that the remaining structure has been overhauled, there's a street-level coffee shop that, unusual for Downtown Detroit, is actually bustling at midday. Access to the upper floors is well secured (a key card is needed to even take the elevator from floor to floor), and, once there, visitors are treated to exposed brickwork, open rafters, and a number of floor-to-ceiling murals. Large windows dominate the space on the south and east sides, offering sweeping views of the Detroit River and the east side of town, including Comerica Park. The loftlike warehouse space—which includes three floors of offices, an auditorium, meeting rooms, and an open-air party deck on the roof—is unlike anything else in Detroit.

And it's packed. The day I visited, workers were crowded into cubes and offices, with many even working at tables in the hall. DVP and its associated companies take up about half of the third floor, with Bizdom and its entrepreneurs crammed together on the other side. Where there aren't startups at work, there are sport-jacketed executives waiting for meetings. In the middle of the space, a stairway leads down to the second floor, with hardwood accent walls giving the stairs an organic, natural feel.

It's a cool space, for sure, but the importance of the Madison goes beyond the smoothie machine and the city views. There is serious work being done here, and it is work that many in the city believe would not be happening locally if the forces behind this space did not exist.

"The whole idea is to help reinvent the urban core," explains Ross Sanders, CEO of Bizdom, in the Madison's glass-enclosed conference room. "You look at other startup ecosystems—we studied Boulder, we studied Boston, we studied Silicon Valley—they all have these accelerators that are doing the real heavy lifting. Detroit didn't have an accelerator, so we've lost a lot of great talent to these other cities."

The short-term goal, he explains, is to help entrepreneurs get their ideas off the ground and start generating revenue, thereby creating jobs and eventually contributing some legitimate economic growth for the city.

At Bizdom, this is being done through a nonprofit model that includes a lot of hands-on business training and mentorship. Many of the entrepreneurs that enter the Bizdom program—six potential companies are accepted into the program per session, Sanders says, with three sessions per year—come with little more than a good idea and a business plan. These aren't experienced entrepreneurs. Bizdom kicks in up to $25,000 in seed funding and, with the support of Gilbert's family of companies, helps the entrepreneurs get their companies set up and running. They come from all over the country—two founders even recently came to town from Silicon Valley, Sanders says proudly—and are required to keep their company headquartered in Detroit once they complete the program.

"Most people know Dan Gilbert because he's the majority owner of the Cavs; he's the founder of Quicken Loans," Sanders says. "But most people don't know he also has this network of sixty businesses that he's associated with. So we heavily leverage this network. So not only do we have full-time trainers out here to work with the businesses, but we pull in experts from this family of companies. For example, the woman who does SEO over at Quicken Loans does a whole thing on SEO [for our companies]. Josh Linkner over at DVP does a whole thing on how to pitch to investors. Rock Ventures, which is Dan's private equity firm, does a whole thing on business valuation."

In exchange for all this support and training, Bizdom takes an 8 percent stake in each business. All proceeds from its various startups are then funneled back into the nonprofit fund for use in other business funding efforts, and as of 2013, two Bizdom companies were making payments back into the fund. Sanders expects the program to be self-sustaining in this way within the next several years.

"If you can go and produce a startup and create a couple of jobs, you're a hero in my opinion, because that's pretty hard to do," he says. "And if you can make a great business out of it, that's even better; that's a huge accomplishment. But if you can do that in Detroit? I think the appeal of Detroit for some startups is that in Detroit you get to affect the outcome. We truly believe that the next five to ten years is going to be a period that historians will write about, about how Detroit came out of this whole tailspin with manufacturing. And there will be certain businesses that they write about that are going to be startups."

Go to Silicon Valley and start a business; that's great and more power to you. But doing the same thing in southeastern Michigan is about more than just your own startup and your own personal goals. "Here you're really affecting a whole city and a region. With Detroit's success goes the region's success," says Sanders.

DVP's Ted Serbinski agrees, singing the Madison's praises and calling the building one of the best locations in Detroit for what he and the others are trying to achieve.

"The startup ecosystem was very fragmented in Michigan," he says. "There was a lot of stuff going on around Ann Arbor, some stuff in Birmingham, which is one of the nicer suburbs. But Detroit was really in disarray. Dan Gilbert's whole premise is what he calls the 'big bang theory.' It's that we need everything at once. We need high-tech jobs, we need residential units, and we need commercial spaces. And the impetus for a lot of that is the fact that startups create the most change. We have to build a brain economy, and we need tech jobs."

It's all about connectivity, between companies, between entrepreneurs, and between investors. The physical space of the Madison and the community it has nurtured has, many in the city believe, raised the probability that this will all pay off in the end.

Most of Downtown Detroit still consists of vintage steel and concrete office towers—including a collection of beautiful gothic skyscrapers—and a handful of parking garages. Street-level activity is all but nonexistent (though I'm told it is quite a bit better now than it was just a few years ago), and unless you're walking to a Red Wings or Tigers game, it's unlikely you'll spend much time on the sidewalks, especially after dark. This is a block-by-block city. Near Comerica Park or the General Motors headquarters at Renaissance Center you might as well be in Chicago or New York, but stray too far off the beaten path and things get rough. Quick. There are few restaurants and bars, or anything else that would draw people downtown in the evenings, and it has been that way for years.

The blocks around the Madison, however, are strikingly different.

Coming up the block to the building, located directly across the street from the half-moon-shaped Grand Circus Park, the "differentness" of the Madison is obvious. There's a small plates-style restaurant a few doors down, complete with New York–style sidewalk seating, and an organic bakery on the corner. It's different, and it's a welcome change compared to the gritty urban canyons that surround it, but it's just the start of what Gilbert has in mind for Detroit.

Gilbert's end goal is to overhaul the entire downtown core, updating existing buildings, improving retail and restaurant spaces, and even adding new residential units between Grand Circus and the Detroit River.

It's a huge project. It's at least seven blocks of Woodward Avenue—nicknamed "Webward Avenue" due to all of the tech startups moving into the area—much of which is currently all but abandoned, and capital investment in the millions to bring these buildings not only up to code but also up to modern-day standards of desirability. Most of these buildings, which Gilbert is admittedly picking up for pennies on the dollar, need wiring and electrical updates, but they also need structural improvements, new ceilings, new paint, and all sorts of other renovations.

But it appears to be working, if slowly, and the neighborhood is already visibly changing.

In order to get a better view of this entire project, I caught up with Eric Randolph, a manager with Gilbert's real estate firm, Bedrock Management, for a tour of the "new" Downtown Detroit. Starting at the Madison, Gilbert's companies have bought more than a dozen existing structures in the immediate area, all the way down Woodward Avenue to the river, with plans to pick up additional properties to the east and west as the project progresses.

It starts at Grand Circus, which is immediately adjacent to the Madison. The thirty-five-floor Broderick Tower is one of Detroit's iconic skyscrapers and, until recently, was one of the better-known emblems of the city's decline. Completed in 1928, the Broderick was at one time the second-tallest building in Michigan and, until renovations began in 2010, had fallen into disrepair and sat empty for years. Now it, and the 1997-era humpback whale mural that's painted on its side, is one of the hottest residential addresses in the city, with some 125 apartments on the upper floors, many of which are occupied by Madison-related tenants. In fact, it's becoming something of a "dorm" for Detroit's young entrepreneurs.

Detroit Labs cofounder Dan Ward, whom I met while touring the Madison, lived downtown for about two years prior to this most recent overhaul and says urban life in the city is definitely doable, despite what many outside the area might think.

"You miss out on some things, service things like groceries and laundry," he says, "but it's getting fixed. You adapt how you live a little bit, but it's a city, so you're going to do that anyway. But it's great. You can go out, walk around. It's a city like any other."

Back on our tour, Randolph and I stop at 1527 Woodward Avenue, the future home of Bizdom. It's a nondescript, six-story steel and blue structure. Certainly nothing that would be out of the ordinary in any American city, though a little dated and maybe a bit rough around the edges. Up on the second floor, however, Bedrock has dramatically overhauled the space, opening up the once-cramped offices, creating a large open workspace, and bringing in new light from the street-facing windows. It's an old office, to be sure, but the promise here is clear. Once complete, it will be every bit as nice as any modern office space and at least twice the size of Bizdom's cramped quarters at the Madison.

"So all of this is brand new," Randolph says, pointing around the room at all of the new installations, "and it just shows you what you can do with these spaces. We kept the ceilings the way they were, the walls the way they were, and we kept the columns here and just fixed them a little bit. But as far as power, networking, nothing was here."

And that's just one example. Two doors down, a three-story 1960s-era office building is getting a similar overhaul, with restaurant space slated for the ground level and a handful of smaller offices upstairs. Next door to that, Randolph points out a turn-of-the-century red stone structure on the corner that could easily have been a bank or private home back a century ago. It is now being restored to its former glory, with loftlike offices slated for construction above a large open retail space on the first floor. Similar projects are under way across the street and up the block, as Randolph points out building after building that Gilbert now owns.

But it's still a work in progress. At the moment, there isn't much street-level retail or a single restaurant to speak of within two blocks on this particular stretch of Woodward, though Randolph is optimistic that this area will be a Midwestern version of New York's West Village in just a few years' time. Part of the delay, he explains, has to do with a new light rail project that will eventually connect Downtown Detroit with some of the popular Midtown neighborhoods a few miles to the north. Once construction begins, Woodward Avenue will be torn up for a few months, which could make it difficult for retailers and restaurants in the area in the short term.

"The last thing we want to do is have these businesses move downtown, and then Woodward gets ripped up and they don't do well," Randolph says. The plan is for these businesses to move in after the light rail is complete.

We walk another block, past several buildings where the "Gilbert effect" has already taken hold. In one, we see a series of chain stores and some real signs of life. Across the street, there's a rough-looking convenience store that clearly is not part of the master plan. On the corner, a shiny new Moosejaw Outfitters store anchors another Gilbert-owned building, with another Madison-like collaborative space set to go in nearby. It will eventually rent out space to small startups that might need just a few workstations instead of a full office, Randolph explains.

"We want to get people out on the streets," he says. "We want to make this a destination. So we're working with some urban planners to make sure we plan this the right way and get the right people in the right spots. We only get one shot, you know."

At the time of my visit, the real meat of the project was happening around Campus Martius Park, where the Quicken Loans offices are located in the modern Compuware building and where several of Gilbert's larger corporate tenants are moving in. The twenty-five-story First National Building, for example, is anchored by Midwest law firm Honigman Miller Schwartz and Cohn LLP, complete with a snazzy New York–based coffee shop called Roasting Plant in the lobby. Across the street, at 611 Woodward, stands the Qube, a modernist structure where approximately 4,000 Quicken Loans employees are now located, as well as JPMorgan Chase Bank's Detroit offices. Originally built in 1959, the building was overhauled by Gilbert and company in 2011.

Oddly enough, the Qube is also home to the Quicken Loans "command center," which provides security services to the whole Campus Martius area. The company operates a series of more than fifty security cameras on all of its buildings, all capable of facial recognition, and it monitors them 24/7 from this glass-enclosed "eye in the sky." This is in addition to the private Quicken security force that patrols Campus Martius on foot and provides shuttle service to employees.

"This area is the safest area in Detroit," Randolph says. "People always say these negative things about Detroit but considering what goes on in New York, Chicago, Miami—all cities—the same things happen, but here it's just further out. This is the safest part of the city, and we're trying to make it even more secure."

As part of this effort, Randolph explains, every time they buy a building they make a point to "light it up"—installing new lighting on the façade, the sidewalks, even the alleys. Everything. He says, "Before we came downtown, it was dark down here, and people were scared. Now people are coming back because they're seeing that things are happening."

It's an impressive project, to be sure, and a valuable service to both Gilbert's employees and the city in general given Detroit's well-documented crime problem. But the very existence of such a high-tech security operation raises questions about the sustainability of the downtown core over the long term. Sure, Quicken Loans can afford this kind of system right now while business is good, but what about its neighbors? What about the startups? And how long will Quicken Loans really be interested in bankrolling the security of Downtown Detroit? What happens if they leave? If the city's public services are so far gone as to require a private police force, which is what this Quicken Loans system really is, what chance do less well-funded companies have here? When we get to the point that private enterprise feels the need to subsidize its own police force to make its workers feel safe—well, clearly this is a dysfunctional city.

It's all still a work in progress, though. At the time of my visit, Woodward Avenue was still essentially a ghost town of half-empty office towers, limited retail space, and minimal foot traffic. But a change is happening, if slowly. The chain stores are moving in, there is construction all around, and the sidewalks are legitimately more crowded than those in many other parts of the city. Boarded-up storefronts are noticeably less common.

And Randolph is excited to get the word out.

"One of our interns who was here this past summer went back to U of M [the University of Michigan] and brought 150 of her sorority sisters to Detroit for a visit," he says. "We broke them up into groups of about twenty to twenty-five girls and, of the group that I had, only one was from Michigan. The rest were from Texas, New Jersey, New York. And they had never been downtown; they had only heard stories of Detroit."

Needless to say, they were surprised by what they saw, he says. This past summer, Quicken Loans brought some 1,200 interns in to work at its downtown offices.

"The feedback we've gotten from the interns has been incredible," says Randolph. "They love the city, and downtown is not what they expected. That's what it's all about."

For their part, the entrepreneurs on the receiving end of all this development are upbeat when asked about Detroit's long-term chances for success.

Michigan native Greg Schwartz returned to the city in 2012 to start his company, UpTo, a service that makes appointment calendars shareable on social networks, as part of the DVP portfolio. He and nine employees currently work out of the Madison building.

"For me, trying to do a startup in New York seems crazy," Schwartz says. "From the office space, to the cost of doing business, and all the different distractions and people trying to do the same thing. Why do it there when I can come back to the Detroit area?"

The key selling point for him was hearing about everything that's happening downtown and how many other startups are based in Detroit now. The ecosystem is starting to become self-supporting, he says.

"Here's an opportunity where we can actually make a name for ourselves. It was both a personal decision but also a cost-effective decision in terms of access to resources and access to talent. I had a hunch [that this would be a great place for startups], but I discovered that it was reality."

Of course, after growing up in the area, Schwartz was hesitant about the downtown location at first.

"I was skeptical," he says. "I met with DVP and still didn't believe it. But after kind of a week of being down here and living, I realized that Detroit isn't what it was twenty years ago. Now restaurants are opening up. Part of it is how much has come up in the past twelve to eighteen months. The thing that really blows me away is not just working down here but living down here. A large chunk of [employees in] this building lives around here and hangs out all the time in Downtown Detroit. And that was never the case growing up.

"It's cool to be in Detroit. It used to be cool in the suburbs, but now there are cool restaurants, cool bars down here. It's the thing to do. A really cool sort of cultural shift has sort of happened."

For app development shop Detroit Labs, its downtown location has turned out to be a significant competitive advantage. Headquartered on the second floor of the Madison (at least it was at the time I visited; the company was set to move into its own space around the corner in summer 2013), the firm is a technology services provider specializing in advanced mobile apps for brand-name clients like Domino's Pizza, Stryker Corporation Medical, Caesars Entertainment, and General Motors. It has also been on a growth kick of late. Only a year into its existence, Detroit Labs has thirty-two employees, is self-supporting, and has developed a reputation as the go-to mobile development shop for much of the Midwest.

Locating in Detroit has played a large role in this success, explains CEO and cofounder Paul Glomski.

"There is some competition in the metro area," he says, "but downtown we're the largest, and that's given us a lot of press and attention that we wouldn't otherwise get in just some random city in Silicon Valley where we'd be one of many. The fact that we are *the* mobile shop that is growing fast and is now very quickly the largest in the city of Detroit has definitely given us an advantage."

Detroit Labs was also one of the first major tenants in the Madison, giving its founders a front-row seat to the growth of the local scene and the redevelopment of the downtown core.

"Where else do you get the kind of support and attention that we get here?" asks Glomski. "And not from just Josh [Linkner, DVP managing partner] and Dan Gilbert. But you can see that there are a lot of other startups here. We've got a community here, a real community, so there are tighter connections and more support than is typical."

And, according to cofounder Dan Ward, there's that whole Midwestern work ethic at play as well.

"This might offend folks on the coasts, but I like to say we're blue-collar technology here," Ward says. "Automotive was here, the whole blue-collar movement was here. This is where the hard-working part of the country was. And I think it translates really well to technology because creating a startup is hard as hell. It's glamorized in movies and people think that's what it's assumed to be. And here it's just a little bit different. Not to knock on the coasts, but here they're willing to put the time in; they're willing to sweat it out. It's definitely blue-collar tech here."

But can this blue-collar vibe extend beyond the walls of the Madison and make waves nationally? It did for Jay Gierak and Nathan Labenz, the cofounders of online business referral platform Stik, who after raising funds and launching their business in Silicon Valley moved it all to Detroit in 2012 in order to work with DVP.

The company has done well since moving home—both Gierak and Labenz, who met in college, grew up in Michigan—adding eleven employees and recently closing a $2.3 million round of fund-raising led by DVP and a group of non-Detroit investors.

The reality, however, is that Detroit is a city torn in two.

It's the urban core versus the suburbs. The unemployed, largely African American downtown neighborhoods versus the upscale, college-educated suburbs. And neither side is happy with the situation.

But, when speaking about the Detroit suburbs, it is important to be clear about what we mean. The city of Detroit is made up of three major zones: the downtown core, the ring of older neighborhoods just beyond that, and then the true suburbs. The suburban areas are the same as they are in any area across the country—malls, chain restaurants, highways. It's the older neighborhoods in that mid-outer ring where most of Detroit's problems lie. That's where you'll find the abandoned buildings, the burned-out homes, the empty streets.

DVP's Ted Serbinski sums it up best when he compares the city and its suburbs to a doughnut.

"The center of the doughnut where we're at is good and becoming very good," he says. "The ring is where there's a lot of abandonment. And then when you get outside of that you get in the 'burbs and it's nice and it's fine. It's the ring and that sprawl that needs to be improved, and once the core is solid that will happen."

As far as tech startups are concerned, there are still some interesting things happening out in the Detroit suburbs, beyond that "ring." Sure, the density outside of town isn't the same as it is at the Madison and the downtown core, but there is enough going on outside to justify a visit anyway.

So, one morning I drove north on Woodward Avenue, through the historic neighborhoods of Highland Park (home to Ford's original Model T factory), the funky and young Ferndale, and then Royal Oak, to the upscale suburb of Birmingham. It's about twenty-five minutes outside of the city limits, with tree-lined residential streets, a low-rise commercial district, and even some light industrial space.

But for Jeff Epstein, who founded Ambassador—a company that helps corporations create, track, and manage their custom referral programs—in 2010, setting up shop in Birmingham just made sense. He had grown up nearby in West Broomfield and wanted to be close enough to the city for meetings, but didn't want to sign on for "the big gamble" before the downtown tech community really got established.

"Birmingham is a cool place and there are a lot of young people here," he says, in Ambassador's small office space off of a residential street. "The whole Woodward Avenue corridor from about 9 Mile to about here is all where the young people who are staying in the area live, so I wanted to be close to that. It's a really great spot. It's easy access to downtown and you can get to pretty much anywhere in southeast Michigan pretty quickly."

What's happening in Downtown Detroit is "awesome," Epstein says, but it's still too early for him to consider moving down there full time.

"In the past year it's gotten more interesting to move down there and a lot of people are doing that," he says, "but a lot of people still don't live down there and it can be sort of challenging, especially when you're working twelve to fourteen hours a day. What they've done downtown is amazing, and it's nothing about what they're doing, but the infrastructure just isn't there. It's tough. In the past six months there's been a lot more to do down there, and Gilbert's been buying buildings, and I think in five years it's going to be great, and you'll be able to walk around at night and not be nervous. It's definitely getting there; it's pretty exciting."

For Epstein, however, picking up and moving his company downtown just doesn't make sense yet. He and his employees all live out in the suburbs anyway and, for a scrappy startup like Ambassador, it's easier for them to be located near everyone's homes. An hour-long commute over the course of a week can be an extra day of work that's not getting done otherwise.

But, as far as local entrepreneurs are concerned, Michigan native Epstein is blazing a path nonetheless.

"My peers, my generation, all went to other cities," he says. "Even if they stayed to go to U of M or MSU [Michigan State University], they went to Chicago or New York or LA after graduation. Nobody, *nobody*, stayed. It was a sort of a lost generation. And those people are starting to come back."

There remain a lot of political hurdles in Detroit, he explains, and figuring out transportation and fire and police for the city are top priorities. But it's happening. If nothing else, there is money flowing into the city now, more employees are coming to work downtown, for Quicken Loans or otherwise, and it's making a noticeable difference.

Is the suburban location holding back his growth? Does he wish he had done things differently? Not necessarily. The Internet works from anywhere, suburbs included.

"I think people are rooting for Detroit," he says. "I think Detroit gets an overly bad rap in the press, and that has people rooting for it. Detroit was really bad when I was growing up; in the eighties to maybe 2000 you'd go there for a show or a sporting event and basically that was it. It wasn't a cool place to go. It's way better now, and people are coming in with a fresh perspective. Yeah, it's a little gritty, but that's sort of cool."

And with jobs come people.

"People will start coming here," Epstein says, "but at the end of the day, the companies need to offer a compelling reason."

Just beyond the Detroit suburbs, about forty-five minutes from downtown, lies the small city of Ann Arbor, home to the University of Michigan and many of the state's traditional innovation industries. In fact, for a college town of just over 100,000 people, Ann Arbor is well connected. There's quite a bit of venture capital in town, mostly focused on biotech and the life sciences, as well as a small but growing community of more traditional tech entrepreneurs.

Erick Bzovi and Lance Carlson cofounded HealPay Technologies in 2010 to develop online applications to support billing and collections services. Based out of a small, walk-up office in the middle of Downtown Ann Arbor, the company now has a roster of clients ranging from collections agencies to attorneys to real estate investors, anyone who can benefit from online billing tools. Bzovi and Carlson still run the operation with a staff of about five total employees.

But it ended up in the shadow of U of M almost by accident.

"Lance has been an Ann Arbor guy his whole life," Bzovi says, "and when we got together he was like, 'Dude, Ann Arbor is so much more techie than Detroit.' And it is. You can go to any of these cafés around here—Starbucks or Sweetwaters—and you hear people talking about JavaScript or Ruby or cloud computing. And you don't often hear that in Detroit. So Ann Arbor has that tech cluster feel. It's kind of cool."

But that doesn't mean it's an easy place to start a company. Having a major research university in town—particularly one as well regarded as Michigan—is theoretically great for recruitment and great for talent, but convincing a twenty-one-year-old computer science major coming out of a school like that that he's better off staying in southeastern Michigan than trying to make his name in San Francisco or New York is almost a losing proposition. Most of these graduates feel like they can do better.

"There are so many smart kids here," Bzovi says, "but we just have a window [to keep them around]. We had an intern who was a data scientist and we would have loved to have kept him, but he left. Ann Arbor has a window and then they leave."

Still, HealPay is making its mark on the fledgling "fintech"—financial tech—space. They're traveling the country to attend banking and collections conferences—"I actually got licensed as a collection agent," Bzovi says. "It's not something I ever wanted to do, but it helped me understand how these companies operate and how they make money"—and have recently expanded into residential billing and big data services. The goal is to help collections agencies and other clients better understand their own customers via the reams of data that HealPay processes for them.

"What we do is a business solution, and it's actually a legit business model that makes money," he says. "It's not about downloads or shares or apps or whatever. Enterprise is not sexy, but in enterprise just being visible is the most important thing. You don't need an elaborate setup."

As in many university towns I visited across the country, the university is "sort of but not really" part of the local startup discussion. Michigan, however, is actually trying, if in no other way than by encouraging current students to consider working for a startup after graduation. The student-backed MPowered tech entrepreneurship organization, for example, hosts a startup career fair that, in 2013, attracted more than 100 small companies from all over the country and hundreds of qualified soon-to-be graduates. And that was in addition to the 1,000-plus business ideas that competed in its recent elevator pitch contest, or in what has become the world's largest student-run hackathon.

I sat down with Scott Christopher, the president of MPowered, at Sweetwaters coffee café in Downtown Ann Arbor to learn more about the university's interest in entrepreneurship and how Michigan students are getting involved.

"Staying in Ann Arbor is becoming a lot more likely than when I first came here," he says, referring to his freshman year in 2010. "I remember when I was a freshman I saw a talk where the speaker said, 'When you graduate, the school should give you a plane ticket to either the East Coast or the West Coast,' because nobody stays in Michigan."

But there's been a real push in the last few years, he says, to try to get U of M students excited about the possibilities of a career in Detroit. The startup career fair is part of that, as is the army of Michigan interns that now work locally each summer.

"People are realizing that you can make a difference in Detroit," he says. "A lot of people come to Michigan, want to get a good education, want to enjoy the big public university scene, but also want to make a difference in the world after they graduate. Detroit is the perfect place for that right now, because there's not a lot going on there yet and there's plenty of opportunity."

Big talk. Big opportunities. And what is Christopher himself planning to do after graduation? He was just a junior when we met, but he had already secured a summer internship at Google, in Mountain View, California. More than 2,300 miles away from Ann Arbor.

The fact is, Detroit is still a huge city. It's more than 140 square miles in total, encompassing dozens of distinct and contained neighborhoods, some of which are doing better than others. In the upscale Grosse Pointe area to the east of town, you can still drop $300,000 or more on a country club home. But on the west side? And to the north? In these areas there are almost more foreclosures on the books than people, and arson has become a nightly problem for the city's fire department as abandoned buildings keep going up in flames. There's just no one around left to care.

Homes across the city—and these are nice, large, historic structures on picturesque streets—are selling, when they sell at all, for five-figure prices and less.

To learn more about the city itself and the macro problems it is still facing, I sat down with Leslie Smith, president and CEO of TechTown, a research and technology business park and accelerator program located near the campus of Wayne State University north of Downtown Detroit. And this is the real Detroit. Her office is located in a converted General Motors research and development facility, the actual building where the original Corvette was designed, and we could see the abandoned shell of GM's first headquarters building across the street through her window as we talked.

We started off discussing the ongoing tech renaissance, but the conversation quickly veered to the city's larger problems.

"The challenge with Detroit is that there are so many pockets of despair," she says. "We have the riverfront, downtown, midtown, here at TechTown, and the north end. Really, the entire downtown area runs from the river to Grand Boulevard and even just getting connectivity between those districts has been a thirty-year challenge. And they're still not really connected."

One of the mysteries of Detroit is what happened with the city's freeways, she says, which cut through the heart of downtown and take away many of the walkable areas.

"We broke up all of our neighborhoods, broke people apart, and created all of this segregation and the racial challenges that go along with that. That still faces us today. What started as a central business district approach has broken up into all of these different neighborhoods, so we still have some infrastructure and walkability challenges."

As a result, her work at TechTown, which was originally designed and funded as a fairly straightforward technology accelerator program, has taken on more and more traditional economic development projects (though the tech incubator still exists and works with a limited number of companies each year). Right now, Smith says, the organization has become the "last stop before dying" for all sorts of people who really have no business calling themselves "entrepreneurs," let alone tech entrepreneurs.

The problems began when "entrepreneurship" became the answer for anyone who had anything to do with the dying automotive industry, she says. You spent twenty-five years fitting frame rivets? Start a company. Your career was in design and fabrication? Start a company. You shipped tires for a decade? Start a company.

"For some people it was, 'I finally get to do this thing that I've always wanted to do,' and that was great," Smith says. "But for many people, we took them on this really weird path to creating a company when all they really wanted was a job, and we weren't helping them find jobs."

So TechTown has begun to go into neighborhoods, doing work that is well outside its technology portfolio, if for no other reason than the fact that there is really no one else willing to do it. It offers retail boot camp programs to help storefront shop owners launch and maintain their businesses. It works with small-time service providers to make sure they have the resources they need to succeed. It goes in, solves problems as needed, and then leaves.

"It's been really humbling work," Smith says. "We just go in and ask them what they need. We have some team members who are really passionate about this mission, so they're embedded in the neighborhoods, have offices there, but most of this is basic stuff. Getting them QuickBooks. Getting them access to suppliers or other resources that they need."

And it's surprisingly capital efficient, especially for an accelerator that usually works with tech companies. In the four months that TechTown spent working in the Brightmoor neighborhood— "which has abject poverty, and disinvestment, and population shrinkage, and crime, and I think is just a really horrifying place,"

Smith says—it added four new jobs, stabilized fifteen local businesses, and added two new businesses to the economy.

"We've kind of become integrated in a neighborhood that kind of felt forgotten and now doesn't anymore," she says.

Inspiring stuff, for sure, but what does any of this work have to do with technology? Very little, admittedly, but the real key here, according to Smith, is shoring up the Detroit economy from the ground up and laying the foundation for future growth. Without those stable local neighborhoods, without a city that really wants to improve, it will be all but impossible to ever get the tech ecosystem in Detroit off the ground.

"The challenge of the Detroit experience is that it's pretty wonderful," she says. "It's very satisfying at the end of every day to say, 'OK, I made a difference.' But there are elements of this work that are simply exhausting. And if we can't figure out stickiness, I think what we'll do is we will attract them, and we will get a lot out of them, but we won't be able to keep them. Technology companies, specifically, still don't have in the state of Michigan a real venture capital industry. We have a lot of state support for startups, but we only have a small group of investors. So you almost ultimately have to leave if you grow a significant business here, because the answers are not here. We're going to grow these fantastic companies, and we're going to lose them."

Part of the problem isn't even unique to Detroit; it's common across the Midwest: You don't move to the area unless you have a good reason to be there. Of the two dozen people I talked to in the area, all but one of them either grew up in the region originally or had married into a Michigan family. Transplants just don't stay here. They rarely come here in the first place. Sure, many transplants have been moving in to be a part of "the great Detroit comeback," but the reality is they generally don't stay for long. It's just too big. Too overwhelming. The problems are too numerous. And if you don't have a built-in reason to stay, it just makes too much sense to hightail it back to wherever you came from and start over there.

At least you tried, right?

Amid all this doom and gloom, does tech in Detroit really stand a chance? It's complicated.

During my visit, I kept a list of "things I'd never seen in the US before," and it ended up running to more than a half dozen legal-sized pages.

Marked city streets that peter out into nothing or turn into dirt? Detroit has those, and they're surprisingly close to downtown.

Blocks worth of broken streetlights? Tired, old police cars with mismatched, mid-nineties graphics? Yep.

Abandoned libraries and torched elementary schools? Saw several of those, too.

Graffiti on occupied homes? Lines on the road that don't match up after intersections? Collapsed buildings immediately adjacent to open businesses? Yes, yes, and yes.

And that was all before the city was forced to declare bankruptcy in July 2013, kicking off the largest metropolitan rescue effort in US history. That's still a work in progress.

Despite the problems, there is a lot of optimism in and around Detroit these days. The city has struggled for more than a decade, but many in the area now see technology as a way to bring at least some of Detroit's lost glory back. No, it likely won't erase the images of the abandoned and crumbling old train station in Corktown anytime soon, and the wasteland between downtown and midtown will probably linger for a while, but at least now the city has a plan. It has hope. It finally has some economic growth on the horizon.

"When you think about other places and what they're going to be like five years from now, it's hard to think about anything that's going to be [more] different than Detroit," says DVP's Stasik. "San

Francisco is going to be San Francisco, except they'll probably put lights on the Bay Bridge. New York is going to be amazing for all the reasons that it is, but it will still be New York. Chicago is going to be Chicago. But I think Detroit is one of the cities where I think the next five years are going to be transformational."

And, at the end of the day, that's the big selling point for entrepreneurs in this town. Sure, you can come to the city, find some funding, and get your own personal dreams and aspirations off the ground. There is a community and a support network in place to make that happen now. But startup life in and around Detroit is about more than just individual goals and individual aspirations. It's about the fortunes of the city and the region, it's about contributing to something bigger than yourself, and it's about getting in on the ground floor of what, many hope, could be one of the largest civic recovery projects in US history.

For entrepreneurs, particularly in the tech space, it's an intriguing opportunity, not only to contribute to this rebirth but also to carve out a new niche in the regional economy, with the backing and support of everyone from the state government on down.

Everyone there wants to see you succeed. Everyone there loves your ideas, simply because it's something new and different, and many are prepared to put up cash to back your startup. The economy needs solutions, and tech startups are very much on the radar for the future of Detroit.

And the message to entrepreneurs is clear.

Come to Michigan, do interesting work that makes sense for your career, and enjoy the quality of life that comes with it. Weekends at the lake house (which you can afford, since the Michigan real estate market is in shambles), private school for the kids (which is pretty much required, given the state of public education in the city), and a beautiful house . . . in the suburbs. It used to be called the American dream and it's still possible—at least for some people, in certain ways—in and around Detroit.

3

New York City

"I believe that more and more Stanford graduates will find themselves moving to Silicon Alley, not only because we're the hottest new tech scene in the country, but also because there's more to do on a Friday night than go to the Pizza Hut in Sunnyvale."

—*Former New York City mayor Michael Bloomberg, Stanford University commencement, January 2013*

MICROSOFT'S NEW YORK CITY office is in Midtown, not far from Radio City Music Hall and the NBC studios at Rockefeller Center. It's a sleek, modern space on one of the building's upper floors, highlighted by walls of windows, long straight hallways, and the well-known red-green-blue-yellow color scheme from Microsoft's logo played out in everything from artwork motifs to carpeting. The lobby downstairs is marble—white walls, gray floor—with vertical lighting and soaring, twenty-foot ceilings.

And for the monthly meeting of Ultra Light Startups, one of the oldest startup-investor pitch meetups in the city, the office space is packed to the gills. There are probably 300-plus entrepreneurs, investors, and other technology pros in the Microsoft auditorium when I arrive, all there to hear from a handful of founders and VCs and to debate the latest-and-greatest in digital currency innovations. The night's discussion is centered on bitcoin and the New York–area startups that are working to make sense of the fast-emerging digital currency.

"So here's what we're going to be seeing," explains Graham Lawlor from the podium. Lawlor is the founder of Ultra Light Startups as well as BrightMap, a service that leverages technology to connect event MCs and potential sponsors. Prior to founding this series of startup pitch events, he spent a decade as an IT project manager in the financial services industry, including positions with UBS and Deutsche Bank. He continues, "You'll hear pitches from nine startup companies, all of which are built with or for bitcoin in some way. Once we hear from them, we'll hold the contest and give out prizes to the winners."

Standard stuff. But the interesting thing about this particular event is that it's bringing together several different parts of the New York City economy. There are tech enthusiasts and startup watchers here, to be sure, but there are also representatives from the financial services industry—attracted by the focus on a digital currency that at the time was poised to shake up the business of money management—media representatives, and a variety of non-tech investors. At first, that might seem pretty unique. But the ability to access multiple industries and bring them all together in one room is a hallmark of the New York business world, and is one oft-cited advantage that the city offers its startup founders. Since the region is home to so many different companies in so many different sectors—just about every firm of note has a New York–area office, even if their headquarters and primary businesses are far away from Manhattan—it's not difficult to reach out across industries when looking for new clients or potential partners. Want to sell your product or service to the fashion industry? Great, everyone you need to talk to essentially works within in a few square miles of Midtown. Want to expand your financial technology business beyond the banks and mutual funds? No problem, there are dozens of other industries to reach out to in the city, all just a subway ride away. It's that whole "crossroads of the world" effect in action, and it can make life a good bit easier for growing startups.

Afterward, Lawlor explains to me that the New York startup ecosystem has been on a strong growth trend since about 2008, as evidenced by the large crowd that came out for the Ultra Light Startups event on bitcoin. (And his events are not alone in this, by the way. The New York Tech Meetup is generally considered to be the largest meetup group in the world with some 33,000 members.)

"I would say there was something of a dead period for startups [in New York] probably about after the tech bubble burst from 2000 to 2001," he says. "And back then, there really wasn't a startup community at all. It was all very, very limited. You know, if you told people back then that you were involved in startups you'd get a lot of blank stares. The attitude was kind of, 'wasn't that over in 2000 when the bubble burst?'"

That's all changed now, Lawlor says, with growth happening in both the number of overall startups in the city (counting all five boroughs) as well as the number of people founding companies and working for them:

> Everything is growing. The number of investors, the number of angels, the numbers of VCs, the number of local VCs as well as the number of outside VCs that are opening offices in the city. There's also more diversity in the set of startups and the projects that they're working on and the sectors that they're working in.

Not surprisingly, given these various trends, he is very optimistic about the city's long-term prospects.

"I think it's entirely possible that [New York City] could even overtake Silicon Valley at some point as a hub for startups," he says, "just because the city is bigger and the economy is bigger. And if tech grows in parallel with the size of the economy, then it will be. I think a lot of it is driven by the size of the city itself and the size of the economy. Tech is a trend that's just going to span everything. I think it's kind of inevitable. Big cities are hubs of economic activity, so just by virtue of the fact that New York's as big as it is, it's almost inevitable [that entrepreneurs will play a major role in the city's economic future]. Every big city is going to be this way."

As far as technology is concerned, New York City is already in the big time.

In fact, the city ranks behind only the Bay Area itself and Boston-Cambridge in terms of metro areas by venture capital investment, according to the National Venture Capital Association, with more than 8 percent of the overall VC market and 10 percent of the deals as of 2013. And the New York City startup ecosystem is massive, easily dwarfing every other metro area that I visited as part of this project in terms of number of startups, amount of venture funding, numbers of mentors, and support organizations.

The fact is, startup life in New York is intense. While it's easy to see the appeal in many other cities (including the Bay Area) where success seems within reach if you have a novel idea and the right kind of business sense to make it happen, entrepreneurs who set up shop in America's largest city are cut from a different cloth, given all of the challenges that come with doing business there. It's expensive, it's competitive, the market is crowded, and no matter what you're doing, there's a good chance the city has seen it all before and is far from impressed with your latest version.

In short, it's New York.

But, across the board, the city's entrepreneurs don't see it that way. When they look at New York City—the massive, overwhelming, challenging, hyperactive city that it is—they don't see the same hurdles and challenges that I do. All they see are the opportunities that being in this city at this time in history affords them.

"I mean, the difference between New York and San Francisco really is that in San Francisco technology is just ingrained in everything you do," explains Alex Taub, the cofounder of Social-Rank, a startup dedicated to helping brands find their most valuable social media followers. "So, you know, unless you're someone like a Drew Houston or Brian Chesky, the founders of Dropbox and Airbnb, you're still small potatoes compared to these big tech titans."

Whereas in New York, he says, the scene is still early enough in its development that a founder can still make their mark and "be somebody" in the tech community pretty much right away. Meaning you don't need to start a $4 billion company to get noticed. Even as of 2013, an entrepreneur can get something started, do a really good job with it, and be considered one of the founding fathers and mothers of the New York tech scene. The city's ecosystem is just at a different point in its development than Silicon Valley is.

"When a company in San Francisco starts and then sells itself for, you know, $100 million, it's great, but they're not the new kings and queens of the Bay Area tech scene," Taub says. "They're just someone who sort of just cashed out. In New York [with an exit like that], you would really be somebody."

This trend has not gone unnoticed in City Hall, where former mayor Michael Bloomberg (who was New York tech's chief cheerleader during his time in office) long promoted the city as a high-tech destination and fertile breeding ground for startups. By the end of his third and final term in office in 2013, the city was home to a growing technology sector that had already seen its first

$1 billion–plus exit when Tumblr sold to Yahoo. In fact, according to a report released in September 2013 by Mayor Bloomberg's personal foundation, there were at that time 262,000 workers in the New York tech/information sector, including those at startups, those at more established tech companies (like Google and Facebook), and those working for "major information companies" like Reuters and the *New York Times*. Economist Dr. Michael Mandel, the author of the report, estimated that those jobs contributed almost $30 billion annually to the New York economy in the form of wages.

"Despite the aftermath of the financial crisis, New York City's share of the nation's private sector employment stands at the highest level since 1992," Mandel wrote in the study. "The reason: In an era of massive convergence, New York City rapidly reinvented itself as a world-class, urban tech/information hub, uniting tech startups with the city's publishing, media, design, and entertainment companies, all of whom are rapidly digitizing themselves. A key catalyst of this reinvention was policies undertaken by the city itself to improve the tech infrastructure, build and promote a tech/information community, and provide training and support for entrepreneurs."

The data is staggering. According to the Bloomberg report, the tech/information sector is now the second most important part of the New York City economy, behind only the financial services industry, and was reportedly responsible for one-third of the private sector job growth in the city since the start of the Great Recession in 2007. And that's in a metro area that saw its number of private sector jobs increase by about 4 percent between 2007 and 2012, compared to a 3 percent drop in those jobs nationally. In fact, since the beginning of the recession, New York tech has added about 26,000 jobs worth some $5.8 billion in wages to the city's economy.

This growth extends beyond Manhattan, as well. Brooklyn's tech/information sector alone has reportedly outpaced almost every other large startup area in the country—including Austin, Seattle, Boston, the Research Triangle, and even Silicon Valley itself. Only San Francisco has been growing faster.

"The mayor, himself being an entrepreneur but also focused on ensuring the economy is diversified, has devoted a ton of focus and effort into growing the tech sector here," explains Eric Gertler, executive vice president and managing director of the New York City Economic Development Corporation's Center for Economic Transformation, the office charged with keeping the city's economy prepared for the next century. "It's been a major focus of ours to ensure that, you know, we're involved in making sure that we've got a very vibrant tech community. And I think we're pretty proud that, if you look at the statistics, you know New York has become now the number two geographical area in the US for most venture capital invested in all these tech startups."

The fact is, he explains, New York is a city that has incredible economic diversity at its disposal. It has a huge talent pool of creative and high-level "knowledge" workers—thanks to its long association with industries like advertising, fashion, media, and finance—and offers an urban lifestyle that appeals to many young workers.

According to a study by Made in New York City, the city's tech-focused economic development office, there were 593 Internet companies operating in the five boroughs as of August 2013, 324 of which were "actively hiring" at that time. And, by its count, employment in the city's total tech sector—which in this study included high tech, biotech, health sciences, and general technology—has been growing at an average rate of more than 7 percent per year.

"So we're seeing really fast and vibrant growth," Gertler says. "And just in terms of highlights, I mean, when Yahoo went to go buy its next company, it [bought] Tumblr here in New York for a billion dollars. So that has been one of a number of acquisitions, but it just gives you a sense of New York's emerging status as a high-tech center."

"So we got our start in 2008, the second half of 2008, a week before the market crash," laughs Owen Davis, managing director of NYC Seed, at the early-stage venture firm's offices in New York's downtown SoHo neighborhood. NYC Seed is a partnership program dedicated to investing in New York–based technology companies, providing "funding, mentoring, and support to create the next generation of companies in New York City." The partnership includes backing from the Industrial + Technology Assistance Corporation; the Partnership for New York City Fund; the New York State Foundation for Science, Technology, and Innovation; and the Polytechnic Institute of New York University.

New York is a great place for this, Davis explains, given the value of the city's deep media experience and the many talented people that are already living there.

It was the availability of all those things, combined with what was at the time a lack of local seed capital, that led to the beginnings of NYC Seed. Today the organization has some thirty companies in its portfolio, and it runs an accelerator program focused on enterprise software companies called SeedStart.

It's all about making "real companies" happen, he explains; that's the whole idea behind the funding that NYC Seed offers, as well as the mentorship and direction it provides its portfolio companies. Not just putting capital behind ideas, but also working with founders to make sure their companies are structured properly, that they're following the right corporate governance practices, that they know what they're doing with recruiting, and that they're getting the right introductions and making the right connections with those first customers. The goal is to make sure they have a solid foundation in place on which to grow.

"Tech is an important industry in New York now," Davis says. "I mean, it's incredible. But this [funding mechanism] needed to be created to sustain it. There were a lot of good companies in New York that needed to be funded that weren't being funded by either anyone or by the right people."

Interestingly, this plays into another unique advantage that New York City provides for its startups. As arguably the global center of the financial world, there is plenty of money and investment capital in town in the form of individual wealth, small funds, large funds, and the banks themselves. With this comes experience and expertise with money management that few other cities can match.

One example of this in action is John Frankel, the founder of New York–based VC firm ff Venture Capital. Before starting the small firm in 1999—it had about $75 million under management as of 2013—Frankel spent twenty-one years in financial services with Goldman Sachs, handling a series of responsibilities for the bank and spending more than a decade directly managing accounts on the firm's trading floors. These days, he oversees ff's portfolio from a modern office space near Bryant Park.

"I think that a lot of people that who end up being VCs ended up there for whatever reason," he says, from ff's "fitness office," which is filled with standing desks, healthy snacks, and fitness balls instead of desk chairs. "You know, when I look at the skill set that I think is really helpful, the one that's not the top of most other people's lists is experience managing other people's money. Right? You hear about operations, you hear about people that come in as analysts with an MBA background, but what about portfolio construction? What about risk management? I never hear those terms really talked about that much among VCs."

That's the trick, he explains, and it's something unique that the New York ecosystem can offer founders. In many cities, venture capitalists come to the industry out of the tech sector or after finding success as entrepreneurs themselves. In New York, there is money management experience to spare, meaning Frankel is far from the only former Wall Street pro to have found a second career in venture capital.

"Because I've worked with people who manage money, I have a real sensitivity to portfolio construction and risk management," he explains. "A lot of people who are VCs either come from either an operational role or an MBA role. So they're either much more theoretically or operationally focused; they're not necessarily focused on 'how do I construct a portfolio?'"

This skill set has proven successful for ff Venture Capital—Frankel tells me that the fund's returns have averaged more than 30 percent since inception—but it also contributes to his outlook on the venture capital industry, both in New York and beyond, as a long-run play. In his view, this is not the place to go looking for quick profits.

"You know, I think there's also a sense here—I think it was Gus Levy who came up with the term 'long-term greedy,' the idea being that if you look after relationships and you shade transactions to the other party, over time you do well," he says. "And that's what we're really looking to do. If we look after our founders and we look after our LPs [limited partners], everything else will solve itself out. We think that this is a long-term game; it's a reputation game. And if we try to squeeze a particular transaction, that's not going to help anyone."

Fellow New York–area VC Charlie O'Donnell with Brooklyn Bridge Ventures agrees.

"The interesting thing was, whereas people were expecting in 2008 with the financial crash that everyone would just stop investing, it actually did just the opposite," he says. "A lot of people were looking for alternatives to the stock market to invest their money. And, you know, after the whole Madoff thing it was like, shit, I'm not going to give my money to some guy at a club who promised these returns anymore. I'm going to hand my money to these two startups founders, where I can see them in their offices. I can see that they have shitty Ikea furniture, so I know they're not overspending, and I can help them. So I'm actively managing my own money.

"They were, like, shoot, if I'm going to lose my money in the public stock market, I might as well lose it on these two guys who might be the next Google. Besides, it's more fun than just handing your money to some money manager, you know?"

O'Donnell himself has particularly deep roots in the New York venture capital industry, having moved in 2004 from the General Motors Pension Fund to Union Square Ventures, one of the city's oldest VC firms. He likes to remind people that he was one of the first 100 people to join the NY Tech Meetup, number 71 in fact. His fund focuses on smaller, seed-stage deals.

It's not complicated. Obviously, the dollar you put in when the company is worth $3 will be much higher returning than the dollar you put in when the company is worth $100, which is why it can be tough for large funds to find good returns when they have so much to invest. That's why O'Donnell likes to stay small. "If the company is already valued at $500 million, how much bigger is it going to get from there? Whereas I have a tiny little fund at $8.5 million and 100 percent of my dollars are going into the seed round. We're going in at valuations where, if this thing wins, it's going to be a twenty-five times returning deal."

It wasn't like this when O'Donnell first got his start in the city. In the late nineties, there was some media technology going on, along with some financial tech, but the infrastructure wasn't in place yet to support much else. There just weren't enough investors, there weren't enough engineers, and there weren't enough spaces for two- and three-person startups to set up shop. When the dot-com bubble burst after 2000, what passed for a startup ecosystem in New York at the time all but disappeared.

That has changed.

"There's a density thing going on here now," O'Donnell says. "There's the fact that we didn't have pedigrees [in tech], so it wasn't like, 'Ooh, you work for Facebook; you're cool and I'm not.' There isn't any of that here. People just said, OK, well we have a lot of the pieces here. We have the industry, and fintech, and e-commerce, so we have enough critical mass of people who know how to code because they've been working at banks and agencies and stuff like that."

Also importantly, he says, New York itself has become a more interesting and safer place to live. The outer neighborhoods, like Brooklyn, have been developed and gentrified in recent years so that folks who can't afford the West Village rents can still find cool places to live and create a reasonable lifestyle for themselves. It's just become a more livable city.

"These days you have people coming in from out of town and saying, 'You know what, I do want to be able to go get Thai food at one in the morning.' That's important to the developer who's doing the overnight shift, and it's not an easy lifestyle amenity to find."

As a result, many involved with the city's startups are optimistic that this time is different. That this time, unlike before the dot-com crash, the technology ecosystem in New York is now resilient enough to weather a downturn. That this time tech isn't going away.

That certainly seems to be the case so far. New York is already home to the largest Startup Weekend event in the country, the largest tech meetup in the country, and just about every major tech company in the country—Google, Microsoft, Yahoo, Facebook, Apple, etc.—now has an East Coast office in New York. Google, in particular, has been very involved with the local startup community, with its $100 million Google Ventures arm stepping in to fund a number of local companies.

I met up with Andrew Young, the organizer of New York City Startup Weekend, at a coworking space in the Financial District called WeWork. Young is the CTO for a startup alcohol delivery service called Swill, which delivers booze to users anywhere in the city by connecting customers and local liquor stores via an app-based ordering system. It's kind of like Seamless for cocktails.

"Startup Weekend here is amazing," Young says, as we lounge on couches in an office overlooking the southern tip of Manhattan. "We can touch on topics and themes that normally other cities wouldn't want to do or don't have the population to generate the interest. This is New York. We want to be able to do a lot more and push more initiatives here, everything from connected devices to the Internet of things. It's a lot more than just finance and mobile. People have done that. People do it all the time."

There's just so much opportunity in New York tech that's waiting to be explored, he says, in everything from fashion, to health, to media, to art. His goal as an event organizer is to get people involved with entrepreneurship that might not have considered it before, since it may not be in line with their traditional East Coast–centric career goals. His hope is that Startup Weekend and other high-profile events will spread the message that tech is in the city to stay and help expand the audience.

"Especially in the last two years there is a lot more opportunity; there's a lot more growth in every sector," he says. "You see a lot more tech companies building apps because the cost of building something and getting it to market is a lot cheaper. But at the same time it opens up different areas as well—in fashion, in health tech, and even for people opening up their own restaurants and bakeries. Now they're building a bigger audience through social media—like the Cronut guy [at Dominique Ansel Bakery in SoHo]. So there are a lot of new and different ways for people to get out there and just start doing business, whether it's directly in tech or just complementing something else that they're doing."

As a result, the audience for startup events in the city has been evolving as well. No longer are they reserved for entrepreneurs and their employees—now New York has a whole population of potential investors, future founders, hackers, tech wannabes, and other startup hangers-on to populate its various meetups. It's not unlike the vibe in other cities—the drive to strike out on your own is universal—but, this being New York, the audience for startup events here is that much bigger and that much more diverse.

"It's a total mix," says Frank Denbow, another organizer with New York City Startup Weekend and the curator of the city's Startup Digest email newsletter. "For Startup Weekend, about half the people are working nine-to-five; definitely a lot of people in finance and other industries that are looking for a bigger category.

"We're all trying to figure it out at the same time," he says.

Still, the nexus of New York tech has been centered on Wall Street for years, where an army of quantitative analysts (a.k.a. "quants") toil away on their computers for banks like JPMorgan, Goldman Sachs, Morgan Stanley, and others. But, instead of developing consumer apps and creating new software programs for start-ups, they are tasked with creating the algorithm-based trading programs that drive much of the market activity in the modern financial markets. The quants began coming to the city in the mid-1990s, drawn from engineering and math programs at Stanford, Caltech, the Massachusetts Institute of Technology, and others by the promise of big paydays and the opportunity to put their computer science skills to work for banks instead of technology companies.

Their reputation since, in the city and beyond, is mixed at best.

Wall Street Journal reporter Scott Patterson described the quantitative analysts' influence on world financial markets in his 2010 book, *The Quants: How a New Breed of Math Whizzes Conquered Wall Street and Nearly Destroyed It.*

"At Morgan Stanley's investing powerhouse Process Driven Trading on Monday, August 6, founder Peter Muller was AWOL, visiting a friend near Boston," Patterson wrote. "Mike Reed and Amy Wong manned the helm, PDT veterans from the days when the group was nothing more than a thought experiment, its traders a small band of young math whizzes tinkering with computers like brainy teenagers in a cluttered garage.

"On Wall Street, they were all known as 'quants,' traders and financial engineers who used brain-twisting math and super-powered computers to pluck billions in fleeting dollars out of the market. Instead of looking at individual companies and their performance, management, and competitors, they use math formulas to make bets on which stocks were going up or down. By the early 2000s, such tech-savvy investors had come to dominate Wall Street, helped by theoretical breakthroughs in the application of mathematics to financial markets, advances that had earned their discoverers several shelves of Nobel Prizes."

Not surprisingly, most of these analysts and the traders they work with remain well outside the realm of New York's startup ecosystem—no founder is going to be able to convince a Wall Street developer, no matter how promising or how interesting their business idea, to give up the multimillion-dollar rewards that come with life on the front lines of the financial services industry and take a chance on an unproven startup. But the rise of the quant class did something else, perhaps even more important, for the New York tech ecosystem: It brought a generation of tech-minded developers and engineers to the area *en masse* for the first time. It also helped seed the city's growing financial technology industry. Those startups focused on serving the banks and other financial industries, as wave after wave of Wall Street layoffs sent thousands of former quants packing following the 2008 downturn. These "fintech" companies have become a particularly large part of the city's technology ecosystem, primarily because of finance's traditional role in the New York economy and the opportunities that exist in the city for entrepreneurs in the sector. Their clients are all nearby.

"It's tremendous," says Greg Neufeld of the fintech segment, which has been a cornerstone of the New York tech scene since the 1990s. "Everybody wants to make that changeover, or at least wants to get their finger into the cookie jar. It's a very interesting dynamic right now."

Neufeld is the managing partner and founder of ValueStream Labs, a fintech-focused accelerator and investment fund in the city's Meatpacking District. The firm's offices were sparse when I visited—just a few open offices carved out of a converted loft space, with exposed brick walls, plank flooring, and windows overlooking the midday activity on Fourteenth Street. The Hudson River is about a block away.

"They all want to get out," Neufeld says of the bankers he talks to regularly who are interested in going to work for the city's startups. Layoffs on Wall Street have only accelerated these calls, he says. "And the guys who are higher up the food chain, they want to invest in these companies and stay in the cushy managing director roles where they are now. We're kind of appealing a little bit to that group by allowing them to invest in the rounds for the companies that we work with here at ValueStream. So basically, we're looking for the guys who can be the triple threat: the customer, the advisor, and the investor. And there are a lot of them floating around."

The fintech sector itself is changing, too, he says. Although entrepreneurs have long targeted Wall Street firms with their innovations—dating all the way back to Bloomberg's original computerized market data terminals in the early 1980s—the natural progression of technology has accelerated in recent years, bringing mobile, tablet, and other options to the wider world and putting pressure on financial firms to catch up and bring their notoriously conservative back office operations into the twenty-first century.

"The consumerization of IT is a big trend now," Neufeld says, "so people are saying, 'OK, I can do this on my smart phone; why can't I do this in my work?' And so you're going to see more of those Web-enabled platforms that are less expensive to build going on top of the already existing infrastructure. For most companies that just means, you know, a Web site. It goes without saying that mobility is a big part of that. And the 'bring your own device' movement gets some of these consumer platforms that are already working in consumer markets and we can actually reposition them for the institutional side. Figure out licensing deals and ways to create a new source of revenue, which tends to be a lot higher than in the consumer space."

Technology on Wall Street is no longer just about the middle and back offices, he explains. Now banks are bringing tech front and center—from consumer apps for mobile account access to new communications systems between brokers and clients. Big data is even coming to the table, giving analysts and traders a whole new set of numbers to play with. "It's 'what can the quant guys do with the data to kind of manipulate it better?'" Neufeld says. "Now we have the tools; they are kind of like the pickaxes in the gold rush."

That's a big part of the idea behind Estimize, a ValueStream Labs–backed company that aggregates buy-side and independent analyst stock estimates, allowing users to crunch this data in order to extract useful justification for their investment decisions. It's a little like "the wisdom of crowds" for stock market investors.

"We ran some interesting strategies that looked at earnings acceleration and analyst estimate revision models," explains CEO Leigh Drogen, who himself came out of a quant trading back-ground more than a decade ago and has multiple hedge funds on his resume. "And out of that came really the understanding for why the sell-side analyst estimate data set was so inefficient and skewed because of the incentive structures on that side. So we built an open platform to crowdsource all this data. We basi-cally built a whole machine learning apparatus to chew through all of the different attributes of an analyst and their estimates and their track record and figure out which of those attributes are correlated to give us confidence that that analyst will be more accurate in the future. So we can weigh his estimates in the con-sensus more heavily and other people's less."

Turns out, the company's data-focused approach is actually more accurate than Wall Street's human professionals, beating the pros about 70 percent of the time when analyst expectations are compared to actual portfolio performance. And, since it's a Web application, it's all free and open to anyone, allowing users to participate and contribute as they like, Wikipedia style. The system's algorithms on the back end take care of the filtering and curating to ensure that only the highest-quality opinions and most-reliable predictions float to the top.

"I basically woke up one day and said, I could be doing this when I'm forty and it would have been great, but I never would have built anything of any value," Drogen says of his hedge fund career. "And I told myself, 'Look, you're young enough to actually go and take a shot at building something.' There was a huge hole in the market for this type of data set. There was a lot of inefficiency in the way it was created and, you know, crowdsourcing structured financial estimates and data was just something that hadn't been done from the buy side, and I felt like social finance was breeding all of this."

This was all before the more recent incarnation of the New York startup ecosystem had really gotten started, so there was nothing at the time really like Estimize in the city. In fact, when Drogen's previous employer, StockTwits—a Twitter-based social finance network—got its start in 2009, there were no meetups, no hackathons, nothing really at all going on in New York. Nobody was getting funded. In fact, StockTwits was funded primarily by West Coast and Boulder VCs, as there was nobody in New York looking at those investments at the time.

And this was in 2009.

By comparison, when Estimize raised its round in 2012, things in the city had changed dramatically.

By the time Drogen raised his round in August 2012, the market had gone "bonkers," with interested investors flooding the tech scene. All of a sudden everybody wanted to be in fintech, everybody wanted to invest in startups, and it's just gone crazy from there.

Of course, the New York City economy is about more than just finance. The city is also the center of the media, fashion, and advertising worlds and home to some 1,700 corporations in a wide range of industries. For example, the online craft sale site Etsy.com is based in Brooklyn and is fast becoming one of the city's major tech success stories, as is 3D printing pioneer Maker-Bot and Rap Genius (now called Genius), a Wikipedia-type site that allows users to notate and explain rap music lyrics. (As oddly specific as that sounds, Rap Genius scored a $15-million invest-ment from Bay Area venture capital firm Andreessen Horowitz in late 2013. In a blog post explaining the somewhat surprising investment, firm partner Marc Andreessen wrote: "It turns out that Rap Genius has a much bigger idea and a much broader mission than [creating a community of rap aficionados], which is to generalize many other categories of text . . . annotate the world . . . be the knowledge about the knowledge . . . create the Internet Talmud.")

To find out more about what "else" is happening in this city of 8.3 million people, I stopped by the offices of Betaworks, a sort of incubator and startup funding operation based out of a stylish, red brick building in the Meatpacking District that it shares with several high-end fashion houses and design agencies. Founded by a group of investors in 2008, Betaworks is perhaps best known as the company behind news aggregating site Digg, as well as the developer of Dots, one of the most popular games in the iTunes App Store ("#1 game in 21 countries, top 5 iPhone apps in 30 countries"). It also owns Instapaper, a service that allows users to clip and save online articles for later reading offline, and a handful of other companies all based around the idea of the social Web.

"So we are a little different, and we don't like to really call ourselves an incubator or an accelerator," explains Nick Chirls, who heads up investments at Betaworks. "So instead of building a simple product or a VC fund, which didn't interest us, as a lot of those structures are very rigid, can you build a structure where you have just building, just investing, just operating? There are usually founders on one side and investors on the other, but what if those investors come from an operating background and don't want to sit at a VC fund and write checks all day? They want to get their hands dirty. So that's the central thesis of Betaworks."

In short, it's a holding company. Chirls and the firm's partners go out and acquire startups in their focus niche—the social Web—set them up with offices, and provide them with everything they need to be successful in the long term. The founders and other employees stay involved with their own projects, but get everything else they need from Betaworks—corporate administration, finance, legal, business development—so that they can focus on building their product and developing their market. The firm also serves as a funding backstop to keep its companies going.

Everybody in the office essentially works for Betaworks, so they are wholly owned internal businesses rather than just investments. In terms of the model, it's closer to IAC (InterActiveCorp) than it is to an accelerator or a VC fund.

Many of the people in the Betaworks "system" are very senior, talented engineers—developers who likely would have no problem finding work at established companies like Google or Facebook or even running successful companies on their own. But the firm basically exists to fit a certain risk profile that, for a lot of people, has largely gone unmet. The only other option is to go work for one of the giants—where the pay is good and the perks are reliable, and where the software stack is amazing, but fundamentally, it's still a corporate environment. For a lot of people, that doesn't work. They want the challenges and stimulation of startup life. But maybe they're in their thirties, maybe they've started a family, maybe they don't want to do the whole startup thing again and eat nothing but Ramen for eight months straight. Betaworks fits somewhere in the middle of both extremes in the sense that it's a startup-like environment, where engineers are able to build new things and work on their passions, without the financial sacrifices that usually go with that.

As an investment model, it's a unique approach, and Chirls admits that it has started to attract copycats—including a holding company based around e-commerce and backed by the former president of MySpace and another focused on hardware startups. The firm itself has also begun investing outside of its network on a limited basis with investments in more than 100 companies, including most of the big names in the Web 2.0 space like Tumblr, Kickstarter, Twitter, and others.

"Rather than do this as a little insulated product studio, how do we extend our tentacles and network into the ecosystem and participate beyond our companies?" he asks.

"I think that for us the main goal is how to best boost cash flow outside of investment returns on a more sustainable, predictable basis. That's what we're trying to do. And to the extent that we can do that, there's no reason that Betaworks won't be around for a very long time and could even be a public company. Some of these companies might be spun out, some of them might not. Like Digg is starting to become a very good cash-producing asset, so there are some like that where increasingly we're very happy to hold onto them and just operate them."

Startup "holding companies" and subsidiary social Web arrangements—these are not descriptions that you hear much around the country yet, but in financially savvy New York, they're becoming borderline common.

Take the Hatchery, for instance. Based out of an office tower near Times Square, the Hatchery describes itself as a "venture collective," a unique type of incubator/community/entrepreneurship organization that sponsors a number of coworking spaces and pitch night events across the city. In theory, its model seems pretty straightforward.

But in reality, the Hatchery operates sort of like an inverted VC firm, CEO Yao-Hui Huang tells me one evening in the group's near-deserted offices, as what appears to be a support group for out-of-work actors meets in the conference room across the hall.

"Traditionally, you build a product, you sell a product, you go get investment funding once you have a little traction, and that may take as long as three years," she says, sketching me a model of the startup investment cycle on the whiteboard. "Instead of going this way [from product to investment], we go this way [investment to product]. So first we get the funding, [and] then we get the customer. The last thing we do is we build the product. So by the time we've finished building the product we already have sales and funding."

This approach allows the firm to boil down the product-to-market process to as little as six months, Huang explains, and takes a lot of the uncertainty out of deals from an investment perspective. The Hatchery isn't working on random ideas that it hopes will find a market. Its companies only build products that are directly aligned with specific markets and often at the request of the firm's industry partners themselves. When I visited, the focus markets were cybersecurity, fintech, big data, and health care—"Big-boy businesses," Huang says. "They don't necessarily have to be doing the sexiest things, but they do need to solve a problem that exists within a large corporation. We build these products alongside them."

The firm accomplishes this by effectively operating as, like Betaworks, a holding company for the startups in its portfolio. Huang has a network of experienced, proven entrepreneurs that she works with, bringing them in on projects that she feels suit their background and providing them with a team of people to help make each project happen. Private industry requests a product, the Hatchery essentially assigns it to an entrepreneur, and the process begins. The firm puts in a single round of funding—no dilution for the investors, Huang says—and remains involved as sort of a "cofounder" until the company exits (which had not yet happened for a Hatchery company as of my visit).

"I really don't care about your beautiful idea," she tells me, smiling. "I want to know what other companies want to buy. I want to know that you're thirsty before I pour you water. I don't want to just come up with the concept of water and hope that someone might want to buy it."

Aside from this inverted VC model, the Hatchery also functions as an incubator in the sense that it's hatching new companies alongside its founders; it somewhat resembles a VC's entrepreneur-in-residence program. And the money is there. The Hatchery funds its products with up to $5 million dollars of upfront capital, if that's what it takes to make it a success.

"We're not throwing $20,000 at them and saying 'good luck,'" Huang says. "No. We like this idea, we're going to do it, we're going to make a full-on run at it."

The trick for New York is finding a way to take all of its inherent talent—all of those career changers from financial services, media, fashion, and advertising—and convert them into a tech-ready workforce that the city's startups can use. As a result, the city is home to more than a few training centers dedicated to educating workers, many of whom are changing careers from other industries, on the basics of Web development and mobile app programming. Perhaps the best known of these is General Assembly, a trade school/coworking space in the Flatiron District that offers a wide range of part- and full-time classes in everything from product management, to user experience design, to data analysis. But there are many others sprinkled across the city, each focused on its own niche, its own market, and all trying to resolve the city's shortage of qualified developers.

A big part of this push these days is happening on the campus of Cornell University's New York City outpost, Cornell Tech, which when I visited was located in the Google office in Chelsea but is set to move to a new, two-million-square-foot campus on Roosevelt Island in 2017. Located in a former Port Authority shipping terminal building at 111 Eighth Avenue, the Google office is better known (in some circles) as one of the most connected buildings in the world; the spot where much of New York's Internet traffic enters the island of Manhattan. It's easy to see the clues once you get in there. Like the data center it is, the halls of the eighteen-story, 2,900,000-square-foot Art Deco building are quiet and cool, with cable and pipes running overhead. The red-blue-green-yellow Google color scheme is hard to miss.

This is one of the places where the East Coast Internet lives.

Cornell Tech's space is on the third floor and consists of a collection of classrooms, group meeting spaces, and cubicles for faculty and administration. There are two large classrooms in the space—one at either end of the office—with faculty and staff seating taking up the rest of the room. A wall of windows runs along the north side.

"Most of our students are techies," explains Jennifer Ellison with the Office of the Dean and Vice Provost, as we walk through the open, colorfully designed space, "but they also may have had some experience with a startup, or have that entrepreneurial spirit that we're looking for. You're not looking at things from one perspective or one lens; you're looking at how you can change the way that things are being done. How can we enhance societal good with what we're doing? And it takes a certain type of mind to be that kind of entrepreneurial person."

The goal for Cornell Tech, she tells me, is to prepare students for leadership roles in the New York technology ecosystem, while providing the city with a pipeline for much-needed engineering and development talent. The focus is on real-world experience and multidisciplinary training—a large part of the program, for example, involves local founders lecturing to students about what life in a startup is really like.

A lot of this simply involves giving students different perspectives of what this work really is about and what being in a tech ecosystem actually looks like. For example, the school brings MBA faculty down from its main campus in Ithaca to teach the business courses, so there's a lot of crossover that students wouldn't necessarily get if they were just in a straight computer science program or an MBA program.

And that crossover experience is what the school is trying to bring to the city's tech ecosystem, explains Cornell Tech Dean Dan Huttenlocher.

"We look at these students as being equipped to take technical leadership roles in companies of all shapes and forms and sizes," he says. "But really what they're learning here is how to combine their technical know-how with the ability to really make a difference in an organization. I think a lot of technical programs are focused only on the technical knowledge and that's it. So our students take a business class every semester, they engage every week with people from industry through projects that they're doing. So they're really learning how to interact with people who aren't all other software and engineering people. And we think that that combo of skills will prepare them for technical leadership roles in pretty much any size organization, from startups up through large corporations."

It's a skill set that's very much in demand, he says, both in New York and beyond. Workers who can bring a technical skill set to whatever they're doing will be better off, whether it's in media, or marketing, or even finance; if they can combine this with honed business and personal skills, even better. Still, these can be difficult attributes for companies to find in the job market.

"It's sort of like, everybody can write but that doesn't make everybody a journalist," Huttenlocher laughs. "The similar analogy is a lot of people can write code but that doesn't make them all computer scientists. And so I think it's important to have that deeper know-how coupled with the ability to work outside of the purely technical domain. I ran a startup company for a while and I was at Xerox for a while on the technical side, and the hardest people to hire were the ones who had real technical depth but also had acumen for really engaging with customers and the business side of the company. It's just the hardest thing to find. And that remains true today."

The fact is, just about every job in the economy has become technical on some level, and every company is now a technology company whether they want to admit it or not. The trick for workers is finding a way to weave new technical skills into their existing resume in a way that makes sense for their employers and their career goals.

That's the approach that Avi Flombaum is taking at his coding startup, the Flatiron School, which moved from the Silicon Alley district near Union Square to the southern tip of Manhattan in late 2013 as part of a city-backed program to bring hipper, more growth-oriented companies to the Financial District. After working on a series of startups, he created the Flatiron School in 2012 after teaching a few programming classes on Skillshare (which is run by a friend) and helping out at General Assembly. The whole operation is self-funded and it charges about $10,000 for a three-month, full-time course that promises to teach normal people how to code, regardless of their background.

"I found that in every class there would be three or four students who would form a study group and take it really seriously," he tells me, reclining on a couch in the middle of the bustling workroom while a class meets nearby. "After five weeks, they would really be able to code and I would either take contract work and subcontract it out to them and mentor them through it, or maybe get them a job or just recommend them for interviews. And that was my favorite part of teaching. It was always the people that took it really seriously that I could really like, you know, change their life."

Taking it seriously probably isn't a problem anymore, at least according to the numbers that Flombaum shared with me. The school's acceptance rate, which was only at 10 percent to begin with, was down to 5 percent as of late 2013—at the time, he expected to get more than 900 applications for the forty-four available program spots in his next class—and that still won't be enough to meet the city's demand for developers. According to Flombaum's estimates, there are about 50,000 computer science majors coming to New York City every year to fill as many as 150,000 jobs.

"There could be a hundred schools like us and we'd still have a shortage," he says.

The situation is likely just going to get worse. The startup scene in the city continues to grow, and high-profile companies like Foursquare, Tumblr, Facebook, and Google continue to hire more and more developers. But for entrepreneurs like Flombaum, the citywide talent shortage has actually turned into welcome news, for more reasons than the simple fact that it's driving demand for his services at the Flatiron School. Now, local engineers are able to do the work they want to do in the city where they want to do it.

"I'm from New York and I've always wanted to work here," he explains. "I was never interested in moving to San Francisco, but I've been out there a bunch, and one of the differences I see is that I've always seen technology in a supportive role and not necessarily an industry within itself like it is out there. It's more about how do you help other industries integrate this and understand how to leverage these technologies to do something better or faster. And when you have such a diverse economy like in New York, that's really helpful, right? Because all of our end users are right here."

This is a common refrain in the city, where the message is commonly "what else can we do with these technical tools to make our existing industries more competitive?" It is tech serving fashion, and tech serving finance, and tech serving media, all coming together to create a more vibrant, more diverse business community in the process.

"[In the Bay Area] it's like this bubble with this kind of rebound effect," Flombaum says. "It's like, 'Ooh, I'll tell you my idea and you'll tell me the exact same idea.' Here it's more like, 'I'm speaking to a banker and I'm solving his problems.' And I really like that."

Down at the southern tip of Manhattan Island, literally across the street from Battery Park, is the office of the Partnership Fund for New York City (PFNYC), a private organization dedicated to developing the local economy in New York by identifying and supporting what it deems the city's most promising entrepreneurs. It was established in 1996 as a network of sixty-seven local industry leaders and has raised more than $120 million since investing in a series of startups at around the $1 million to $5 million level.

"We have a mandate to create jobs in New York and increase economic activity," PFNYC President and CEO Maria Gotsch tells me in her office, looking out over the Statue of Liberty. "So that's a very broad brushstroke."

When the fund was set up in the late 1990s, there really was no tech sector in New York to speak of. So at that time the fund functioned as an early investor in a number of seed-stage companies, stepping in to provide funding where no other capital was available, essentially serving as a backstop to get money around deals and encourage the area's then-developing tech investment community.

Fast-forward fifteen years and New York today is a very different place, Gotsch says.

It has a robust tech sector in digital media, e-commerce, and ad tech. Entrepreneurs are getting funding. Experienced entrepreneurs are becoming angel investors. People are coming in from out of town to invest. And the fact that 85 percent of the startups in New York have to date been focused on digital media, e-commerce, and advertising tech led PFNYC to pull out of those markets five years ago, since that segment of the market has become self-sustaining and doesn't need their support anymore.

"So we looked around," Gotsch says, "and asked, what are the assets that New York has? You always want to start as much as you can from a position of strength, so what we're now doing is focused on three verticals: financial technology, digital health, and life sciences. And the theme that cuts across all three of those is we have a lot of something here that we can leverage. So in New York we have the largest concentration of financial services firms, we have the largest concentration of hospitals and patients and doctors, and we have one of the largest concentrations of biomedical researchers at our universities."

That's what the fund does; it brings the expertise and resources of New York to the table for the good of New York. It does it with investments of time and money; it does it by offering connections and networking help to startup founders (like connecting health IT startups with some of the largest hospital systems in the world to work on pilot programs—access that would be all but impossible for the founders to secure on their own). The idea is to try and capture the innovation that's happening in New York and put it to work on a commercial basis right at home.

For example, the city does not have a biotech industry. So whenever intellectual property exits the city's universities and research facilities, it generally has to go somewhere else to be commercialized, taking the jobs and potential tax revenues that come with that to another city. As it stands now, New York's research institutions are doing great work and are great anchors for the city, Gotsch explains, but they're also nonprofits that don't pay property taxes and so are able to do that hard work under the "protected nonprofit" banner.

"It's interesting," she says. "New York has always been very long in technology, it's just been within corporate walls. It's not like there haven't been technology companies here; the banks on some level are technology companies that happen to make money. I mean, there are some very sophisticated consumers of technology in this city."

There is still room for growth in many areas as well, she says. The numbers tell the story. For example, in biomedical research, if you look at any metric that measures the field—National Institutes of Health (NIH) dollars, number of Nobel Prize winners, Howard Hughes Medical Institute investigators, National Academy of Sciences members—New York City itself, even without the New Jersey suburbs, ranks in the top two or three in each of those categories. That's in the same realm of traditional powerhouses like Boston and the Bay Area, and yet New York is not thought of as a biomedical center because it doesn't have the industry and ecosystem in place to back it up.

"It's still about building an ecosystem, right?" Gotsch says. "There's not any one thing that will make that happen. But we need to work together with the city, the business community, and the academic institutions to make everybody aware that we have the sciences here, that we have technology here. Because in New York, sort of like how oil swamped Venezuela's economy, Wall Street swamped New York City's economy."

The challenge now, she says, is to spread that message and get some of those other industries back.

"I grew up in Maine," explains Ben Fisher, the cofounder of New York–based Alchemy, a social sharing and help network based around users' own personal connections, "which is sort of a strange place. And then after college, I came to New York City to specifically work in advertising, because I always thought I wanted to start an ad agency. But then, I guess it was a combination of timing as well as the market and stuff, I realized that I didn't want to work in advertising, but I did want to return to starting other types of companies, specifically building products."

So that's what he did, tapping New York's experience base as a media center to find engineers skilled in social media and enterprise networking to help build his company. But what he learned along the way is that it isn't the company's address that matters anymore, it's the attitude the founders are able to bring to the project.

"There's a lot of opportunity," he says of the New York ecosystem now. "It's certainly not the Bay Area, but you don't really need it to be. There are a lot of advantages and disadvantages. I think it just comes down to where will you do your best work? And a large part of that is, where will you personally be happiest? At least that's the way that I've approached it and thought about my environment."

The thing about startup life in New York City, as improbable as it sounds, is that there really is just a small tech community at work in the city. Sure, the meetups are large and the industry mixers are numerous, but the fact remains that the most active part of the community—the entrepreneurs on the ground, as well as the mentors and VCs that they work with—is a small, core group in New York, just as it is in any ecosystem. That's one of the reasons that many in the city are so high on tech's future here. Despite the rapid growth in recent years, there is still quite a bit more room to grow, in terms of both investment dollars and startup numbers, as well as overall involvement in the ecosystem.

That's one of the reasons that Reddit cofounder Alexis Ohanian told Yahoo Finance that he expects the tech industry's next billionaire success story to come out of New York. The first one, Shutterstock CEO Jonathan Oringer, whose company offers millions of royalty-free stock photos via the Internet, was outed by Bloomberg in 2013 as the city's first bona fide tech billionaire with a net worth of $1.05 billion.

"I think [in] the Valley and the Bay, there is always going to be a hub there and an amazing place to start a company," he told me after his Yahoo appearance, "but there are going to be different places for different types of companies to thrive. I'm just excited about all the stuff that's coming up in New York."

The key, he says, echoing the comments of so many others in the city, is that the area needs to embrace the industries that have made it great—finance, media, content, and advertising. As Ohanian explains it, when he and cofounder Steve Huffman started Reddit out of their dorm room at the University of Virginia in 2005, social media wasn't yet a "thing." Facebook was still restricted to college campuses, and Twitter, Pinterest, Instagram, and the like weren't even close to existing yet. Now, however, we have nearly reached a kind of critical mass in terms of individual Web users sharing things online—from photos, to videos, to blog posts, and other written materials. As a result, he says, we're seeing a renewed appreciation for content creation.

"And this is where I think New York is so well positioned because of its history in media and content and design and art—all that stuff," says Ohanian. "Basically, tastemakers have always flocked to New York. And a bunch of us now have built these platforms that allow tastemakers to get their ideas to the world effectively, but what are we doing to encourage and nurture these creatives to make and do more with them?"

4

Las Vegas

"A lot of city revitalization projects depend on having an expensive sports team or building an expensive stadium or having a Harvard or Stanford nearby . . . we want to show there's another way. If we can do it in Downtown Las Vegas, the place typically voted as least likely to succeed, and make it a place of learning, of inspiration, of entrepreneurial energy, then really there's no excuse for any other city."

—*Tony Hsieh, CEO, Zappos.com*

"**S**O, I HAVE TO WARN YOU, Tony's apartment is pretty weird." There are about fifteen of us packed elbow to elbow in an elevator on our way up to the top floor of the recently restored Ogden residential tower in Downtown Las Vegas to tour, of all things, Zappos.com CEO Tony Hsieh's apartment. Our guide for the day, a twentysomething employee with pink-purple-blue streaks in her hair, had suddenly dropped her smile, turned off the charm, and got down to brass tacks.

"Seriously, it's really strange. You've never seen anything like this."

Ha, ha. Sure. The eccentric Vegas billionaire, ensconced alone in his massive penthouse lair overlooking downtown, complete with a bizarre animal obsession, singular decorating style, and odd personal scheduling habits. I've read all about Howard Hughes, seen *Diamonds Are Forever*, and pretty much know the drill when it comes to Vegas' legendary characters.

But, unlike Willard Whyte and his ilk, Hsieh is a well-known and widely respected tech entrepreneur who cofounded the online advertising network LinkExchange in the late 1990s before taking on the online shoe business at Zappos in 2000. Amazon acquired Zappos in a $1.2 billion deal in 2009. He's also a very public figure in the city of Las Vegas, working tirelessly to not only weave his company into the fabric of the city but also pledging some $350 million of his own money to overhaul and rehabilitate the once-forgotten neighborhood of Downtown Vegas. How strange could his home, the showpiece of this ongoing Downtown Project, really be?

Back in the elevator, eyes collectively rolled.

And then we stepped through the door.

At first, Tony's apartment—which actually started out as three separate condos that have been combined into one massive space—looks just like a regular home, with granite countertops in the kitchen and a living room dominated by a beige leather sofa. Sure, papers are stacked everywhere, there's a massive beanbag chair over by the corner window, color printouts are being used as artwork, and one wall is essentially covered with a flurry of yellow, pink, blue, and green Post-it notes, but it's a guy's place—for example, the liquor collection takes up half the kitchen counter—and essentially a pretty normal condo.

But go through another doorway, walk down a hallway, and things start to get interesting. The kitchen and dining room area of the second apartment have been converted into a jungle-themed party space, complete with fake vines and greenery hanging from the ceiling, multicolored lights, and a frozen margarita machine on the counter. Further back in the space, the third apartment has been repurposed into a loose conference room/teaching space, with rollaway plastic desks and probably the best view in town of Downtown Vegas (and all the abandoned buildings, run-down storefronts, and vacant lots that go with it).

That's about where the whole "really strange place" thing starts to sink in.

"He does live here on a daily basis," our guide assures us. "The first time I gave a tour I walked in and he was sitting on the couch in his pajamas working on his laptop. So yes, he does live here. I don't know why he opens up his apartment to six tours a day, but it's not my apartment, so I guess it's fine. We're not going to my apartment, by the way."

To be fair, Tony's (everybody in town calls Hsieh by his first name) apartment really isn't all that weird. It's just a reflection of its very unique and driven owner, who is committing not just his bank account but his very home to the idea that true community can take hold in Downtown Las Vegas. And, as I'm reminded over and over during my time in the city, Tony is all about community, starting with the co-op space where he lived in San Francisco to the "big happy family" model that he nurtured at Zappos. Now, his focus is on bringing this idea to an entire city.

And it all started with a need for office space.

Zappos' original Vegas headquarters was located on the outskirts of town near McCarran International Airport in a nondescript office park in Henderson, Nevada. But by 2010 the company, by then more than 1,000 employees strong, was rapidly growing and in need of a new facility. But office space—particularly in the form of large, interesting buildings—can be tough to find in the Las Vegas Valley since most construction in the area has focused solely on hotels and casinos for generations. Class A office space is something of a new thing for the city, leaving the inventory lacking.

So the company got creative, studying other corporate campuses like those of Google, Apple, and Nike to find a model that would work for them, as a public-facing, community-driven company.

With that in mind, Tony went shopping for a new headquarters and settled on the old Las Vegas City Hall building, a hulking circular seventies-era structure that takes up nearly an entire city block between Fourth Street and Las Vegas Boulevard in the heart of downtown. The city's offices moved to a new facility nearby in 2012, so Zappos bought the old building, two parking garages on either side of it, and all of the available land from Las Vegas Boulevard to Eighth Street and from Stewart Avenue to the I-95 freeway. When the city was using it, the building held about 800 employees, but Zappos in 2013 moved some 1,400 workers in using an open concept office design.

That's a lot of new people downtown who need places to live, restaurants to eat at, bars to hang out at, and stores to shop at in a neighborhood that, until very recently, was better known for hourly motels and 24-hour liquor stores.

Our tour guide explains: "When we realized that we were buying a building and moving everyone down here, Tony decided he really wanted to do some revitalization work in downtown, to focus the neighborhood on what he calls the three 'Cs': community, collisions, and colearning. Even though we are completely separate entities, Zappos and the Downtown Project, we kind of really got started after Zappos decided to move down here."

It's been a slow process, but Hsieh's Downtown Project—the name refers to the overall downtown revitalization effort, including Tony's $350 million investment—is starting to move forward. A handful of restaurants have opened for business, there are no less than three tech-focused coworking spaces within walking distance of Fremont Street, and the whole area is now safe for foot traffic thanks to a legion of 24/7 rangers, employed by the

Downtown Project, and providing street-level security. Coffee shops, clothing stores, hipster bars—the neighborhood is coming back to life.

It's funny what a few million dollars can do.

But despite all the press coverage over the last few years, the story of Vegas tech isn't really about Tony Hsieh. It isn't really about the multimillion-dollar Downtown Project. It isn't even about the startups that the city has spawned in recent years. It's about the community that's been in place for longer than many people realize.

And there's a lot more going on here than you might think.

Downtown is not exactly what most of us think of when we think of Las Vegas.

Miles from the glitzy, modern casinos on the Strip—like the Bellagio, Caesar's Palace, and the Cosmopolitan—Downtown Vegas is these days best known for the Fremont Street Experience, a sort of outdoor pedestrian mall; older casinos like the Golden Nugget and Four Queens; and former Las Vegas mayor Oscar Goodman's namesake steakhouse (full name: "Oscar's Beef, Booze, and Broads"). It has long been a somewhat tired, run-down part of town, rough around the edges and generally the place to go when you're looking for 99-cent shrimp cocktails, seedy dive bars, and casino furnishings that went out of style during the Ford administration.

But there is surprisingly more to Downtown Las Vegas than just the tourists. Aside from the Downtown Project, the city itself has also been pumping millions in investment dollars into the area to rehabilitate properties, update infrastructure, and generally class up the ten-block core to attract more out-of-towners and locals alike. And that second point is key, since downtown is also the administrative heart of the city. It's home to a shiny, new federal courthouse building at the corner of Las Vegas Boulevard and Bridger Avenue, the new $146-million city office building, and more than a few bankers, lawyers, and other professionals that still commute downtown every day for work.

The key to understanding the city, I learned over nearly a week of living and working downtown myself, is that, despite its checkered past, Downtown Las Vegas is a living, breathing neighborhood that's working hard to overhaul its image.

"There's money coming into downtown from a variety of different sources," explains Andy White with VegasTechFund, the Downtown Project's seed-stage tech investment arm. "Restaurants and bars are opening up, other stores have opened, and there's talk of new residential buildings being developed. All of that is happening around us. Many people have seen the potential of downtown and where things are going, so we've had tremendous support from the community."

The general attitude, he explains, is that the city itself is a startup. (Sound familiar? Detroit is going with the same message.)

But really, how can real business ever get done in Las Vegas?

"The biggest liability is that everyone already knows Vegas," White says. "Everyone's been here for a conference or a bachelor party. It's Vegas. But once we get them here and show them what it's like to live and work here, show them the close community that we have, there's really just an energy here that you don't find in other places. It's a combination of having this big population with the resources necessary to make things happen and so many people working toward this common goal."

That commitment to the Downtown Las Vegas community has extended well beyond the grounds of the new Zappos headquarters. In addition to the Downtown Rangers teams that are securing the neighborhood, Hsieh in 2012 took it upon himself to address the neighborhood's other pressing problem—prostitution—by literally buying up five hourly motels on Fremont Street where the business was going down and demolishing them on his own dime. The site of one of those former motels will soon be home to a medical clinic. Another will house a new primary school.

"The great part of what's happening here is that being part of the community is in the fabric of everything that we're doing," White says. "It isn't rolling out the red carpet or anything like that; we're ready to hit the ground and get to work."

A full $50 million of Hsieh's $350 million Downtown Project pledge is earmarked for investments in startups, with an eye toward companies that will help contribute to the downtown community, playing off of the "return on community" mantra that Hsieh is so fond of. So far, the project has invested in nearly thirty new companies and expects to spend through the full $50 million fund by 2015. (As for the rest of the $350 million, it breaks down into $200 million for real estate purchases and residential developments, $50 million for local small business funding, and $50 million for arts and culture projects.)

"Our primary target is post-accelerator companies," White explains of the fund's startup goals, "and it's worked out really great for us so far. It's the area where we have the most potential to help—the team is fairly solid, they have good products, some good customers, and they just need help growing that into a company. We can really help get that foundation in place."

Certainly, the Downtown Project has brought money and media attention to Downtown Las Vegas for the first time in ages, but the fact is there was an active, if underdeveloped, tech community in the area long before Zappos came to the neighborhood. In fact, many of the entrepreneurs, developers, and local cheerleaders got their start in the area back when the only thing uniting the Vegas Tech community was a Twitter hashtag (#VegasTech) and a dusty coffee shop and arts space on Fremont Street.

"It was right here in this room, a little over two years ago, that we held the first Las Vegas Jelly," Rick Duggan told me over coffee at the Beat Coffeehouse and Records in what used to be a J. C. Penney store on the corner of Fremont and Sixth Streets. The "Jelly" was and is the primary organizing force for the city's developer community, a free monthly meetup where members can swap ideas, dig into code, and just generally hang out with like-minded tech enthusiasts. It started out with just over a dozen members but quickly spiraled to more than 200, outgrowing its modest coffeehouse digs and eventually moving to a regular weekly schedule.

Even in 2011, there was a Vegas tech community on the rise.

"There was definitely technology in Vegas," says Duggan, who, in addition to his after-hours work as an evangelist for the local tech community, works as director of Web site systems at Zappos. "You come here and the average person sees all the glitz and the glamour, but those lights don't move around that way on their own. There's an underlying technology that's been here for a long time. But the challenge in Vegas was that there just wasn't any sort of central place to meet. And I mean that in a physical sense as well as a connected online sense."

The Jelly filled that role, along with the centrally located Beat Coffeehouse, which, for a long time, was the only daytime meeting space available anywhere near Fremont Street. It didn't take long for similar events to spring up in the wake of the first Vegas Tech meetup, including a local edition of Startup Weekend, hackathons, meetup groups, and a whole roster of other related activities. Within months, Duggan says, a bona fide community of tech enthusiasts had sprung up that was, for the first time, centered around downtown. This was about the time that the city's first tech coworking space, /usr/lib, was created above the Beat, charging members just $25 per year for access.

Duggan organized an early pitch night event at the coffee shop to help local entrepreneurs focus their business plans and get comfortable pitching to investors. Five early-stage companies presented and a crowd of maybe a dozen was expected, so Duggan didn't even bother to reserve a room. More than seventy-five people showed up that first night, and it has turned into a regular event since then that reliably draws strong crowds.

Things were starting to get busy on Fremont Street. But the fact that real work was even being done in Downtown Vegas at all, and during daylight hours no less, was still a novel prospect as recently as 2012. The fact that companies, and jobs, and economic growth were coming from this—organic community and all—was just a bonus.

"When I started coming down here, the community was just growing by word of mouth," Duggan says. "I might know you, and you know a couple of other people, so I'd talk to you, and you'd talk to your friends, and everybody would sort of just talk to a couple people. Before you knew it you had sparked this amazing thing."

And this was all happening before the Downtown Project came to town.

"The Tony thing is really funny," Duggan says, "and certainly it's great that he is who he is and gets the press that he does, but he's also supportive in a super hands-off way. Putting his own money in it shows how much he believes in this, but there's no dictating about the how. It's just sort of, yes, he's supportive of it, but he isn't telling anyone what to do."

For the city of Las Vegas, however, the growing tech community surrounding the Downtown Project is serious business.

Like Detroit, Vegas long ago fell into the trap of becoming essentially a single-industry town. Casinos are fine moneymakers in good fiscal times, when visitor numbers are up and everyone is in a free-spending mood. But that industry struggles when the economy takes a downturn, like when the recession hit in 2008 and tourists cut back on entertainment spending and simply stopped traveling. Vegas' casinos, once the lifeblood of the southern Nevada economy, were hit hard. They're still recovering.

According to the Nevada Governor's Office of Economic Development, employment at the state's casino hotels fell by 10 percent between 2002 and 2012, accounting for about 173,000 jobs statewide. Employment at stand-alone casinos fell even further, dropping by 18 percent, while careers in the convention and trade shows space were down 15 percent in the same time period.

Clearly, Las Vegas needed to diversify its economy.

Following the downturn, city leaders got to work identifying industries that would help augment the gaming and hospitality sectors. Technology fit the bill as a high-growth, low-capital industry that could build on Las Vegas' existing strengths—an educated workforce, a diverse business community, and a creative base featuring everyone from dancers, to chefs, to musicians, and more. In addition, the city and state have also thrown their support behind green energy, mining, aerospace and defense, and health care in an effort to bring new jobs to the region.

For information technology, however, Las Vegas has a distinct, if little-known, advantage: the Switch SuperNAP data center.

Located in a series of gray, windowless, and all but anonymous warehouses on the outskirts of the city, Switch is one of the largest, most secure, and efficient data centers in the United States, home to Web clients as diverse as eBay, Sony, and the US Air Force. It's an intimidating place, as each building on the grounds is protected by a troop of armed commandos, 24/7 video monitoring, and God only knows what else.

But what does having all this technology support nearby mean for Vegas startups? Enter the InNEVation Center, a startup incubator owned and operated by Switch, located just a few hundred yards from the data center in Enterprise, Nevada.

"The whole idea is just to build a place where an entrepreneur can have all the resources, funding, and office space they need to have a good startup platform," explains Richard Ethington, general manager of InNEVation, in the facility's glassed-in conference room. As opposed to many of the spaces downtown, this suburban space is sleek and modern—with a dark red and steel color scheme that matches the nearby data center—complete with wall-to-wall carpeting and water coolers in the break room. The hallways are quiet, serious.

"The concept of InNEVation, although it has expansive goals, is that at some point we had to start somewhere," says Ethington. "What we're trying to do is to create one place we can bring in tech startup entrepreneurs, along with leaders, educators, government leaders, and investors, bring all those groups together where they can collaborate and work all their things out. And one thing that gets a lot of feedback from the Bay Area is that, out there, a lot of times when you describe the idea that you have, somebody will say, 'Oh yeah, I've heard of that. My buddy is working on something like that.' You know? There's not a lot of support that way and it's very competitive. But here every startup that comes out, the community really backs it. That's kind of the cool thing about Vegas."

As an incubator, InNEVation is a little like the big brother of the downtown scene, where late-night happy hours are replaced with monthly conference room allotments and separate office spaces. It's a place for those entrepreneurs who are looking for a quieter, more serious environment, with dim lights, long corridors, and minimal noise and distractions. (And the WiFi speeds—wow. Never in my life have I enjoyed better network performance than during my afternoon at InNEVation.) The goal, however, is the same: help local founders get their businesses off the ground.

Of course, the InNEVation Center is just one coworking space in a city that seems to suddenly be full of them. The Downtown Project has backed no less than three spaces near City Hall so far—one dedicated to tech startups, another focused on fashion, and a third dedicated to art and music—and plans are in the works to convert another two floors of a Hsieh-owned office building on Bridger Avenue to serve as shared space for tech startups as well.

"This used to be a law office, so everything in here was really cheesy and bad," explains Josh Bowden as he shows me around Work In Progress, the Downtown Project's first tech coworking space behind the federal courthouse on Sixth Street. Opening the door to the onetime kitchenette, he points out the brass-plated fixtures and granite slab countertop. "Everything was marble and gold. Very classy."

It may have come from cookie-cutter eighties beginnings, but the building is now home to some twenty-plus tech startups and more than 100 individual members, mostly working in the open, library-like room on the second floor. A few office suites are available around the perimeter of the room, but, according to Bowden, those are all leased out to larger companies (like Zappos, which runs its college campus outreach operation out of Work in Progress) or as Vegas outposts for out-of-town businesses.

It's about more than just business development. Like just about everything the Downtown Project touches, community is the name of the game at Work in Progress.

"Really it's more of a collaborative workspace," Bowden says, explaining what the future holds for the space. "We want to have a mentorship program and do lots of classes, and we're working on possibly bringing in a Web development immersive program that we'll offer in-house. We want to have a setup where people can go through the program over four months and hopefully get placed in jobs at the end of it."

At the moment, however, Work in Progress is filling a very simple need for the community: office space. The Las Vegas Valley is, oddly, one of the tighter commercial real estate markets in the country, with less than 20 percent availability on average. It's hard to find office space for small five- to ten-person startups, and when you do, it can get expensive. For founders, that kind of real estate overhead can be a significant liability. That's the niche that the city's coworking spaces are hoping to reach.

"We want to be able to scale as companies start growing, be able to offer space and meet their needs whatever they are," says Bowden. "Small spaces, larger spaces, conference rooms, whatever. So we're definitely looking at doing a lot more."

The Vegas sales pitch worked for Keller Rinaudo and his cofounders when Romotive, his Downtown Project–backed startup that's making iPhone robots that users can program and control on their own, moved their entire company from Seattle to Las Vegas in early 2012 at Hsieh's urging. They set up a makeshift robot assembly line in a condo at the Ogden (a few floors below Tony's penthouse apartment) and, after pretty much trashing the place in the process, grew their business from a handful of founders to nearly twenty employees.

"It turned out that Tony had always had a thing for robots and kind of, like, offered us this apartment where we could build our robots immediately," explains Rinaudo as we sit around what would otherwise be the dining room table. It's like any other apartment, except in this one there are robots, robot parts, and general robot "stuff" scattered just about everywhere. "We were like, 'We should take this.' So we just drove from Seattle and we started working while watching *Wall-E* and James Bond and building robots."

The freedom that the Downtown Project offered has been key to Romotive's success, according to Rinaudo, as it allowed them to tinker with their designs without worrying about the ins and outs of startup life like rent, overhead, and funding. And it's working. In the past year, the robot maker, which now builds its products in China, has gone from shipping a few hundred, hand-built robots per week (which Rinaudo remembers tagging and lugging to the Downtown Las Vegas post office himself) to thousands per month, with plans for upgrades and refinements coming all the time. According to the CEO, their goal of creating the first affordable, personal robot is now within reach.

"The Downtown Project is very, very interesting," he says. "Tony is investing all of this money trying to build a city from scratch. And that's basically what he did. You know, when he was in San Francisco he created this building with all of his friends and they built this little community, and he really loved that part of that.

And then when he invested in Zappos, he built a 2,000-person company around the idea that you can have a shared community with shared values. So the next step is, 'What if I build an entire city around shared values?' So that's what he's doing."

Another Vegas tech success story is LaunchKey, an online security firm that actually grew out of a Startup Weekend idea in July 2012. As of mid-2013, the company has a handful of employees and has just raised a $750,000-funding round for its authentication program that allows for high-level security without passwords; with its technology, the user's smart phone (or other device) can now stand in for the password.

"It's definitely a unique situation here," says CEO Geoff Sanders on the roof of yet another Hsieh-owned building about a block from Work in Progress. "Before we started LaunchKey and the whole monster that it's become, I was definitely considering jobs in Silicon Valley, and I was actually really close to moving out there."

Sanders is actually an old-timer in the Vegas tech scene, having moved to town before 2010 to work on a contract project for his old Web design business. LaunchKey was, at least to start, little more than an interesting idea that Sanders and a few friends decided to take on in their spare time. They've stayed, he says, because of the unique mix of community, talent, and resources that Downtown Vegas offers.

"It was what I found out about this downtown scene that really got me to stay," he says. "There's something unique about it. Even compared to Silicon Valley, and everyone likes to hype up Silicon Valley, but while there are so many resources there, there are also so many takers, so many people who need those resources. Here the 'per capita' is just so much lower, so there's so much more resources per entrepreneur."

The physical proximity of Downtown Vegas is a bonus, too, he says. Unlike California, where you're driving between Palo Alto, Sunnyvale, San Jose, and other cities for meetings (and it can be more than an hour between destinations if you throw San Francisco and rush-hour traffic into the mix), Las Vegas is remarkably compact. The general rule is that you can drive pretty much anywhere in town, from the airport to Nellis Air Force Base north of the city, in about twenty minutes or so, depending on traffic. The downtown core is even smaller, lending itself to those natural "collisions"—chance meetings and random encounters that in the tech world can often turn into new projects or opportunities.

"Silicon Valley is a big place," Sanders says. "Here, you'll literally have everyone in the startup community here in this building and that white building over there where Tony's apartment is. And I think that's unique, to have this close of a group. And then there's just the excitement that comes with a 'new city' project like this. That's built a lot of energy that's translated to a lot of the startups that are coming up."

But, as anywhere, there are limitations, and in the end, those limitations finally caught up with Romotive. After almost two years in Las Vegas, the company was forced to relocate to San Francisco in the fall of 2013 to get closer to the rest of its industry and focus more on what's next. It's about growth, says the CEO, and taking advantages of the opportunities that are coming down the road in the robotics market. By being closer to their competition, Romotive will be better able to recruit talent, sell products, and keep in touch with potential investors.

"The vision of the company has grown a lot in the last year," says Rinaudo. "We want to build the world's first affordable personal robots. We think that that's a huge market that's really untapped. It's crazy when you think about it that mobile and Web in the last fifteen or twenty years have seen this explosion of design; that's what drove Apple to become the biggest company in the world. And that's what's kind of driven Facebook and interest in Twitter. These are companies that have just gotten huge because the divine design is excellent."

So that's where the company itself is headed—to the Bay Area—and Rinaudo is realistic about the city he's leaving behind.

"I do think that right now it's going to be hard for the Downtown Project to recruit bigger companies," he says. "I think that it is possible to outgrow the Downtown Project, because when we came in we were three people out of one hundred that were part of the Downtown Project. But now we're like twenty people out of two hundred, and so the percentage has increased dramatically, and it feels a little like as we grow as a company it will be important for us to be in a bigger area.

"I think that Tony will succeed at what he's doing and, as the Downtown Project grows, it will become a lot more natural to have, like, a one-hundred-person company here that's thriving. That's coming."

The city has certainly come a long way since brothers Frank and Mike Yoder, the cofounders of WinTech LLC, first moved to the area in the mid-1990s.

The pair had owned a software consultancy in Chesapeake, Virginia, for twenty years, but the last economic downturn hit them hard. As Mike, the company's CTO, told me: "We basically said, 'Do we want to build this again after the dot-com bubble burst or do we want to go in another direction, which was what we always wanted to do, which was building products?'"

The brothers chose option number two and, after some market research, decided to pick up and move their new business to Las Vegas. It was the ideal location, Mike says, because they were already doing a lot of work in Silicon Valley as well as on the East Coast, and the travel time alone from Virginia was eating into their profit margins. By locating the company in Nevada, they are barely an hour away from San Jose by air and about three hours from Washington, DC—convenient both ways.

"My brother and I were basically commuting across country every week," Mike says. "After a little while of that, and when it became obvious that our work would be in Silicon Valley in Palo Alto, it just made sense to move out West and service our customers back East from time to time. We had one or two accounts here in Vegas, but we looked at both California and Vegas from the standpoint of tax incentives, friendliness to business, and cost of living, and we really decided that Vegas was hard to beat. It was booming, one of the fastest-growing cities in the country at the time. Lots of opportunity. At that time we were doing work throughout the nation, so location didn't really matter for us that much, not as much as access to flights and direct flights."

Today, WinTech is the force behind ALICE Receptionist, a virtual front office system that, by combining motion capture technology, two-way videos, and a touch-screen interface, allows small businesses and corporations to centrally control their receptionist functions. It's essentially a call center tool for front office services that replaces a live receptionist with a touch-screen and video system.

"I will say that during the dot-com boom in the late nineties and early 2000s, Vegas did have a tech scene, but everyone at that time was doing their own thing," Yoder says. "There were some relatively big tech companies—PurchasePro was one—that were doing quite well, but every instance was isolated."

That's what's different in the city this time around, he says. These days, the Vegas technology community is all about collaboration, about helping each other get their feet on the ground, and about building something more than just a single successful company. It's about the city as a whole staking its claim as a tech hub.

"When I attended my first Startup Weekend, I guess it's been two years ago now, I was just blown away by all these young kids who were excited about what they were doing, but also that there were so many people in my community," he says. "They were not just excited, but also entrepreneurial minded and starting companies. Even though I have been here for a long time and doing various things in IT, just to see that excitement and to see that kind of movement happening locally—I wanted to help them and be a part of that. That is sort of what I see as different now from the first time around."

Not that he's surprised by the recent resurgence. Las Vegas is uniquely situated to take advantage of the tech economy and is changing faster than many longtime residents ever expected to see.

"I used to not go downtown at all," Yoder says. "Why would you? And now I love it; it's one of my favorite parts of the city. It's still got a long ways to go—don't get me wrong, it's not Sixth Street in Austin—but it's starting. There's a lot more going on, and it is much more of a community now; you can walk to restaurants and bars."

It's interesting to watch the downtown change happen from the outskirts of the city, he says, because everyone has a different take on the whole project, from the casinos, to the local government, to Tony Hsieh himself. On one level it's an economic development play, while on another it's an effort at community development in a neighborhood that has long been on the decline. For the casinos, a nicer, more vibrant downtown will help attract more tourists and help keep them there.

"I think they're all overall interested in the same thing, which is making downtown a place that people want to go to," Yoder says. "And so they're all attacking it from different angles, and hopefully in the end they'll merge at the same place—which is a place where people enjoy being and having a good time."

Jennifer and David Gosse, the husband and wife team behind social collaboration and project management tool Tracky, have had a similar experience as longtime residents viewing the new startup community from the inside. The pair moved to Las Vegas in 1996 to start another company and ended up with a front-row seat to the dot-com bubble, watching their high-flying entrepreneur neighbors attract interest from out-of-town investors, move to oversized new offices, and go belly-up within two years' time.

After the tech crash, they say, what was once referred to as "Silicon Oasis" became more like tech no-man's land.

"There really wasn't much here," Jennifer says of those post-crash years; "there really wasn't. There was TBAN, the Technology Business Alliance of Nevada [which still exists], and other organizations like Tech Tuesday, but all of it was with players who were already here. Like, they worked for a security company that worked mostly for the casinos. And that's tech, but it's not what we typically think of as Silicon Valley tech, like software, like apps, like startup culture."

We're sitting on the patio at Park on Fremont, a brand new Spanish-style restaurant at the corner of Fremont Street and Las Vegas Boulevard—right across the street from the tourist-heavy pedestrian mall—that wouldn't look out of place in Santa Monica, California, or Scottsdale, Arizona. Only here, in Vegas, there's a building made to look like a six-story pint of Bass beer directly over my shoulder and everyone at the table gets carded, even at two in the afternoon. A small billboard in the vacant lot across the street, which will soon be home to the Downtown Project's new meeting and event space, displays a message from the project's organizers: "Downtown Vegas makes you smarter (if you know where to look)."

"This is definitely unique and different—what's happening now," Jennifer says. "And we dabbled in those older tech communities, but we were always software, and we were always Internet, so there was never that sense of community, for us anyway, in terms of our business and what we were working on."

But it did exist. Unfortunately, the early 2000s crash laid waste to Vegas' fledgling technology scene, and it's been a long, slow road back to relevance.

The difference this time around, according to the Gosses, is that now it's based on organic growth and on supporting a community that was already in place. Nothing is being forced this time.

"What I think about Las Vegas versus other startup communities is that the founders and the community here really got to know each other early on," explains David. "And that really helped it grow into what it is now. And once it got some critical mass, that's when the outsiders looked in and said, 'This thing's got some merit; OK, let's set up some funds and let's support it with sponsorships and so on.' The cool thing is that this community grew organically from itself, basically, and now it's getting support from external sources."

Jennifer nods in agreement, adding that, "It's sort of like you've been hungry for it for so long, like we have, and there are other people who have been on their own, and suddenly you have all this support, and at least for now there's all this collaboration and community. And those aren't just buzzwords, it really is happening. Then when you have names like Tony and that kind of global exposure, I feel like if I invest my money and my time into this I'll probably see a long-term return on this community."

Hsieh's involvement is key in growing the ecosystem, according to the Tracky founders, in part because of the attention he has brought to the downtown community, but also because of the expertise and excitement he brings. For example, the Downtown Project speaker series is already bringing a steady stream of speakers and tech industry experts to town. And these aren't just your run-of-the-mill Chamber of Commerce–style speakers. These are folks like Ben Yoskovitz, the lean startup expert who was in town during my visit, and Brad Feld, the TechStars cofounder. True subject matter experts who are really there to teach local entrepreneurs something that they would not have access to otherwise. Tony's professional network is now becoming part of the community.

"You can't have startup culture without coffee shops," Jennifer says, "without coworking. And then you have the culture, the nightlife, because people want that. You want to go out and be with other people to offset the crazy work schedule. So this whole thing of building a city and having shops and restaurants and farmers' markets and bars and entertainment and culture and speakers—there is such a concerted effort here to diversify and make sure it isn't just an app-building thing. Because that's great, but to really make this downtown a livable city it needs everything."

But for all the improvements in the area over the last twenty-four months, Downtown Vegas is still Downtown Vegas. It still attracts a rowdy after-midnight crowd seven nights a week, it still has its fair share of shady, run-down businesses, and it's still ground zero for the Las Vegas housing crisis.

The Las Vegas Valley—the 600-square-mile region that contains the Las Vegas–Paradise-Henderson metro areas—was hit particularly hard by the 2008 housing crash, which saw local prices plunge by as much as 28 percent in just a few months. What had been a growing, expanding city was suddenly brought to its knees as the floor fell out on prices and many homeowners were left underwater on their mortgages. Home values in the surrounding suburbs of Henderson, Enterprise, and Summerlin are just starting to bounce back more than five years later, but many of the city neighborhoods remain gutted by foreclosures, short sales, and simple abandonments. Even in downtown's nicer, more historic neighborhoods—filled with the spacious ranch homes built by Las Vegas' early casino magnates—the market is shaky. A restored 4,000-square-foot rambler near downtown could set you back maybe $200,000 in this market. But the abandoned properties next door and across the street? They'll likely go at an auction for less than $75,000. Even longtime Vegas performer Liberace's famed 15,000-square-foot rhinestone palace—complete with two bedrooms, ten bathrooms, and a fresco on the ceiling of what used to be Liberace's bedroom—sold for a mere $500,000 in August 2013 after falling into foreclosure in 2010.

Housing issues like this are hardly a strong selling point for entrepreneurs and companies considering a move to Vegas, but it's an issue that the locals are well aware of. In fact, some consider the rock-bottom real estate market to even be an advantage for out-of-town buyers.

"Obviously there have been a lot of negatives with the local real estate crash," says Mike Yoder with WinTech, "but if you're coming into this market, you didn't experience that and you're finding great deals. It's starting to get better, but when you're coming from San Francisco or New York, the deals are still here."

The community has stepped in to address this problem, with several startups locating in something that's informally being called "Startup Block," a residential neighborhood located about a mile south of Fremont Street in the John S. Park Historic District and where a number of entrepreneurs have set up shop in old rental houses where they can live and work. The plan is to eventually formalize the arrangement and expand it into something of a live-work-play setup, although those plans are still in the very early stages. For now, it looks like a scene out of Martin Scorsese's *Casino* back there, minus Sharon Stone, Robert DeNiro, and the exploding Cadillac.

The potential upside in real estate, coupled with the extremely low cost of living, is what brought real estate broker Jon Sterling to Downtown Las Vegas in the summer of 2013. When I met with him at the Beat Coffeehouse, he was in the process of crowdfunding a home purchase nearby that he was planning to lease out to local entrepreneurs, combining long-term tenants with one-nighters on a lease-free basis. At the time of our meeting he was living downtown, waiting for the purchase of his new house to go through and getting to know the community.

"It's where all the original casino owners used to live," Sterling says of the nearby residential neighborhood. "We're living in [former Binion's Horseshoe casino owner] Ted Binion's old house, and he sold it to the Border's Books family, so there's interesting history with all of that."

Sterling is a different type of entrepreneur. Unlike most of the technology folks involved in the Downtown Vegas scene, he's here for the real estate, the city's traditional bread and butter industry, and is finding a rich vein to explore.

"The returns on these group homes are much better than typical rentals," he explains. "Once you get one or two long-term renters, who are sort of like the managers, and then you can do Airbnb-style for the other bedrooms to make up the difference."

If Sterling is able to pull it off, he plans to set up similar group homes in other tech hotspots—including Palo Alto, Denver-Boulder, Kansas City, Detroit, and so on—and create a network of these "startup houses" across the country, literally meeting entrepreneurs where they live.

"So you'll find in different communities like this around the country—Chicago, DC, New York—there are a lot of people working on cool stuff like this," he says. "The types of people who are drawn to this stuff are similar. But Vegas, it's a non-tech place that's becoming a tech place. Zappos was the first big success, and that created a lot of money to go back into the community, and that's fine. But what it's going to take is another round of successes from the fifty or one hundred startups that Tony invests in. When those guys have successful exits and come back to invest money, that will be the second generation."

For now, however, the Las Vegas tech community is all about getting the word out, bringing attention to what's going on in the city and what the startup scene has to offer entrepreneurs.

"Vegas has always had tech," explains Gabe Shepherd, the director of business development at tech event firm Tech Cocktail and the local Vegas community liaison for South by Southwest (SXSW), while leaning against the brick wall in front of Work in Progress. "We have some great innovators, the casinos are doing amazing things, but it wasn't like a startup culture. So, I went to South By [Southwest, in Austin, Texas] a couple years ago, and I was kind of disappointed. I knew what was happening back here, but I was just disappointed because no one from Vegas was there."

So Shepherd came home and set to work "activating" the community, with the goal of making a #VegasTech splash at SXSW the next year. The idea was to market the city and its growing startup community as if it were a product, generating attention, building buzz, and creating connections, all at the largest annual tech and innovation conference in the country.

"The goal was to put Vegas tech on the map and let people know that we're legit," he says. "Maybe what we lack in numbers we make up for with enthusiasm and what some people might call blind idealism, but we're for real. I've been accused of drinking the Kool-Aid before, but we're building something here."

Naturally, being a Vegas native, Shepherd's first instinct was to throw a party.

And then things got out of hand.

The party plan soon became more a series of events, panels, mixers, and booth space to truly show the SXSW attendees what the city has going on. Then the idea hit critical mass: The best way to show off the Las Vegas community was to, literally, show off the community by bringing them all to SXSW. Before Shepherd knew it, he was organizing a community-wide trip to Austin for SXSW 2013, where 140 members of the Vegas tech community ended up sharing a booth and making headlines as a community (complete with an after-hours party, of course).

It was audacious, it was new, and it was a lot more work than anyone could ever have expected. But it worked.

"Nobody's going to pick up and move to Vegas after seeing us at South By, no matter how good of a time they have," Shepherd says. "But if people knew that there is something besides casinos and tourism, that we have other things to offer, maybe they'll consider Vegas. Just come visit; get to know the community. If it's for you, great. If not, we wish you the best of luck. You're welcome anytime."

The group trip was a big win for the local startups themselves, too. Exhibit space on the crowded SXSW show floor isn't cheap and it's all too easy to get lost in the shuffle of 30,000-plus attendees. But, by combining forces in one large #VegasTech booth, community members were able to maximize their visibility and make far more of a splash than they ever would have been able to on their own.

More than that, the group trip brought the community itself closer together.

"It was like summer camp, man," Shepherd laughs. "Putting people together who didn't know each other, right? They went out there as 140 individuals, and trust me, they all didn't know each other. This was all still new. They all came back knowing each other. And now they're building together, now they're leaning on each other, they're active on Twitter. They've started hanging out in real life. Those are things that you can't put a value on."

Oddly enough, Shepherd's big caravan trip to SXSW preceded another big Austin-Vegas connection by just a few months: the launch of the new SXSW V2V conference focused on startups and entrepreneurship, which held its inaugural four-day session at the Cosmopolitan hotel and casino in Las Vegas in August 2013.

"SXSW V2V is an extension and reimagining of SXSW's twenty-six-year-old Austin event with an emphasis on the creative spark that drives entrepreneurial innovation," the Texas-based organizing group said when announcing the new event. "The startup and venture capital space is of major interest to all the creative industries that are at the core of the SXSW family of events. Featuring four days of informative panels and workshops, inspirational speakers, intensive mentoring and coaching programs, networking events and receptions, pitch competitions, and startup showcases, SXSW V2V offers innovators and entrepreneurs across all creative industries a space to learn the skills, make the connections, and find the inspiration to take their ideas and talents to the next level. If you are involved in building an app, a service, a business, a brand, or a community, then this event is for you."

Shepherd is now working to help organize the event locally and has emerged as the leading SXSW evangelist in the city. Unlike the Austin event, V2V is considered more of a "vertically agnostic" conference, designed to appeal to creative professionals in a variety of different fields, not just apps and software, and aims to bring Vegas' artists, entrepreneurs, and tech experts together in one room.

And, of course, it provides an opportunity for the city's growing startup community to strut its stuff.

"We're going to have a large activation downtown to engage the community and show South By what's going on downtown," Shepherd told me before the inaugural V2V event. "And it's really just providing an outlet for people that maybe don't want to go to Austin or are more interested in different niches. So we're excited. We're cautiously optimistic that we will get maybe 1,200 attendees the first year and build up slowly and organically, much like what's happened with South By."

The Vegas tech community prides itself on being open to everyone, accepting of new projects, and always being on the lookout for that next big thing. Even for out-of-towners like Kyle Kelly, who moved to Las Vegas from New York City in early 2012 to take a job at Zappos, acceptance and place in his adopted home came surprisingly easy.

"It's about getting embedded into the community and making friends," he told me at Zappos' then-office space in Henderson. (That "jungle room" at Tony's apartment? His cube at the office is decorated in the exact same way.) "And I think that's what it really comes down to. You go to cookouts and pool parties and just hang out with the people you like to work with."

But the reality is that the core community that calls Vegas home is very, very small, especially when you just focus on those involved in the city's tech startup scene. Tony Hsieh is there, and he's a rock star, but the rest of the group is still pretty small-time, still working their way up and making names for themselves in this new tech economy. That's not necessarily a bad thing, just an example of where the Vegas community stands on the ladder of tech ecosystems right now. On the plus side, it's a very close-knit group, filled with we're-all-in-this-togetherness, group support, and what in another time might have been called e*sprit de corps*.

But sometimes that kind of tight-knit community can cause problems, becoming insular, cliquey, and closed off to outsiders. The same people end up having coffee every week with the same people, and at the same coffee shop, making it difficult for outsiders to break through. Or the same investors keep funding the same types of projects, trying to address the same types of problems, without considering outside projects or ideas. In that type of environment, pretty soon the innovation engine grinds to a halt as an inward-gazing community forgets to focus on its customers and becomes instead about maintaining the status quo and keeping "the community" in place.

In smaller cities like Las Vegas, this can be a real risk and a real problem. And, despite all of the positive vibe surrounding the Downtown Project, it is still occasionally an issue.

"The mentality can be 'we only want to work with people who are here,'" Kelly says, "and 'we only want to invite people to be speakers who are here,' and all that good stuff. And I would love to sort of get out of that, because New York can't do that. They want everyone from everywhere, even if you are just there for the weekend, to be a part of that. And I think it will eventually grow here."

The key to overcoming it, he says, is addressing that insularity early and often, and then taking steps to avoid it down the road. It can be a community killer. In Vegas, Kelly says, the community is moving past this small-town attitude, and everyone, from the Downtown Project, to the casinos, to the city establishment and so on down the line, has been "extremely, extremely supportive," turning out for events, supporting local companies, and putting up money for activities when needed. It's still just a work in progress.

"When we set up the first Vegas hack, we had ten sponsors for it," he says. "So we knew at that point that this was something that people were thirsting for. I was the MC for the event and I remember getting up there in front of the crowd and saying something like, 'Do you think Vegas needs more hackathons?' and people were like, 'Yeaaahh!' It just reassured me that we were doing the right thing for our very talented community. It's just like giving them the canvas to write on and letting them do their thing."

Kelly's goal going forward is to help spread the word about Vegas tech, both beyond the city limits and locally. "A lot of people still see Las Vegas as a place to travel or a place to live," he says, "but not too many talented developers or businesspeople know about it as a place where they can thrive career-wise."

But Las Vegas has always been about opportunities, dating all the way back to the city's founding as a railroad outpost in the middle of the desert. Today's Vegas is, in fact, a very big place. The kind of city where literally millions of people pass through every year, where its airport is among the busiest in the world, and where every visitor has an opinion. Love it or hate it, for good or bad, everyone knows Vegas.

And that's a huge advantage for the city's tech startups. It means there is a steady stream of new potential customers coming right to their doorstep.

"It's a small enough community where it can be tight-knit in many ways," explains Chad Ramos, cofounder of Tabeso, an event-scheduling and ticketing app, at his InNEVation office space, "but it's all about connections anyway, right? Vegas is a small enough town that if you know people that know people, and they know you're good people, it feels like it's a little easier to get things happening. Whereas in Silicon Valley and other places, it can be a lot harder. It really is all about who you know."

In Ramos' case, his company's app likely wouldn't even exist if it weren't for the founders' personal networks, which got them introductions to potential clients, helped with word-of-mouth advertising, and even lined up funding. All of the founders grew up in Las Vegas.

Still, small cities have their limitations. And, as is often the case, those limitations boil down to dollars and cents. In Vegas, the fact is that the people with the money (a.k.a. potential investors) are not the same people who know technology or are ready to invest in it. They know real estate. They know gaming. They know construction. They don't know software; they don't know Web services.

"You can get $100,000 if you want to build a strip club, because people know that," Ramos says. "But with tech, they have to go through this vetting process and it's almost antiquated doing it, because the people who have the money usually can look at the deal and go, 'Snap'—done. We don't have anyone here who can cut a check [for a tech company] in two weeks."

Still, as a lifelong resident, he's optimistic that the city's tech ecosystem can make a go of it long-term.

"Sure, if I had an investor in New York or in Silicon Valley saying, 'We love what you're doing, it's great, but we need you here,' yeah, I'd move," Ramos says. "I wouldn't hesitate. And there are not a lot companies that would say, 'No thanks, we're staying in Vegas.' But the nice thing about being in Vegas is that it's not an expensive place to live. It's not an expensive place to do business. And there are millions of people who come to our town every month to spend money. There are plenty of worse places to be in business."

5

Austin

"My mission is [to help] make Austin a better Silicon Valley. . . . We don't aim to be better than Silicon Valley. We aim to be a better Silicon Valley. And by the phrase 'Silicon Valley' I'm referring to the bloodthirsty, take-no-prisoners, swing-for-the-bleachers, free enterprise, venture capitalism that I enjoyed during the seventies, and eighties, and nineties and prospered under."

—Dr. Robert Metcalfe, professor of innovation at the University of Texas at Austin, founder of 3Com, and co-inventor of Ethernet, at the UT McCombs School of Business Masters in Technology Commercialization Program commencement, May 2013

IT ALL STARTED WITH THE DEAN.

Before Dr. George Kozmetsky became the dean of what is now the McCombs School of Business at the University of Texas at Austin (UT), he was a technology entrepreneur, cofounding global conglomerate Teledyne with Harry Singleton in 1960 and the IC² Institute think tank in the late seventies. He later served as a mentor to both Michael Dell and National Instruments founder Dr. James Truchard. Former president Bill Clinton awarded Kozmetsky the National Medal of Technology in 1993.

But back home in Austin, Texas, he is probably best remembered for his unique weekly schedule.

For years, Dr. Kozmetsky held office hours for his students every Friday morning at 5:00 a.m., when the print edition of the *Wall Street Journal* was delivered. During those sessions, Kozmetsky would go over the business news of the day with his students, sharing with them his thoughts on the economy at large, as well as career advice, business strategies, and any other topics that came up in the hour-long discussions. For the students, it was a can't-miss appointment.

"I had the good fortune of having Dr. Kozmetsky as an MBA professor at UT, so he was kind of the guy who seeded the whole venture capital and technology idea into my head," remembers Austin-based venture capitalist Rudy Garza. "And it was pretty humbling, you know? He had built this $60-billion company and he would let any student come meet with him. You could just go. Any of his class students, any MBA student, could go and visit with him and talk about any topic. I was just fascinated. So I took advantage of that and became a regular participant in those regular 5:00 a.m. Friday meetings."

Garza is far from alone in this experience. Kozmetsky is something of a local legend in Austin, a name that comes up in conversation with entrepreneurs and business leaders all over town, especially if they've been working in the area for more than a few years.

Take John Harkey Jr., the CEO of Houston-based Consolidated Restaurant Companies Operations and an '83 UT graduate, for example. In a 2013 profile in the McCombs School alumni magazine, *McCombs Today*, Harkey mentioned the role that Dr. Kozmetsky had played in his own business education. "He would say, 'Meet me at five in the morning,'" Harkey told the magazine. "So, I would be up at 5:00 a.m. banging on the dean's office window [to be let in]. He was just a great visionary; he really kicked off the beginning of the preeminence of the UT business school."

Jason Seats, the current director of TechStars' Austin accelerator program, calls Kozmetsky "the guy who pushed the rock down the hill" to get the Austin technology community up to critical mass. Many of the young students and campus leaders he mentored back in his UT days are still in town, Seats tells me, working on startups, investing in new technologies, and leading many of the tech companies in the area. They are the city's founding generation of entrepreneurs and tech investors.

When I met with Seats at the TechStars Austin office in Downtown Austin, he shared a story with me about a man he had met shortly after arriving in the city in mid-2013. He was a "crumpled-up old man" that Seats ended up sitting next to at a Chamber of Commerce dinner. Not surprisingly, this old-timer was right there with Dr. Kozmetsky in those early days, too, stopping by the office in the predawn hours along with a long line of students and well-wishers every Friday morning, all coming to get business advice from the "oracle of Austin." Everyone from timid undergrads to the governor of Texas made their way through that office during his tenure at the McCombs School, which extended from 1966 through 1982.

Dr. Kozmetsky died in 2003, but his impact on the Austin-area tech ecosystem remains as vital as ever. At his memorial service, UT president Larry Faulkner called Kozmetsky an "innovative pioneer," citing his vision and creativity when it came to both business matters and education. "He was the father of Austin's entrepreneurial spirit and a prominent presence in the business community worldwide," Faulkner said. "His accomplishments reflected brightly on this city and helped to place Austin's name on the global register. Whenever I travel throughout the nation and overseas, I discover that business leaders are keenly aware of George Kozmetsky and what he has achieved here.

In fact, many speak to me with reverence about what George had done for them personally."

Chances are he would not be surprised at all by what the Austin-area technology scene has become.

Not to put too fine of a point on it, but Austin is perhaps the most active and most successful small city for tech entrepreneurship in the country.

According to a 2013 report compiled by Praxis Strategy Group, the Austin–Round Rock–San Marcos, Texas, metro area has generated more jobs in technology fields than any other region in the county since 2001, including the Bay Area. Tech employment in Austin was up 41 percent in that time, and the number of local workers in STEM fields (science, technology, engineering, and math) is up 17 percent. Austin also ranked first in the country in all of these same areas between 2010 and 2013.

The capital city of Texas also tends to do well in terms of both venture capital investment and angel funding, ranking in the top ten nationally in both and generally outperforming similarly sized smaller markets. The city's population was about 842,000 as of 2012.

None of this is an accident, says Julie Huls, president of the Austin Technology Council, explaining that the technology sector currently supports about 26 percent of the jobs in Austin, accounts for some 110,000 local workers, and contributes $21 billion in direct value to the regional economy annually. Tech employment in the area is expected to increase by 9 percent by 2017, adding about 9,000 new jobs, and one out of every five new tech jobs in Texas in that time is expected to be in Austin.

"I think we've been fortunate that we have a super-friendly business climate," Huls tells me in her office about fifteen minutes outside of Downtown Austin. "And obviously tech is enjoying that, but there are other industries that are enjoying that as well."

That pro-business reputation is spreading beyond Texas. Huls says she takes at least one phone call every week from people in New York and California who want to know more about doing business in the area because they're thinking about moving to Texas to start a company. That's in addition to the business owners who reach out to her when planning a corporate move to the state. Dell is headquartered in the nearby suburb of Round Rock, and organic grocery chain Whole Foods was founded in the city in 1980 and maintains its headquarters and flagship store on Sixth Street downtown.

"I think that everyone outside of Austin understands that Austin is different," Huls says. "So we have a lot of people coming in. And then we have a lot of executives that have been here for fifteen or twenty years and have had a series of companies and successes, and they just like living in Austin so they've stayed around."

Certainly, more than a little of this has to do with the city's reputation as an affordable, easygoing place to live and do business, as well as its standing as one of the great live music and entertainment cities in the US. Having the University of Texas in town, as well as the offices of Texas state government, certainly don't hurt, either. According to *Forbes*, Austin was the fastest-growing city in the US from 2010 through 2013, with a 2012 population growth rate of 2.8 percent and a total metro-area population of 1.8 million. More than 30,000 people moved to the city in 2012. Unemployment during that period was just 4.9 percent, compared to about 7.7 percent nationwide, and the job growth rate clocked in at 3.1 percent. The median salary in the area for college-educated workers is a solid $63,200.

Everybody wants to live in Austin; *Forbes* calls it "Austin envy." It's the best place to start a small business, according to the Business Journals newspaper chain; the most popular city for college graduates, according to the Brookings Institution; and was number one on Kiplinger's list of the nation's ten best cities for the next decade as of 2013.

"People are moving to Austin in record numbers," said Austin realtor Shannon Schmitz when the 2013 Forbes report was released. "Our current sales reflect the surge in demand. We're getting multiple offers for new home listings, on their first day on the market."

The city is riding the same wave of success that has made Texas America's fastest-growing state. Some 106,000 people moved to Texas from other states in 2012, according to the US Census Bureau, and since 2000, 1 million more people have moved to the state than have left it. Most pointedly for our purposes here, more than 4 million people have moved directly from California to Texas over the last twenty years. And, from a purely economic perspective, it's easy to see why. The state's economy has been on a tear for the better part of a decade, despite the 2008 recession that still lingers in many parts of the country. It's not a problem in Texas, though. Since August 2012, Texas employers have added more than 274,000 new jobs, according to the Texas Public Policy Foundation (TPPF), outpacing the next best-performing state, California, by some 51,000 jobs and accounting for a whopping 13 percent of all new jobs added nationwide in that time period. The state's 6.4 percent unemployment rate in 2013 was well below the national average of 7.3 percent, and that's despite a 1.4 percent increase in the workforce over the twelve months studied in the report.

And here's the kicker: According to the TPPF report, there are now 661,000 more Texans working than there were before the recession started, due in large part to the state's massive job growth over the last five-plus years. Nationally, 1.9 million fewer Americans are working today than there were at the end of 2007. So that's Texas as of today.

Austin's entrepreneurs, of course, know all of this perfectly well; it's why they're in the state in the first place and it's why they're working in Austin in particular. They know it's a nice place to live. They know it's a good place to start a business. They know it's a great place to raise a family. And they don't (necessarily) want the rest of the world to move to town and ruin it for them. But, on a more direct level, all this civic pride has been spilling over to the business community, helping startups with recruitment, luring more established companies to town, and in general just making life easier for entrepreneurs.

"A huge part of why people love Austin has everything to do with our creative scene—mostly music, because everybody knows Austin is about live music," Huls says. "So we're starting to work with other music organizations now to just make sure everybody knows how important it is to protect that affordability factor. The creatives really are fueling the rest of us."

It doesn't come cheap, however. Sure, Austin boasts a fairly low cost of living, at least when compared to the Bay Area and other coastal cities, but it's far from a low-cost place to be. According to *Forbes*, the city's cost of living is 8.9 percent above the national average and the median housing cost is just over $204,000. And, when compared to the rest of Texas, Austin looks downright pricey. According to FindTheBest.org, the cost of living in the Austin–Round Rock area is 14 percent higher than the rest of the state. When narrowed down to simply the cost of housing, Austin is easily the most expensive place in Texas to buy a home, 48 percent higher than the statewide average.

Chances are, this situation is about to get a lot worse.

Affordability is a difficult thing to maintain, because as a city becomes more desirable, out-of-towners start moving in and driving up demand for housing and services. Prices soon follow. But at this point, Texas is still a far cheaper place to live and work than many parts of California, and that, coupled with the area's quality of life reputation, make it an easy place to recruit technical talent and retain them.

What's more, GoBankingRates.com ranked Austin at number four on its list of US cities that combine high salaries with lower costs of living—calling it one of the most "cost-effective" cities to live. (New York City is the opposite, by the way, with pay that averages $6 more per hour than national rates, but living costs that are a whopping 216 percent higher than average.)

Still, Austin's place on the cost-income ratio compares favorably to many other parts of the country, especially the big metro areas where most tech jobs are located.

"Austin has, I think, a lot of really nice solid assets that we can build on," Huls explains. "The university has been great, and it's not just UT. We have actually within the span of maybe 100 miles several awesome universities and colleges that our companies can choose from for talent, or choose to commercialize technologies from.

"And I think people read the headlines and have a tendency to think that we've got it all figured out. And we probably aren't there yet. But there is a growing awareness, not just through tech but through traditional business and public leadership, that we do have a lot of model components here in Austin. Or if not that, then maybe we have sort of a formula for success in the new information economy."

Serial entrepreneur Josh Kerr certainly thinks so, and he credits the city's general help-me-and-I'll-help-you vibe with helping get his career off the ground. When he first moved back to the city from New York, after having graduated from UT and moving away for a number of years, he was working on a new startup and decided that he needed help getting it to the meaningful exit stage. He asked around town, got connected with the folks at the UT-backed Austin Technology Incubator, and eventually found a local CEO to advise him on business development matters. Fast-forward a few years and Kerr has since built multiple companies, had his share of solid exits, and now mentors other founders in the city via the Capital Factory accelerator and TechStars.

That's just part of the life of an entrepreneur in Austin, he says.

"The community here is really unique in that it is very open. It's accessible. Like I could call the CEO of a company that in New York or the Bay Area would never give me the time of day, but here will not only meet with me but actually look at my sales deck and give me feedback. And that's pretty amazing."

This attitude has remained intact even as the city has grown in recent years. The ecosystem has created a number of famous and very wealthy and successful businesspeople in the last few years, Kerr says. There have been five tech IPOs in the last five years, including enterprise IT software firm SolarWinds in 2009, nonprofit fund-raising software developer Convio in 2010, online vacation rental marketplace HomeAway in 2011, shopping data network Bazaarvoice in 2012, and coupon code aggregator Retail-MeNot in 2013. The key factor for the Austin ecosystem is that all of these entrepreneurs (and many of their employees) have emerged from these companies and others with the attitude that they want to give back to the community that helped them get to where they are. This can take the form of angel investments, board participation, or even just basic mentoring.

"I'm pretty sure that there are other cities like that," Kerr says, "but Austin is really very much about the community. It's very easy to get involved. The bar to get in is very low; it's really just about showing up. And that's pretty cool."

Attitudes in the city are changing, too. For a long time, and for a lot of founders, just making a run at an idea and keeping it afloat for a while was really the dream. In a city like Austin, where it doesn't take a seven-figure payday to make a good life for yourself, it can be easy to fall into the "good enough" category and not shoot for the stars. As far as Kerr is concerned, that's just fine if that's what the entrepreneurs want. If it's just about making enough to go on vacations, send their kids to a great college, be able to afford great health care for their family, and just do the things that they want to do, there's nothing wrong with that at all. That attitude has become a major part of the Austin ecosystem and a big reason why entrepreneurs like the city's less-intense feel so much.

But a growing ecosystem like Austin's also needs to have a few of those big-time, "winning the lottery" kinds of exits—think Instagram, think Tumblr, think Twitter—to really maintain its trajectory, according to Kerr. It's not just about inspiring future entrepreneurs (the "you can do this, too" approach). It's not just about attracting new blood in the form of new talent and new founders. It really has a lot to do with having enough money to keep the scene up and running and growing.

The Austin ecosystem, Kerr says, has finally gotten to that point.

"So what's really cool about winning the lottery is you can invest it back. And we're seeing a lot of that here now. Like employees from Bazaarvoice have all gone and started new companies. And it's the same for HomeAway employees. And they're not just investing money in startups, but they're creating jobs. It's really cool. I just did a round for my current startup, Written.com, and I raised a lot of it from Austin. I mean, I only had one VC from California; the rest were Austin VCs and then all angels from Austin. And a lot of them were people that had made money from an IPO here in the last few years. So that was really cool."

Ask most people what they know about Austin and it generally boils down to three or four things: the University of Texas, the Texas state capital, the Austin City Limits Music Festival, and the weeklong South by Southwest music/film/interactive conference (SXSW).

But to the locals, the city is about a lot more than that. To find out more about the local community, I sit down with Damon Clinkscales, a software developer and community manager who is perhaps best known around town as the organizer of the Austin On Rails technology user group that he started nearly a decade ago. Clinkscales is notably soft-spoken, with shoulder-length gray hair, and I have to lean in to hear him over the din of the coffee shop.

"The thing is, almost everyone here has some kind of side project," he says. "It's just, you know, that Austin is about life balance. So there are plenty of hobbyists, like there are people who do music, and people who do tech. So it's like, yeah, you've got a job or something so you can pay your bills, maybe you're a consultant or maybe you'll have a job, but on the side maybe you're trying to get something going.

"We've got all the kinds of things you find at South by Southwest; Austin has all those all the time. It's just that South by Southwest takes everything to eleven for a few weeks."

There is no shortage of ideas floating around town, he says, and plenty of fledgling entrepreneurs looking for technical cofounders to make their dreams a reality (in addition to Austin on Rails, Clinkscales is also the Austin organizer for FounderDating, a networking event series that brings technical and nontechnical entrepreneurs together). Bootstrapping is not uncommon.

"In terms of the meetup scene, it has really kind of exploded in the last year or two," Clinkscales explains, "to where now if you're planning a new meetup you have to check various calendars to see who you're going to be stepping on. Tuesday nights have been popular in the tech community in Austin for a long time, but now it's really like whatever night it is."

The 2009 founding of the seed-stage mentoring program Capital Factory has helped a lot with this, giving entrepreneurs and other interested parties a central place to gather and meet in the downtown core. Beyond that, however, meetups still happen in bars and restaurants across the city, wherever organizers can find enough space for their events.

In terms of Austin-area events, however, the conversation has to begin with South by Southwest (SXSW) Interactive, the massive multi-industry conference that transforms Downtown Austin into the center of the tech and entertainment world for ten days every March.

"I talk to people all the time about Austin who tell me, 'Ooh, I've only been there during March,'" says Chris Valentine, the producer of the South by Southwest Startup Village, the conference's accelerator program, when I met him at SXSW's sleek, modern office space near the Colorado River. "And I'm like, 'Oh no, we have a vibrant economy and we're growing a lot as a city.' It's just different. But I never want to take away the importance of Austin, Texas, and what the community brings to the bigger picture of what we're trying to do [with SXSW Interactive]. This city is a big part of the reason people do come to South by Southwest."

The interactive part of the conference has actually been around for much longer than many people think—it celebrated its twenty-first year in 2014—and has grown into a showcase event for just about every niche in the technology sector, from hardware, to software, to Web design, to health IT. More often than not, before new technologies hit the mainstream they make their debut in Austin at SXSW Interactive. Examples include the CD-ROM, Twitter, FourSquare, 3-D printing, and even Siri, which was later acquired by Apple and incorporated into their mobile devices.

And it's big. What began with just over 1,000 attendees in the mid-nineties has ballooned into a massive technology industry event, with more than 30,000 registered participants in 2013. That year, there were more than 1,000 conference sessions featuring some 1,800 conference speakers. And that's just the interactive portion of the conference.

The film conference brought more than 16,000 industry participants to town, while the music event attracted some 2,200 US and international acts. Even SXSWedu, a conference that brings together teachers, professors, and policy leaders from the education industry, attracted more than 4,200 people in 2013.

It's a major annual event for the city of Austin, as well. In 2012, SXSW claimed to have been responsible for a $190 million boost to the local economy, thanks in part to the 56,735 hotel rooms that attendees booked at more than seventy "official" hotels, and the fact that Austin's music venues reported a 45 percent boost in revenues during the conference. The media valuation of the attention that SXSW (including the music, film, and interactive portions) brings to the city was worth almost $34 million, according to conference organizers.

For startups, all this activity and all these people crammed into Downtown Austin's bars, restaurants, and event spaces means that it can be easy to get lost in the shuffle, so founders often get creative. Startups have tried everything from running shuttle services to and from the airport, handing out free food to attendees, renting out temporary storefront spaces near the convention center, slapping their brand on pedicabs, and, of course, throwing massive parties every night in order to get their names out there.

It makes for some entertaining media coverage and never fails to delight attendees, but it can turn into a big-money game for founders; those that can afford to pull out all the stops can make waves, while those that don't have such deep pockets are out of luck. In an effort to level this playing field, SXSW Interactive has over the last several years launched a series of startup-focused events, including an accelerator pitch program, a Startup Village expo, and startup-minded events associated with the music, film, and education conferences.

In addition to the Startup Village, Valentine produces SXSW Accelerator, which serves as a platform for early-stage companies to get up in front of big-name industry experts—Tim Draper, Craig Newmark, and Tim O'Reilly have all served as judges in past years—and pitch their products. The idea is to put early-stage founders in front of an audience and get some Q&A going in hopes of helping them iron out their ideas and develop their pitches.

"It's almost like the *Shark Tank* model," Valentine says, "but obviously not as intense."

To date, more than 600 companies have gone through the program and Valentine says that more than 50 percent of them have since secured funding, totaling about $600 million. Startup Village, which takes up an entire floor of the Hilton Hotel in Downtown Austin for the duration of the conference, grew out of this success, as did the startup components that now exist as part of the Music, Film, EDU, and ECO conferences. All of this led to the creation of V2V, an entire event based around startups and entrepreneurship, that was launched in 2013 in Las Vegas.

"The main point of what we do in this business is connections," explains Christine Auten, who produces the V2V program. "It's education, inspiration, and connections, but those connections always kind of rise to the top. And when people come to these events, especially South By, they come out of it with five or six more connections than they had before. And these connections could mean business, it could mean funding, it could mean future inspiration, it could mean partners, it could mean cofounders, it could mean anything."

The key for South by Southwest as a startup-friendly event, she says, is making sure the conference touches on enough topics and enough subjects to bring different and diverse people together in the same room and get them talking.

"What's kind of cool about it is how you can have, you know, a tech developer sitting next to a health-care provider who's looking for a certain solution," she says. "And these two can get together. That mash of different industries and different ideas that are kind of forced together during this 'spring break' week makes them sort of think outside of the ways that they would normally think and meet people that they wouldn't normally meet. And if we can, you know, sort of spur that along, it's really cool to watch."

The thrust behind all of SXSW's various startup events, everyone in the room agrees, is that it's all about who you meet and who you connect with. That's the whole point of any startup ecosystem. You have the incubators, you have the mixers, you have the meetups, you have the crawls, but all that really matters is who you come out knowing and working with. That's something that SXSW has been working hard to focus on, making sure that their entrepreneur attendees are getting what they came for when they make the trip to Austin.

Interestingly, it has taken some work to get the Austin tech community itself on board with all of this. When I mention to Valentine that, doing the research for this book, a number of Austin-based entrepreneurs suggested avoiding the city entirely during South by Southwest because it would be impossible during that time to get a real sense for what Austin tech is all about, he nods knowingly.

"So, you know, I see this as a global event but with the understanding that our roots are still in Austin, Texas," he says. The fact is, the South by Southwest organizers have had to make a concerted effort to reach out to the local startup community over the twenty-plus years of the Interactive event, trying to take care of their neighbors at the same time they were taking care of the global growth of SXSW. The local ecosystem was for a long time just too small to take advantage.

"It's interesting," says Hugh Forrest, who has been the director of SXSW Interactive since the very beginning, "that with our growth within startups as well as our general growth, in a fashion we became more popular with people outside the city first and then it grew a little more internally.

"I remember when we were much younger and trying to establish more of an audience or a following in Austin and we always felt that it was difficult. It was difficult with anything beyond the very small tech scene at the time, and I think a lot of our growth came from, you know, this crowd of folks in San Francisco kind of came in, discovered us, quote unquote, and then pushed the agenda. What's interesting is this was not a top-down agenda, meaning there weren't city leaders saying, 'There's a startup scene here now; you guys should cover it more.' It was more like, 'Well, maybe this will work and will stick.'"

Times have changed, of course, and now local entrepreneurs are more apt to get involved with SXSW, recognizing the event as a chance to show off their work for the whole industry. For a week, it's like the technology world comes to them. And city leaders are very much on board now as well, Forrest says. His office these days works closely with the Austin Chamber of Commerce and a variety of government agencies, all of which are more geared to what he calls the "startup economy" than they were even just a few years ago.

"Four or five years ago I would have thought, this is crazy, they never would have paid attention to these people," he laughs. "And now everyone's trying to court this thing."

For entrepreneurs, the appeal is obvious.

"It's a time when everyone can kind of come together and just be a part of a larger conversation," Clinkscales says of SXSW. "It's really hard to miss. When it comes it kind of takes over everyone's mind-set there for a couple of weeks . . . It's a very active time for all of us."

As far as the Austin tech community is concerned, it's impossible to overlook the role that Capital Factory plays in the ecosystem. Part incubator, part coworking space, part startup education center, the facility bills itself as "Austin's entrepreneurial center of gravity," 50,000 square feet of work space spread over two floors in an office tower adjacent to the Omni Hotel downtown. "Take classes, find cofounders, rent desks, or apply for funding and mentorship"—the sales pitch is pretty straightforward.

"Austin's at a very unique place right now," Capital Factory cofounder and serial entrepreneur Josh Baer tells me over lunch at the facility's cafeteria/bar space some sixteen floors above Brazos Street. "There are lots of up-and-coming startup cities, but

Austin, of all the ones I've visited, really seems to be in a unique spot. It's got a lot of energy behind it; it's just big enough to matter and small enough to actually be cohesive and be able to get your arms around it. You know, in Silicon Valley a place like this wouldn't be that special. There's a bunch of them. And you can't create a center of gravity in Silicon Valley; it's the whole thing, it's everything. But here we can. And when we do it's significant, it's impressive."

The whole idea behind Capital Factory is density, Baer explains. How many interesting, like-minded people can he bring together and get them interacting, all living, and working in close proximity? Once that happens, all sorts of good things often come out of it.

"That's what causes [journalists like] you to come here, and every week we have different press people coming through wanting to see what's happening," he says. "Every government official that comes through town wants to come here, all the way up to President Obama and down to senators, congressmen, and representatives from other countries. Any kind of investor group or strategic partner, too. So big companies that come through Austin, they come and they say, 'Hey, show us the startups.' You know? GM shows up and they go, 'Hey, show us startups doing stuff with auto.' Samsung comes by [saying], 'Show us people doing stuff with mobile and other technologies we can use.' And so that density truly creates a synergy. It makes it better for founders to be here than to be on their own."

The Capital Factory program started out in 2008 as a standard three-month accelerator boot camp, similar to TechStars, Y Combinator, or any of the others. What Baer and his cofounders discovered, however, is that most of the time over those three months was spent on fund-raising and getting that initial boost going. They wanted to develop more long-term relationships with these companies, helping them more with growing their businesses and tackling all of the issues that come after an entrepreneur raises their seed round. As a result, Capital Factory now operates more like an index fund of the Austin startup scene, bringing all of the major players together in one place and finding them all the resources they need to succeed. When I visited, there were about 500 affiliated members and 200 different companies at work in the Capital Factory space.

"Any great Austin startup," Baer says of his long-term ambition for the place, "I want all of them. Every single one of them. I want them touching this community in some way."

On the flipside, DreamIt Ventures, an incubator program based in Philadelphia that recently expanded to Austin (among other cities), runs a more traditional three-month program that's designed less to nurture homegrown talent than it is to bring new entrepreneurs into the system.

"So whereas Josh's model at Capital Factory is very much all about Austin born and bred, we actually draw companies from around the world to specific ecosystems, to, like, immerse them in all this stuff," explains Kerry Rupp, DreamIt CEO, over coffee near the Texas state capital building. "It's not our mission or goal necessarily to have them end up in Austin. While we'd love to have them nearby and we'd love to have alumni around, it's not part of our mission."

It sounds a little self-defeating for the Austin ecosystem overall—bringing entrepreneurs to town for a few months, supporting them while they're there, and then watching them scatter to the wind once their time is up—but in fact this model has proven popular in Texas and elsewhere because, Rupp explains, it brings "fresh blood" into the scene. Every time DreamIt launches a new class of companies it's bringing new talent into town from elsewhere, along with new ideas, new skills, and new ways of doing things.

"There is a lot of exciting and good stuff happening here [in Austin]," she says, "but it is also a small enough city where everyone knows all of the startups. So if you are an investor looking for unique new opportunities, [the DreamIt program means] there are new people coming to Austin for you to meet. It's new talent and skills with a different perspective. So when they come into the ecosystem, they're meeting with other startups and sharing experiences: 'Hey, I've lived in San Francisco for the last six years; this is what I learned there.' It's actually nice to have new thought and people injected into the system."

It's a different approach, but Rupp says it has proven particularly effective in Austin, where the community is already so collaborative. If she sees a new company that, though promising, doesn't necessarily fit the DreamIt model but might work for Capital Factory, TechStars Austin, the Austin Technology Incubator, Tech Ranch, or one of the other local incubators, she's quick to pass them along to the others, and vice versa.

"It's a really cooperative kind of ecosystem," she says, "because we all know that there are lots of Venn diagrams, and they come together a little bit, but no one's spot is on top of the other person. And at the end of the day the idea here is we're all trying to help the entrepreneurs be successful. We want to have different kinds of tools that are available for companies at different stages."

As if in a deliberate effort to put this ethos into practice, the office of the TechStars Austin branch (which was launched in 2013) is literally located in the Capital Factory space, right downstairs from its maybe-competitor. It hasn't been a problem, though, says Jason Seats, the managing director of the Austin-based program, because the work is about more than just each individual program and each group of investors. They're really all just trying to develop the local ecosystem, and the preconceived notions that many people have about Texas in general.

"Probably the biggest negative to being here is that people who haven't experienced Texas or Austin have a perception that we have to rewrite," Seats says. "This is not Dallas. Sometimes Texas doesn't do itself any favors. So Austinites will think, 'Well, it's a good thing we have this little island of saneness in the middle of this insane state.' Which is equally as wrong. Like, if you go and spend time in West Texas, there's cool stuff there. There are totally normal people there. This is not like an outpost in the Wild West. There's not a fortress wall around the city."

In terms of the startup ecosystem, however, the fact is Austin is still building things out. It needs "more rungs on the ladder," according to Seats.

"I think in my opinion the thing that's most important, the biggest ingredient that's necessary for ecosystem development, is role modeling," he says. "[There are] other things like mentoring and whatever else, but the way I see it is you have to demystify what it takes to do this."

San Antonio, Texas—an hour south of Austin—is a good example of this, he explains. When San Antonio–based Rackspace went public in 2008, it minted a billionaire and a couple hundred new millionaires. "And those guys will sit down with anybody," Seats says. But the problem is that the gap between the experience of those Rackspace veterans and that of brand-new startup founders, maybe three guys just out of college who are starting something, is just too wide. They can't relate to each other. The three guys starting something need to talk with three guys who started something last year. And the three guys who started something last year need to talk with three guys who just finished raising a Series A funding round.

"It's not about inspiring people," Seats explains; "it's about making it accessible. I mean inspiring someone is good to do once in a while, but a much better feeling is to see someone's IPO and go, 'I know that fucker and he is not that smart. I mean, if he can do it, anybody can do it.' That's much healthier, that invites people to participate. And it's really hard to jump-start that when you have just pockets of success."

That's where Austin is at the moment, he says. The ecosystem has all of the rungs on the ladder filled—it has massive success stories like Dell, recent IPOs like Bazaarvoice and RetailMeNot, established startups like RealMassive, and plenty of early- and mid-stage companies—but it doesn't have much depth at each of those stages yet. It's very active, and deals are happening frequently, but, as Seats explains it, given the various companies and successful entrepreneurs that he knows in the city, he would be hard-pressed to go out and find too many more. There aren't many hidden success stories in Austin. Once you start meeting the Austin tech community, it's not long before you know everyone. And that means there is still room to grow.

"One thing's for sure," he says. "I don't feel like Austin's crested yet. I still feel the upswing right now. I'm nervous about market cycles because I just haven't seen one here yet. The dot-com bust really hit Austin hard. Really hard. And that really changed the mind-set locally around startups and tech. The reputation that Austinites, especially long-timers, like to portray about this being a bootstrap city, that's where it comes from. Because those are the people that were like, 'You know what, I'm not going to go anywhere. I'm just going to go find something that I can do that makes money.' It's like having a Depression-era grandparent. That 'generation' of people here are so cash conscious because of that moment in time in Austin. But it's a very stable foundation."

In terms of filling out the rungs of the Austin ecosystem, the twenty-five-year-old Austin Technology Incubator (ATI) has been stepping in to help later-stage startups find working capital since the 1990s. Not a venture capital fund, ATI is a UT-backed organization and its staff reports up to the university's vice president for research (the office is in fact part of the IC^2 Institute that was founded by Dr. Kozmetsky). The group's tagline: "We get you funded."

"The value proposition with ATI has evolved over the years as Austin has evolved," explains Isaac Barchas, ATI director, at the group's offices in a UT research park on the north side of town. "At the beginning it was really about business infrastructure, and now it's almost exclusively focused on helping companies compete in the capital markets."

Startups generally find their way to ATI—the incubator was working with about forty-five companies as of the end of 2013 in industries ranging from software, silicon, and wireless tele-communications, to energy, clean technologies, and health care—focused life sciences—when they are what Barchas calls "between stages." They've exhausted all of their very early-stage funding options, whether it's personal savings or friends and family loans, and need to get serious about raising some outside capital if they hope to scale their idea. ATI helps them do that. And by doing so, they help very early-stage companies get some foundation under them to move up the ladder.

"You know, there are sort of three narratives on how Austin became Austin," Barchas says. "One of them is the sort of public-private partnership narrative with MCC [Microelectronics and Computer Technology Corporation] and all that. The other is the Austin Ventures narrative. They've deployed $1.8 billion dollars in central Texas companies over the past twenty years. The third is sort of the South by Southwest narrative. It's a cool place to live, and people who are good at building stuff want to live here. I grew up in Palo Alto in the 1970s and 1980s and Austin right now feels a lot like Palo Alto then, before everybody got rich. It's got a lot of the same things—big university presence, it's an attractive place to live, people want to move here, it's a tolerant place."

Of course, there is also the whole countercultural artistic side of things that, in the Bay Area, resulted in the 1967 Summer of Love and everything that grew out of that.

"And all that was pretty big here, too," Barchas says of Austin, "where you had Wild Willie and that whole line."

Counterculture or not, though, the smart money has been finding its way to Austin for years. In fact, according to the Austin Chamber of Commerce, the area drew some $621 million in venture capital investment in 2012, with software and semiconductor companies pulling in 43 percent of that total.

Austin Ventures (AV), for instance, has been a dominant player in the local market for more than thirty years, having raised nearly $4 billion in its history and funding more than 250 Texas companies, including the now-public HomeAway, Bazaarvoice, and RetailMeNot, as well as software development shop Spiceworks, Mass Relevance, Map My Fitness, and CompUSA. In 2008, the firm launched a $900-million fund dubbed "Austin Ventures X" with a focus on emerging startups.

But AV is far from the only game in town anymore. LiveOak Venture Partners recently launched an early-stage fund, as did Mercury Fund and Silverton Partners. S3 Ventures is an earlier-stage Austin-based fund. The Central Texas Angel Network (CTAN), headquartered about twenty minutes west of Austin in the Hill Country suburb of Bee Cave and established in 2006, is one of the most active angel groups in the country, investing some $8 million in 2012 via about 100 members. Overall, the Angel Resource Institute, Silicon Valley Bank, and CB Insights ranked the Texas angel community fourth nationally in terms of investment dollars in their 2013 quarterly Halo Report.

Rudy Garza with G-51 Capital Management has been in venture capital in Austin since the mid-nineties, focusing his small fund on emerging deals and companies in Texas and beyond. Interestingly, his firm employs a small army of MBA students as deal-screening interns, allowing them to look at literally hundreds of deals every year.

"So after I got my MBA I went out and raised some capital for our family business," Garza remembers about his early days as an Austin VC. "We ultimately sold the business and my parents retired, but I had gone through the whole process of developing a plan, marketing the plain, raising the capital, closing the capital, operating the business for two to three years, and then making the transition and exiting the business. I wanted to try it again."

So he started G-51 with $2.5 million of personal capital and started making investments based on his personal philosophy of looking at companies locally but finding investment partners nationally, making Austin a destination for out-of-town investors.

Early on, he found himself at a VC conference on the West Coast, where he recalls "a real nice guy from Hawaii" introducing him to a man who was, unbeknownst to Garza at the time, one of the biggest players in the venture capital industry.

"So I walked over and went, 'Hi, what's your name?' 'My name's John Doerr.' 'Well, hey, John, what do you do?'" Garza laughs. "Right? I mean, hayseed in the city."

Six months later, thanks in part to that awkward first meeting, Garza syndicated G-51's second-ever deal with Doerr's Silicon Valley–based firm, Kleiner Perkins Caufield & Byers. "All of the sudden it helped put us on the map, so to speak, and then that kind of kept happening with Kleiner and NEA [New Enterprise Associates] and IVP [Institutional Venture Partners] and Bain Capital and all the big national firms. So we kind of felt like, you know, by that point we had a good knack for finding and investing in really high potential startups."

But it's been a long road for Austin since the early 2000s, he admits, adding that the local scene has changed "radically" over the last fifteen years, even more so in the last thirty-six months or so.

"So going way back, there were just a handful of players in town with sort of a dominant Austin Ventures presence," says Garza. "I think as the city started to develop and we started getting more funds coming into town more regularly, it began to broaden the market in terms of access. And then fast-forward to today, there's much more funding that's more accessible from a broader range of sources than it ever has been in the last seventeen years. So it's a really exciting time in our market here."

But not everyone is convinced that the city has all the pieces in place yet. Venture capitalist and former CTAN executive director Jeff Harbach told me that "the venture capital scene in Austin is active but it could be better. Certainly Austin Ventures is the dominant player and it sets the tone, but we don't have a Foundry Group–type of firm that's kind of just a catalyst in the ecosystem. And I think the world of Brad and Jason and those guys [with Foundry Group], so frankly that's what I want to create here. That type of fund."

In Harbach's view, Austin lacks a venture firm with a true open-door policy, a place that reaches out to entrepreneurs as a resource beyond just working capital. That's truly just there to help and is based around the "give before you get" philosophy. "We need to have more VCs with that mentality," he says.

"You know, I think maybe AV kind of sets the tone [in the Austin VC community]. But none of the AV guys are bad guys, they're good guys. I think they're just more internally focused. They're not bloggers; they're not guys who go out and put their face in front of the community like Brad Feld does. So it's more about personality, I think, than anything else. We haven't had a firm come here and just kind of go, 'Let's shake it up a bit.'"

Harbach expects the next ten years to be big for Austin, though. It takes time to build an ecosystem; it's a long-term game. "But it's happening." He nods. "It's happening slowly and surely. There's enough happening now that I think we're poised for big things. So I'm trying to solve the funding piece. But the funding piece means so much more than just bringing more capital to the table. Capital is a commodity. It's how you deliver that capital that really counts."

When Karen Bantuveris founded VolunteerSpot in 2009, she didn't have much of a background in Web development or Internet tech. She had spent her career up until that point as a management consultant. But, as a working mom, she knew there was a market for a basic, simple-to-use service that would allow volunteer-run organizations to schedule their work shifts and enable volunteers to manage their commitments online and via mobile. At the time, nothing like that existed.

"So VolunteerSpot is an online coordination tool," Bantuveris tells me over drinks at Lance Armstrong's bike shop on the west side of Downtown Austin. "It's mostly for busy moms who coordinate all the activity that happens in the community. So it's a very intelligent sign-up engine that makes it easy to sign up, schedule, and remind volunteers of their service. On its most basic level, it's Evite on steroids."

And it has hit on a serious need. Bantuveris tells me that the service grew almost organically to 3.5 million users in its first four years of existence, and it's still adding about 120,000 new users per week. It's an unseen market, she explains, that many people, investors included, don't think about or understand . . . unless they have school-age kids at home. "Then they're like, 'Ooooh,'" she says, laughing.

But VolunteerSpot is also a consumer app operating in what, according to all accounts, is generally an enterprise-focused town. Bantuveris says she "wasn't savvy enough to know that" when she launched the company.

"What I've often told people is that Austin is an incredibly networked town. I don't know that I could have started up anywhere else, because of how open people were about meeting with me. I mean, I got to meet with Brett Hurt when Bazaarvoice was still at 150 employees. And he would take a meeting with me, and have coffee with me, and talk about what I was doing. Or meet with the guys over at Mass Relevance, Sam Decker. So for us it was to have access to the kind of mentoring that I had. I'm not sure I'd have that access in the Bay Area, because it's just so big. People here really take the time."

The city also has the built-in advantage of South by Southwest, she says, which brings the entire tech world literally to their doorstep every spring. Bantuveris even met one of her backers, John Frankel with New York–based ff Venture Capital, when he came to town for SXSW a few years ago.

"I had met John by phone when we were doing our seed round and we were too early at the time," she says. "But later on he was coming to town for South By and so he called [and said], 'Can I get a meeting?' He just sets up and holds meetings all day long at the coffee shop at the Driskill [Hotel, on Sixth Street]. It was just so easy. The whole world comes to us. It's sort of like when people look at your Web site and they assume that you're much bigger than you might be. And it's the same thing with Austin. Because of South by Southwest we carry a much bigger footprint than a city of our size would necessarily have otherwise."

It's true; by city standards, Austin is fairly small. The greater metro area is home to nearly 2 million people as of the 2012 census, but the downtown core only includes 800,000 or so. Not a small town, but certainly not a massive city on the same scale as New York, Chicago, or Los Angeles. And that scale has played out in the city's tech ecosystem, according to Jason Cohen, the founder of WP Engine, a Wordpress plugin development shop based out of Capital Factory.

"Austin feels like a really small town and people know that," he says. "Someone who would jump around [between companies] every eight months [in the Bay Area], that wouldn't work here. There's some of that personal reputation thing at play, that you can't take a crap everywhere and have that not stick."

As a result, at least anecdotally, workers are less likely to jump ship in Austin than they would be in a larger city. According to Cohen, that makes for better workplaces, better salaries, and better lives from top to bottom because companies here have to be invested in their workers and their long-term success, since it probably won't be easy to replace them if they do leave. That means there are career paths in Austin companies; people want to grow without jumping ship. For entrepreneurs, Cohen says, it means that they are forced to think about their employees' careers, not just the bottom line, because they aren't going to be able to go out and fill seats with the next hot class of developers.

"Austin has this attitude that you can be whatever you want to be and there's support around that," he explains. "It's not just 'go big and go public,' though we have had plenty of tech IPOs. But you don't have to go that route. There's freelance work, there's full-time, there's in-between work. Whatever your interest is, whatever your goals, there's something here to feed it.

"The city itself is a variety of things. You have the largest university in the country, so that brings a diversity of human beings. There's stability from things like the government center here and large companies like Dell and IBM. Austin prides itself on the fact that there's variety here, and we want to support that. Not diversity for diversity's sake, but like, 'Hey, we're all going to try and do something here.' It's a full city attitude."

RideScout CEO Joseph Kopser agrees. He even moved to the city specifically with the intent of starting his company there after he retired from the army.

"Austin does a lot of things well," he says, "though there are a couple of things that Austin can still work on. What it does really well is this town is as all-inclusive as any community I've ever been in. It doesn't matter if you wear a three-piece suit or if you like to hang out in flip-flops and a T-shirt; everybody's welcome in Austin. It's a very collaborative environment. It probably has a lot to do with Willie Nelson, who came here back in the seventies and did a great job to unite the cowboys and the hippies together through his music and his lifestyle."

For Kopser, as a nontechnical founder, he has learned to appreciate this aspect of the Austin community in particular. After all, it's not every day that a former army officer turns up at Capital Factory with a consumer startup idea.

"I think that early on people were a little skeptical of me," he says. "You know, what's this forty-two-year-old entrepreneur dad with three daughters doing going to all of these pitch competitions and cofounder meetups? Often I was the oldest person in the room easily. And a lot of times I found myself pitching alongside people who were young enough to be [my] son or daughter. So that I think initially had people a little leery."

But over time, Kopser's vision for RideScout took hold and he found his place in the ecosystem—age and background be damned. Now, he says, he feels welcome wherever he goes in the city.

It's been a similar experience for Josh Alexander, another non-technical local founder, and his company, Toopher, an online authentication firm that controls access to a user's online accounts via their mobile device. No phone in your pocket, no logging into your company's private network. Alexander founded the company in 2013 with fellow UT alumnus Evan Grim, who developed the technology behind the Toopher product while working on his PhD in software engineering at the school.

"We love Austin," Alexander says. "We think Austin is an incredible town in which to be a growth-stage company. We've got access to great venture capitalists; we've got access to incredible talent that's coming out of the university. And then there's the cost of living here. I can say it definitely gets hotter here than it does in Palo Alto, but my house cost one-fifth of what it would cost if I lived in San Francisco. So, there's that. The ability to grow a company quickly with the right type of talent can actually be done very well in Austin."

Who would have thought it would have taken this long for me to bring up the city's famous motto: "Keep Austin weird"? It's impossible to miss when you're in the Sixth Street downtown entertainment district—on T-shirts, on hats, on shot glasses—but after spending a few days in the city, it's clear that "weird" is just one part of Austin's identity.

"Austin is a very well-positioned city no matter how you want to measure it," explains Capital Factory's Baer. "You know, low crime, best place for young people, best place for cost of living, best place for lifestyle, best place to raise a family. Whatever it is, we're going to be on that top ten list, and probably near the top of it. So that can make [the city] attractive to anybody.

"It sure helps that we're centrally located, we've got good weather, there's a nice music scene, it's a nice place to live, there's lots of space, there's a good cost of living. Just generally the city's doing well, and that makes it attractive for all kinds of things, including startups."

Dell deserves a lot of credit for driving tech in Austin, he says, despite its recent ups and downs (company founder Michael Dell had reacquired his firm in a private equity deal shortly before I arrived in Austin). But the company has long been a major force in the Texas ecosystem, creating wealth in and around the city, attracting technical workers to the area and spinning out a number of entrepreneurs. That's in addition to companies like Tivoli and Trilogy, two Austin-area software firms that brought a new generation of talent to town in the 1990s before going their separate ways. Tivoli had $50 million in revenue and 300 employees when IBM acquired it in 1996 (today, IBM employs more than 6,000 people in Austin), and Trilogy laid off more than a third of its workforce after the dot-com bust and lives on as a much smaller company.

Trilogy, in particular, however, was known for outrecruiting even the big Silicon Valley players in the mid-nineties (thanks to high-flying salaries, bonuses like sports cars and motorcycles, and even a company-wide trip to Hawaii), bringing smart, talented graduates from schools like Harvard, MIT, Stanford, and Carnegie Mellon to Austin for the first time. It literally imported bright tech minds from the East and West Coasts to seed the ecosystem. They got to Austin, worked hard, got some great work experience, and laid down roots. When the company imploded after 2001, that talent was released into the ecosystem, and many of those alumni are today leading startups in the area. Baer, for example, worked at Trilogy early in his career.

"It's not like California is a bad place to do a startup," he says. "It's arguably the best place. But if for some reason that's not right for you, there are a lot of benefits to being here."

For sure, the Bay Area is home to the best technical talent in the world, Baer says, but with that supply comes incredible demand, meaning that it can be hard for founders to get and hold onto that talent. In Austin, people are "less flighty." Startups in Texas don't see their top developers getting poached too often, at least not over small salary increases or better stock option deals.

"The reason I came back to Austin actually was not as much for entrepreneurial ambition, although I knew I was starting a company. It was a family decision," explains Brett Hurt, the founder and former CEO of Bazaarvoice, one of Austin's more recent tech success stories, which went public in 2012. "We decided that we wanted to go back to an area where my parents were, and [my in-laws] are just right down the road in San Antonio. It was a family decision, so I came back here with that kind of basic mantra."

Hurt, a UT grad, had spent his career up until that point in the Bay Area, where he founded Coremetrics, a Web analytics and marketing optimization firm that is now part of IBM. Once he got back to Texas, however, he was disappointed. The downtown core was nearly empty, office space was being offered up for next to nothing, and startup activity in the area was all but nonexistent. It was the dot-com hangover, and it hit the Austin market hard.

Now entrepreneurship is "very much in the water," he says. Incubators are taking off in the city (and not just in tech; Austin also has incubators focused on fashion manufacturing, culinary services, and even the "creative" sector, a market niche that reportedly employs nearly 50,000 people in and around Austin and contributes more than $4 billion to the local economy annually, according to a 2012 report commissioned by the city's economic development office), UT is taking an active role in the ecosystem, and the local VC community has never been so crowded. It is all still expanding, he says.

Take Bazaarvoice, for example. Since its IPO, former Bazaarvoice employees have gone on to create 15 new businesses, supporting about 100 local jobs so far. And that's in addition to the 800 or so Austin-area jobs that Bazaarvoice itself supports. It is the same thing with RetailMeNot, a four-year-old company that is already adding more than $330 million per year in value to the Austin economy and employing some 900 people.

"This is the capital cycle, right?" says Hurt. "You think big. You swing for the fences. You may build a big company and then people get the inspiration they need. They get the know-how they need because they were part of making it a success. They get the capital they need to think big. If you leave a company and you only have $5,000 in the bank, you're going to take another job immediately. If you leave a company and you've got half a million or a million in the bank, you can afford to think much bigger than you ever have before about what to do next."

It's impossible to overlook the role that Texas culture plays in the Austin startup scene as well. People in Texas are very transparent, Hurt says, and they're humble, surprisingly so for an ecosystem that has seen such growth and success in recent years. In the eyes of many Austin entrepreneurs I spoke with, the city is doing well but could be doing better. It has seen some success, but that could be fleeting. According to Hurt, this is par for the course for Texas.

"One of the things I disliked about Silicon Valley, and one of the reasons I moved back here besides wanting to start a family, was I really like the people here. It's not that I didn't like the people out there. I made some very close friends, people I still call very close friends today. But everybody in the Valley, not everybody but most people in the Valley, are so work obsessed that it's all they think about. I think it's the Maslow hierarchy thing. And I think it's partially because things are so expensive there, so people are just kind of in survival mode trying to afford shelter that's comfortable. But I really believe the more I travel internationally, the more I realize that people are just people. We all want the best things in life. Austin is this place where people are people."

And Hurt is bullish on the city long term as a tech hub and a growth economy, calling it, like others have, an incredible place to be for the next ten years.

"I actually think you can build a much better company here than in the Valley," he says. "I think people in the Valley would ask, 'How can you say that? Look at the billion-dollar companies we're building by comparison.' I would say, 'It's only because you have a hell of a lot more experiments going. More shots on goal.' I think we're building very enduring companies here [in Austin] with very strong souls that are focused on developing the whole person, not just the work person. It's really, really special."

CHAPTER

6

Kansas City

"What Kansas City's growing tech density demonstrates is that the metropolitan area had a strongly growing technology sector prior to recent milestones, such as the advent of the high-speed Internet service potential of Google Fiber."

—*Dane Stangler, former director of research and policy, Ewing Marion Kauffman Foundation*

KANSAS CITY IS A METRO AREA divided in two—one side in Kansas, one side in Missouri—with a small, two-lane residential street (conveniently named State Line Road) running north/ south along the state line. The neighborhoods in this area are vintage—dating to around the 1940s and '50s—and filled with small bungalows and ranch homes: compact two-bedroom kit houses on tree-lined streets complete with sidewalks, gravel alleyways, and the occasional picket fence. It honestly doesn't look like much at first glance—just a normal, suburban neighborhood; the kind of area where most people's grandparents likely live. But hidden in plain sight among the young families, the small-time hair salons, and the retired couples, the neighborhood is, in fact,

153

becoming home to one of the most surprising, effective, and thriving startup communities in the Midwest.

"So two vice presidents from Hallmark purchased this home with their own money," explains Brittain Kovac, pointing to a one-story gray-and-white bungalow with a covered front porch and small driveway on the west side of the street, the Kansas side. Kovac is the semi-official tour guide for the Kansas City Startup Village (KCSV), a loose collection of about twenty-five tech startups that are based out of this residential neighborhood a few miles southwest of Downtown Kansas City. "They don't live there; they have their own families, their own homes, but they purchased it to support the Village. There are four companies that work out of there and one person that lives there. The person that lives there is nineteen; he's from South Carolina."

Just up the block, on the far side of the street, there is a modest, white-and-maroon home that happens to be owned by Boulder, Colorado–based tech entrepreneur and venture capitalist Brad Feld, one of the cofounders of startup accelerator TechStars. He bought the place sight-unseen in 2012 as a way to support the Kansas City startup scene, and, at the time of my visit, was offering the house up free of charge to a startup called Handprint, a four-person team from Boston that was developing an easy way for Web users to arrange for 3-D printing jobs online.

"He has pretty good relations with the Kauffman Foundation," Kovac explains of Feld's involvement, "so I think that just through that trusted network he decided to show his support for the area and the Startup Village. He purchased this home before he ever saw it. He came by about a month later; he did a presentation at Kauffman and they swung him by here on the way to the airport."

Out-of-town VCs notwithstanding, the Kansas City Startup Village is an organic product of the local startup community, an entrepreneur-led, grassroots initiative to solidify the Kansas City ecosystem around a concentrated "neighborhood" of startups, most of which are operating out of what were once residential homes. EyeVerify, a mobile development company working on authentication systems via eye vein biometrics, is based in the area, as is Leap2, a search company looking to challenge Google's dominance of the search market. Hoopla.io is a local B2B event-discovery startup, while SportsPhotos.com is building an online repository of local sporting events photos alongside an e-commerce platform that allows photographers to sell prints of their work and other products. All of them call KCSV home.

It happened, as many things do, pretty much by accident. In late 2012, Kansas City–born entrepreneur Matthew Marcus moved back to the area from Colorado following the death of his mother, and suddenly found himself the owner of her former home on State Line Road. At the same time, a young, local Web designer named Ben Barreth had decided to cash in his 401(k) in order to buy a small house that he hoped to offer up free of charge to fledgling entrepreneurs as a way to kick-start the Kansas City startup scene. By pure coincidence, the house that Barreth purchased—these days known as the Homes for Hackers house—was located just four doors down from Marcus' mom's place. It didn't hurt that the neighborhood also turned out to be the first area in Kansas City to get Google's new ultra-high-speed Google Fiber broadband service in 2012.

Fast-forward a few months and, by the time I visited, the Kansas City Startup Village had ballooned to a handful of houses and commercial spaces on both sides of State Line Road near Forty-fifth Street. It's a busy and active place, full of happy hours and meetups and the free exchange of ideas between founders of all ages. The kind of neighborhood where, if a developer runs into a problem, they can just walk around the corner and get help from one of their peers. If a central hub of startup activity is what Kansas City's entrepreneurs needed, they certainly found one in KCSV.

"As far as the Village goes, it certainly helps attract the talent because there are so many cool people here and so much to learn," explains Hoopla.io cofounder Matthew Marcus in the company's office space on State Line Road (in the basement of what was once his mother's house). "You can say, 'Hey, I want to learn more about 3D printing,' and go to a house four blocks away. If I want to learn about biometrics or eye scanning, I can go to Eye Verify. I think that's cool."

The power of the Village ecosystem, he says, is that with all the knowledge-sharing going on, the area has become something like a brain trust of startup know-how. "All summed up, I think that just increases the chances of success for startups, which have a notoriously high failure rate," Marcus says. In his view, Kansas City founders can effectively lower that failure rate and increase their own chances of success by collaborating and putting their heads together.

"I mean, it's a fact," agrees cofounder Adam Arredondo. "You can't measure it, so who knows what the impact is, but it's a fact that you're more likely to succeed in an environment like this than working in your parents' basement. There are people around, like-minded people, that you can bounce ideas off of. It's just what we always call serendipitous collisions. You never know what conversation is going to lead to a connection or a customer that you just won't get if you're sitting by yourself or with your team in a basement somewhere. I mean, shit, we're still working in a basement, but still . . ."

For Arredondo and Marcus, the power of this community is very real. The Village has played a direct role in their success, they explain, by putting them in touch with both local and out-of-town clients, allowing them to grow both their B2B and consumer-facing businesses much faster than they would have otherwise. And it's true for the media, too. If you want to engage with the startup community in Kansas City, you contact Brittain Kovac and go check out the Startup Village. It's convenient for out-of-town reporters, but that concentration of activity also gives the companies working in the area a powerful advantage when, say, Sprint or Garmin comes calling with product questions or business needs or, perhaps, with their checkbooks open for a potential acquisition.

"One of the toughest things about entrepreneurship is, like, you're busting your ass all the time and it gets heavy at times," Marcus says later over a beer in the Hoopla.io basement. "And there are times when you're just banging your head against the wall and, it's not like you want to give up, but just like, 'I'm done.' And when you do it here, you see other people doing it and busting their asses, [so] it's like, 'All right, I'm not alone.' You know? I feel like I'm doing this with other people who are also struggling—'If I give you a hug, will you give me a hug?'"

Oddly enough, it was Google that really put the Kansas City startup ecosystem on the map when it announced plans in the spring of 2011 to bring its then-new Google Fiber high-speed broadband service to the city. With the announcement, Kansas City became the first metro area in the country to benefit from the service, which offers 1 Gbit/s Internet speeds along with high-definition television service and add-ons like the ability to use an iPad to control your TV. It's cool, it's impressive, and it was in Kansas City first (though the service has since been expanded to other cities).

"Why did we pick Kansas City?" Milo Medin, Google's vice president of Access Services, said at the March 2011 event announcing the decision. "We wanted to find a location where we could build quickly and efficiently. Kansas City has great infrastructure. And Kansas has a great, business-friendly environment for us to deploy a service. The utility here has all kinds of conduit in it that avoids us having to tear the streets open and a bunch of other stuff that really differentiates it from other places in the country."

Following the announcement, Google spent more than a year rallying individuals in more than a dozen Kansas City–area neighborhoods, known in Google lingo as "fiberhoods," to commit to the service before the build-out began. Once 25 percent of a fiber-hood's residents committed to signing up, by putting down a $25 down payment, everyone in that fiberhood was guaranteed access to Fiber. And it's cheap. At the time of my visit, homeowners who qualified for service were able to sign up for the 5 MB package, on par with many cable broadband offerings, for free after the $300 installation fee. Gigabit service cost $70 per month with no installation fee.

But this is far from the first time that the Kansas City metro area has stood in for the US consumer as a test market. The city has a population that pretty well represents the average demographic makeup of the country as a whole and has been used for testing purposes many times in the past, according to Ryan Weber, president of KCnext—the Technology Council of Greater Kansas City.

And, for technology businesses in particular, the city's location in the middle of the country makes a lot of sense.

"Kansas City has been a tech center for a long time," Weber says, in his office overlooking the atrium in Kansas City's historic Union Station, "and you can really start to understand that based on how the fiber optic map of America is really drawn and where those lines intersect. And it's right here in the middle of the country. Most of that runs along road and rail. If you look at a map of the fiber optic infrastructure in America, you can see that it goes to Chicago and it goes to Kansas City. Well, we're the two largest rail hubs in the country."

That built-in advantage has long attracted technology entre-preneurs to Kansas City. Telecom giant Sprint, based in Overland Park, grew out of Brown Telephone, a local phone company in Abilene, Kansas, while DST Systems grew up locally to become a major player in back-office systems and workflow processes. More recently, electronic stock trading service BATS Global Markets has emerged as the second-largest equity trading platform in the country, based in the Kansas City suburb of Lenexa, Kansas.

As for Google Fiber, it may have gotten the national conversation started about Kansas City and tech, but it's far from the whole story.

"The way we look at it is it's a hell of a lifestyle asset that we can add to our portfolio to attract talented people," says Weber. "And it helps. Because all this attention and all this excitement around Google Fiber."

The real problem the city faces now, he says, is that as Midwesterners, Kansas City's residents and entrepreneurs haven't been very boastful about their tech successes to date. In fact, before Google came to town and made a splash with its shiny new gigabit Internet service, few outside of Kansas and Missouri were really paying attention to what was going on here.

The locals hope that is finally changing.

"Especially with the need for talent, more and more companies are not only selling the opportunity of working at their company but also the opportunity to work and live in their city," Weber says. "It's funny. So for the tech council that we run, it's a non-profit membership-based group, and we've got about 115 member companies involved—so everyone from Sprint, Cerner, Google, Microsoft, to a large number of small companies and then a few startups. The thing is, nothing like this really existed before Google Fiber. There wasn't this kind of momentum, and now we're essentially helping share our story with the rest of the world. It's been fun, because no one really knew about all the stuff going on here."

It's not just a Kansas City thing, either. The whole of the Midwest is undergoing a transformation from a manufacturing and agriculture center to embrace a more diverse economy as the manual-labor jobs of the past 100-plus years fall by the wayside and automation and technology replace heavy industry. As a result, high-growth tech is moving in as a key new regional industry in a big way, providing jobs, driving revenues, and providing new outlets for local entrepreneurs across the region.

"I'd say our community is four to five years old," says Jeff Slobotski, the founder of *Silicon Prairie News*, an online publication dedicated to Midwestern startups, and the unofficial spokesperson for the "Silicon Prairie," the tech ecosystem that includes Kansas, Missouri, Nebraska, Iowa, Indiana, and Illinois. "So we're just getting started. We're looking at notable firms like Lightbank out of Chicago investing in [mobile gaming startup] SkyVu Entertainment, and Andreessen investing in a few notable companies, so we're starting to see more awareness and more investment from outside firms. We still battle with that attitude of, 'We love the company and love what you're doing, but you have to move out here [to California].' But the investments are happening and it's all starting to grow, and it does involve some notable firms. Everyone around here sees it, so we're building on it and building on these successes."

In addition to Kansas City, this tech transformation is happening in Omaha, Nebraska; Des Moines, Iowa; Lincoln, Nebraska; and Iowa City and Cedar Rapids, Iowa, as well as a number of rural areas and small towns scattered all over the region. What used to be under-the-radar startups in these cities and towns are now attracting interest from coastal VCs and larger tech firms in Silicon Valley, driving real growth in these small ecosystems and encouraging new entrepreneurs to jump into the fray.

The real challenge for the Silicon Prairie, says Omaha-based Slobotski, is overcoming the ingrained, cultural hurdles that come with doing business in the Midwest. The region still has that heads-down mentality, he says, where work needs to be about creating real value and solving real problems, not necessarily creating the next big Web sensation. The next Instagram is unlikely to come out of the area.

But there's plenty of local pride at work in the area, and with that comes a sense of ownership and responsibility that's somewhat unique in the here-today-gone-tomorrow world of high-growth startups. And there's a boldness in the area that's becoming more common now, too, Slobotski explains, along with a real sense of "we can do this here; we can be successful." It doesn't hurt that upstart entrepreneurs can now look around the Midwest and see other founders who have been successful with their own technology startups—from online payments processor Dwolla in Des Moines, to Groupon in Chicago—as well as an ecosystem that's healthy and established enough now to ensure ample "fallback" opportunities for founders whose own efforts fall short. There's always another job out there.

"It's like, 'Hey, I can make a mark in the startup community and in the region if I succeed,'" Slobotski says. "Whereas in San Francisco or New York you are one of several thousands, here it's still relatively new and the companies feel this sense of ownership. I want to be a part of what's going on out in the Midwest and what's going on in Omaha. I want to be part of that."

So far, the Kansas City metro area has not emerged as a particularly big player in terms of venture capital investment, ranking just twenty-ninth nationally as of 2010.

But that's not to say that there's no money in the area. In fact, Kansas City has a well-ingrained investment community that's especially deep in telecom and mobile development. There are four established angel networks in town, and nearly a dozen venture firms operating in the city (though many of those are based elsewhere and just maintain Kansas City offices). Beyond that, the business community is generally supportive of new ventures, I'm told—though, "how are you going to repay this investment right now, not three years down the line?" is a common attitude among area investors.

"Generally people here are able to get, if they have solid ideas and good founders, they can usually get their early-stage seed money, their first $200,000 to $500,000," explains Lance LeMay, a managing director with Kansas City–based venture capital firm OpenAir Equity Partners. "And then a lot of people kind of hit a wall. Some of it is survival of the fittest, but some of it is, unless you've got a lot of traction with your idea at that point or you're an entrepreneur who's done it before and is a known quantity, or you've got your own relationships with people in more of a broader regional context or other VCs outside of the region, you struggle to get people to go, 'I'm going to come in and lead your Series A in Kansas City.'"

We're seated at the firm's half-circle conference table overlooking the parklike area south of downtown. In addition to me and LeMay, two other firm partners are seated at the table, all former executives with Sprint, Kansas City's marquee technology success story, and seasoned investors both locally and well beyond the city limits.

"[Sprint] PCS today, you look at it as huge," says Managing Director Kathy Walker, the former chief network officer for Sprint Nextel and the executive who oversaw the development of the first nationwide 3G wireless network. "But when it started, you know, Ron [LeMay, OpenAir's fourth partner and a former Sprint CEO] was employee number one there, so the people that he surrounded himself with, that went out and started markets and opened sales and did all those things at the very early stages, those are individuals that I think are the best equipped and the most likely to make that transition to entrepreneurship. If someone has only been in a more mature environment where they're just tweaking, I think they're less suited or less likely to really gravitate to the startup process."

Sprint remains a big source of local talent, she says, and there are always folks coming out of local health-care IT player Cerner as well as Garmin and other area companies in the area that are looking to strike out on their own. Lance LeMay nods in agreement, explaining that these more seasoned, experienced tech executives are what make the most sense in a market like Kansas City. "People just don't understand what startups are," he says of the local workforce. "It's not part of the culture in a market like this."

"I think that for Kansas City, like most markets, you have cycles," he says. "And, you know, kind of like the cycle of the late nineties where everybody got all enthusiastic about startups and entrepreneurship and things kind of got built up, there was a lot of momentum, companies got started, and then the market collapsed. Everything kind of got washed out. And it took almost ten years for this level of activity to come back. I think that of this current crop of companies that have been started [in Kansas City] in the last couple of years, you have to have a couple of those be really successful, otherwise it's not sustainable over the longer period of time."

But that's not unique to Kansas-Missouri. It's the same everywhere. Potential founders have to believe that a tech startup can truly work in a place that's not the Valley, otherwise all of the momentum, all the enthusiasm, and the support of the local investment community and others will just waste away. No one wants to be the first to make the leap; they often need to have that proof of concept before acting themselves. "I think we have another year or so to wait to see how this all plays out, but if we don't have some notable successes in that time it's going to be tough."

There are other hurdles facing entrepreneurs in the area, as well.

"I think it's perfect except for the seed funding," explains Kevin Fryer, another former Sprint executive and the founder and managing director of SparkLabKC, a tech business incubator located in a vintage sandstone office building across the street from Union Station. "It's a gap. We don't have a seed fund in Kansas City. We don't really even have a venture capital firm in Kansas City anymore, that's the sad part. So some of the companies that we're talking to—there's Dundee Venture Capital out of

Omaha that's talking to a few of our companies, there's Cultivation Capital out of St. Louis talking to some of our companies. We've got some VCs from Des Moines talking to us, some from Columbia, Missouri, but very few in Kansas City."

The city does have a fairly active angel community, he says, and many of them are engaged with the local tech startups, but a lot of the local money still isn't savvy when it comes to investing in software firms and Web developers.

"We had a guy in a few days ago," Fryer says. "He owns a humungous trucking company and has for twenty-five years. I mean, he's a gazillionaire. And so he was in here in his shorts and his flip-flops and he told me he's just bored. [He said], 'I hired somebody to run my company and I don't have anything to do anymore.' He's not a technology guy and will tell you he's not a technology guy, but he completely got what these guys [Spark-LabKC participant company Innovative Health Media] are doing and was all over it. So they're out there. It's hard [to find local backers], but it's getting there."

"Something's going on here," says Cameron Cushman, a manager in entrepreneurship at the Ewing Marion Kauffman Foundation, the Kansas City–based nonprofit that works to promote entrepreneurship and small-business development from coast to coast, of the local ecosystem. "I don't know what it is, and that's kind of the fun part. I'm not even sure if I could tell you what's driving it. It's just the attitude has changed, and it's the attitude across the board. People are just thinking of startups in a different way. They're thinking about how they could make a job for themselves instead of just taking a job. It's hard to describe exactly why all that's happening."

We're sitting in a sunny, glassed-in conference room in the heart of the Kauffman Foundation's headquarters in the tree-lined Rockhill section of town. It's a nonprofit, but it feels like a think tank, or a tech company, or the headquarters of some sort of galactic congress. The U-shaped complex partially surrounds a manmade lake, which we can see from our seats; even the parking lot feels like a park, complete with trellising over the parking spaces and flower-lined sidewalks.

"You know, Kansas City was really built by entrepreneurs," Cushman continues, leaning in as he speaks. "And when you think about it, and this is different than other cities; when you think about the big companies that have a huge role in the Kansas City economy, you can trace most of their histories to one individual person."

He rattles them off: Hallmark was created in Kansas City in 1910 by Joyce Hall. Marion Laboratories, the precursor to the Kauffman Foundation itself, was started by Ewing Kauffman in 1950 when he began selling homemade calcium supplements out of his Kansas City basement. Tax preparation company H&R Block was founded by Henry and Richard Bloch in 1955. Garmin, the maker of GPS-based navigation systems, was founded by Gary Burrell and Min Kao—hence Gar-min—in Lenexa, Kansas, in 1989. Software development firm DST Systems was founded in 1969 as Data-Sys-Tance, a subsidiary of Kansas City Southern Industries. Health-care IT firm Cerner got its start as a three-person startup in 1979 when Neal Patterson, Paul Gorup, and Cliff Illig split off from Arthur Andersen, and now claims to be one of the largest providers of electronic medical systems in the US. Kansas City is also home to no less than four major industries— telecommunications (Sprint Nextel employs more than 18,000 people locally), rail transportation, agriculture, and life sciences. It is even home to American Italian Pasta Company, the largest pasta maker in the US. No doubt, the city's entrepreneurial roots run deep, and that's something that civic leaders are counting on going forward.

Says Cushman: "It's not too far of a departure for people who are thinking about starting companies here to imagine turning them into big employers and big top-line revenue guys. It's been done. But I think the difference is which ones are going to be the next ones? How do we foster those along? And it's impossible to pick winners and losers, but you know you do the best you can. You kind of help everybody and you see what happens."

Of course, as a nonprofit, the Kauffman Foundation is in something of an odd spot when it comes to its dealings with the local startup ecosystem. It can't offer the direct financial assistance that most founders need, and it can't take any interest in any commercial activity or organization, like the Startup Village, for example, by providing grants or funding. The solution so far has been to serve the local community by filling in the gaps—offering up Foundation meeting rooms for Kansas City ecosystem events; organizing the wildly popular weekly 1 Million Cups coffee clubs, which bring local entrepreneurs together on the Kauffman campus; and even paying Brittain Kovac's salary to organize the Startup Village's public relations efforts and manage tours of the neighborhood.

"We've been careful to find ways to help them without hurting them," Cushman says. "If you go in and give them a big grant, if you go in and tell them what to do, it will spoil the organic growth and the organic nature of this, so it's kind of a tricky balance that we've faced."

The Kauffman Foundation is not alone in offering support to the Startup Village and local entrepreneurs. The city itself and the Greater Kansas City Chamber of Commerce have embraced the growing startup community, and in 2011 launched what they call the Big 5 Initiative in an effort to "elevate the region onto the world stage and [make] the area one of America's best places to work, live, start a business, and grow a business." The five goals (the Big 5) of the program are to improve the health of the city's residents, boost the local education system, bring in more jobs, increase local investment, and provide a better quality of life for everyone in the region. The end goal? To make Kansas City "America's Most Entrepreneurial City."

"The Big 5 build on strengths we already have regionally," Greg Graves, chair of the Chamber of Commerce, said when the program was first announced. "Taken together, they propel the community forward, enhance our quality of life, and create jobs."

At first glance, the idea of making over a Midwestern metropolis into "America's Most Entrepreneurial City" is almost too pie-in-the-sky to take seriously. But the reality is, even if the city never reaches that specific stated goal, the simple fact that it was included as one of the city's long-term benchmarks has all but ensured it a place at the table when regional leaders discuss economic development or small business going forward. Entrepreneurship has now officially entered the Kansas City conversation.

Case in point: The recent creation of the Startup Village now means the city's young entrepreneurs have a place to call home, whether they live/work there or not.

"Part of the success of the Startup Village is that, when people come to town we now are able to instantly connect them to the startup community," Cushman says. "A lot of cities you go to and you don't know where to find these people. You have to ask around and it takes you ten, fifteen, twenty emails and phone calls to find the right people. Now in Kansas City you can come to 1 Million Cups and talk to everybody you need to talk to in an hour. I've started to use the analogy that it's like entrepreneurial church. It's same bat time, same bat place every week. You know you're going to see some friends. And you're all going to learn something together. You're going to have coffee and you're going to hang out afterward. The analogy's not perfect, but I think it gets the point across."

It's a simple thing, he explains, but it all goes into creating that real feeling of community. As we pack up to leave, Cushman tells the story of an entrepreneur who moved to Kansas City from Boston—itself a very active city for technology companies—and became the first resident of Homes for Hackers. "When he got here he told me, 'So I came here for the free rent and the Google

Fiber, but I stayed for the community.' And that's really what's been different [in the ecosystem recently]. It's just that there's a willingness to help each other out here now. It's not a competitive spirit. And this is what makes the Startup Village so great; it's that they're all in it together."

Mention this to just about any of the entrepreneurs working out of the Village and they'll all agree: The biggest benefit to being located there is the community.

"It's a very open, living laboratory," explains Mike Farmer, co-founder of Leap2, a Village-based startup that's taking on Google, Bing, and Yahoo in the online search market and just happens to be based out of the very first house that Google Fiber connected in Kansas City. Hoopla.io works out of the basement. "There's no top-down agenda or anything. It's just helping one another out."

Farmer himself is no newcomer to the startup game. A veteran of four previous ventures, including another search-market play, he has raised more than $7 million in funding over the course of his entrepreneurial career and authored or coauthored ten patents. He's also a good five to ten years older than most of his peers in the Kansas City tech ecosystem, which gives him something of a wide-angle view when it comes to the culture of the Startup Village itself. Admittedly, with a few dozen recent college grads working in the area, it can take on a college campus feel at times, with cookouts, happy hours, and late-night coding sessions being the norm.

"I have a thesis that [the Kansas City community] is a little bit of a testament to, it's a little bit foreign for me because a lot of it is driven by younger people, but the social media generation," he says. "Share everything; share and share alike. Pay it forward.

"That's a lot of what the ethic of this culture is. And I'm a little bit older than a lot of the startup founders around here, but they all work together, share together, help one another. It's kind of refreshing."

Leap2's director of product, Tyler VanWinkle, working on a demo of the company's Living Search algorithm across the table, nods in agreement.

"Every company acts independently of each other," he says, "but [I'll] be walking across the back driveway sometime and somebody will say, 'Man, we're having a hard time finding talent that knows [the network application platform] Node.js.' And I'll be like, 'Oh, I know a guy, you should check him out.' Or they'll come up and say, 'Mike, we've tweaked our pitch. Do you have twenty minutes so we can run it by you?' And he'll go, 'Yes, let's do it tomorrow at lunch.'"

It's a support mechanism, VanWinkle explains, that can be very helpful to entrepreneurs just starting out, especially as they take their first steps into commercialization, fund-raising, and other they-didn't-teach-us-this-in-school areas.

"And then you have the Kauffman Foundation that's literally maybe sixteen blocks away," he says. "They're coming in and saying, 'What can we do?' There's a ton of support here."

A few blocks away, recent transplant Brandon Schatz has found another advantage to basing his company, SportsPhotos. com, in a converted house in the Startup Village: The speed and power of Google Fiber has finally made his business commercially viable.

"When I lived in Austin, Texas, I contracted with a data center there to do uploads and it was $300 for a day," he says in Sports-Photos.com's dining room/office. "We had a conference room, all the photographers went in and edited the photos, and then I went into the actual data center area and transferred all the files. So yeah, $300."

Schatz's company contracts with freelance photographers all over the country to provide coverage of sporting events like marathons and bicycle races, providing the photographers with a platform to sell their images to participants and media outlets while the site takes a cut of the proceeds. It has proven to be a popular business model, but the scale at which it was growing was taxing Schatz's Internet resources—digital photo files are particularly large and generally take a long time to upload, even over high-speed connections—and he was spending hours per week just transferring files when he could be out developing the business. And that's to say nothing of the sheer cost. Aside from the one-day data center passes, if Schatz wanted a 1GB business connection anywhere other than Kansas City, at the time he'd be looking at a $12,000 monthly bill from his ISP. With Google Fiber, he's currently paying just $70 a month for far superior service.

"Oh man, it's awesome." He smiles, telling the story of the local Color Race that his company covered a year earlier, prior to his Google Fiber connection. They had ten to fifteen photographers at the event, all shooting high-quality photos on professional cameras, and it took him nearly forty hours to get all the images uploaded. That's a hassle. What's more, by the time the photos were ready, most of his potential customers, the runners who had participated in the race, had likely moved onto their next event and were no longer interested in ordering photos.

"And that was just one event," Schatz says. "We can't scale with that. So if we're going to do five events a year, or ten events, or twenty events, or however much, we're going to need the bandwidth to support it. So I was paying, for cable Internet, I was paying like $400 a month for the business package, the best thing that they offered—100 megs down, 10 megs up. So, uh, this [Google Fiber] is amazing."

For Kayla Riggs, who works out of the Homes for Hackers house for a startup called Traveling Nuker, conversations about work often start with the question: "Didn't the FBI come visit you here?" And it's true. The company she works for aggregates scheduling and outage information for all of the nuclear power plants in the United States so that union and labor workers can quickly and easily see what jobs are available and how much they pay. The company was founded by a nuclear technician who travels the country working temporary outages in order to fund the venture, which offers up all of its collected information to users for a $20 yearly subscription.

"It was definitely a quick learning process," Riggs says of her job, which she got straight out of school a few months prior to my visit. "I didn't realize, like, if you look [at the poster] behind you that's all the nuclear power plants that we have in the United States. The ones that have like 2s and 3s on them, that means they have two reactors or three reactors. So there's more than one unit there."

Not surprisingly, the FBI was curious about what a group of twentysomethings in Kansas City were doing with all this nuclear plant information, and stopped by the house in 2013 to check them out. A few explanations later, and the feds left satisfied. But law enforcement interest notwithstanding, local native Kayla, whose job description at Traveling Nuker includes union sales rep as well as UI/UX designer, is optimistic about the future as part of the new local entrepreneurship scene.

"I think that definitely this has raised my expectations in a job," she says. "I kind of dove into the entrepreneurship world so, you know, I was handing out my resume—literally like, 'Here you go, here you go, here you go'—just handing them out everywhere because I wanted it. I wanted in. And I think that it is something new that's going on. Entrepreneurship is definitely something new to Kansas City; it's booming. Everybody wants it. You can control your own life, control where you work, control how much money you make. It's awesome. It's absolutely amazing that people look at me and they're like, 'How old are you?' I'm twenty-one and the cofounder of a company. It's just amazing, you know, that just this community here in Kansas City itself has created that for a lot of people."

The geology of eastern Kansas falls into what's known as the Mississippian Subperiod, marked primarily by marine limestone and other sedimentary reminders of the continent's underwater past. These characteristics are common throughout much of the Mississippi River Valley, hence the name, and mean that Kansas City and its environs sit atop highly shapeable, erosion-prone bedrock. As a result, there are a number of subterranean developments in the area, including SubTropolis, a 55,000,000-square-foot man-made cave a few miles northeast of Downtown Kansas City that was developed by Lamar Hunt, the late owner of the Kansas City Chiefs football team, in 1980 in what was once a limestone mine. Marketed as the "World's Largest Underground Business Complex," the 160-foot-deep SubTropolis boasts sixteen-foot ceilings, seven miles of paved roads, several miles of underground railroad, and year-round temperatures that naturally hover between 65 and 70 degrees. About fifty businesses call the cave home, including the US Postal Service and the US Environmental Protection Agency. There's even a data center located deep in the facility.

And that's not the only cave/office complex in town.

Two miles north of the Startup Village, on the Missouri side of the state line, there is another, similar facility called Downtown Underground that's situated ten stories underground and boasts 1.2 million square feet of office space. Visitors enter through a nondescript beige building next to a small parking lot on Thirty-first Street, and take an elevator down to the main level. It's an easy spot to miss.

But once down in the cave, the floors are carpeted, the ceilings are high, and the rough, natural (but white-painted) walls are some of the only signs that you're actually underground. (That, and the total lack of both windows and cell phone service.) The temperature is comfortable, almost cool, and the sense of quiet is near-total.

It's down in this environment, cut off from the above world, that seed accelerator BetaBlox set up shop in 2008. Entering the firm's offices, it's easy to be underwhelmed by the plain white walls, dull gray carpet, and lack of usual startup-friendly amenities.

But that's just the way they like it, says CEO and cofounder Alex Altomare.

"What we did here was we created the best place in Kansas City to work, and the worst place to hang out," he says as we walk through BetaBlox's entirely nondescript hallways. "So there's no reason to be here if you're going to do anything other than work. And that's been really efficient. We didn't spend any extra money [on the facility], and startups shouldn't spend extra money on their operations. So by acting like a startup, I feel like that's been a key part of being able to teach startups to focus on what matters and just get out of the startup phase."

And that's big, Altomare explains in BetaBlox's dull, drab conference room. The only picture on the wall is a print the founders found next to the Dumpster when they were moving in. ("I'm not fond of it myself," says Altomare.) The thing about startup life, he says, is that it sucks. It really sucks. It takes years off of founders' lives, ruins their finances, and is generally just a miserable experience all around. BetaBlox exists to kill off the startup phase.

"I used to say startups are awesome, I love startups, this is great. And then it was like, 'No, I don't.' Being a startup is miserable; it's the worst. So this exists just to make that time shorter and more efficient. If we could make the startup phase one day here before you have a small business that's growing in revenue, perfect. That's what I want."

BetaBlox operates differently from most traditional accelerator programs. Altomare and his partners don't write their companies checks, don't offer any up-front funding, and instead provide entrepreneurs with all of the back-end support they need to get off the ground in exchange for a small equity stake in each business. They get office space, mentoring, marketing and branding support, legal help, a business education, and access to BetaBlox's network of investors. In essence, Altomare and his partners become cofounders in all the businesses that they bring into the fold. To date that means the group is involved in more than fifty Kansas

City–area companies, and has not yet seen a dime of return for their efforts.

It all grew out of simple boredom, Altomare explains.

"I'd sold my company and was looking for something to do," he says of the firm's beginnings. "Basically I didn't want to get a job. And so I invested. OK, I give this company $25,000 and now I'm watching them spend it on rent for an office space and a lawyer and Web design. It's so inefficient. So we got to thinking—what if we paid for the office space? And paid for the lawyers? And bundled all these services together and created a community of entrepreneurs? And then just took 5 percent equity, and we paid for it all and provided it all upfront."

That's essentially what BetaBlox is, though Altomare admits that from their point of view it's an investment model that just happens to look a little like an incubator. "Actually, starting out we were calling it just 'heaven for entrepreneurs,'" he laughs, "and it turns out heaven is underground, I guess."

In many ways, the BetaBlox program is the opposite of the Startup Village and many other community-based entrepreneurship programs, and Altomare is quick to admit this. Its program exists to create businesses, to get viable companies off the ground and generating revenue. Not to sponsor happy hours and meetups, or to serve as fill-in employment for aimless college grads. In his view, when working on a startup gets to be too comfortable it can end up being counterproductive to business success and economic growth.

"It's a funny thing because there's a group of people, and I think there is in any city, that enjoy being in a startup," he says. "And they like the attention that comes with it, the promise, the hope. But they kind of hesitate and don't end up growing, or they never put their product out there or they're constantly developing it, because they're afraid to fail. The startup community is an amazing catalyst that tells people, 'Let's go.' Just try it. Jump in and give it a try.

"I want to be the one to hold their hand and say, 'Let's jump. I'll do this with you.'"

On the flipside, Think Big Partners in the hip, artsy Crossroads neighborhood operates more like a traditional accelerator program—accepting a set number of startups into its nine-month program, taking an equity stake in each business, and helping them get established in the marketplace before pushing them out the door. Its office is the opposite of the BetaBlox space—open, airy, and located over several floors in a loftlike former Walt Disney film library building—but it comes with a similar goal in mind: helping new companies solve real-world problems.

"You know, I think the common joke that we say is that we're not going to invest in the next Angry Birds," explains Blake Miller, one of the firm's partners. "While we'd love that exit, it's just not something that we can provide value to. So we really look to be able to provide value to the companies that we work with, and we know we can provide value to solving a problem because some people will pay for that solution."

Adds Senior Partner and cofounder Tyler Prochnow, who began his career as an attorney before veering away into sports representation and was even the owner of the now-defunct Kansas City Brigade arena football team for a time: "What we want is for people to be able to stand on their own two feet when they walk out the door. Not just have a viable product and not just have tested a market and say, 'Yeah, I think there might be something there.' We want them to know that there is something there, that there's something solid. They're either profitable on their own or they're on a clear path to profitability, and, like Blake said, they're solving real problems. So there's a scalability and viability to it."

More than 100 companies have come through Think Big's doors since the space opened in 2012, some for the accelerator program, some for business mentoring, and some simply to take advantage of the firm's coworking space, which has proven popular in a downtown where small, flexible office options are in short supply.

"Google Fiber obviously has been a huge catalyst for this town," Prochnow says as we tour the facility. "Not practically speaking, because it's still fairly limited in its rollout, but what it has done not just for Kansas City but for the companies that we work with is it's created a 'what if' mentality. So the idea is, 'OK, I have a gigabit of Fiber. What can I do with that?' It may not be practical today to say, 'I'm going to build a company solely around Google Fiber,' but it has created an environment where lots of people want to get together and talk about what's possible. And when they start talking about what's possible they find the things that bind them together, and communities start to grow and the collisions start to happen. But, that being said, what it's done for the creativity and just the willingness of people to commit resources and time and effort into building a startup community in this town has been probably the single biggest incubator or accelerator event to date."

We end up on the roof deck of the Think Big building to take in the 360-degree views of the downtown skyline and the surrounding neighborhoods. It's a beautiful spot, and it certainly appears popular with the startup founders downstairs, but the longer we talk the clearer it becomes that Kansas City still has some structural hurdles to clear before its entrepreneurs can really take off. For starters, the local economic development agencies are still focused on luring big, established companies to downtown, and there remains a never-ending state-line battle happening between Kansas and Missouri over tax credits and incentives to attract new businesses.

"There was an article the other day griping and moaning about how the city hasn't attracted any big companies to downtown," Prochnow says. "'They're spending all this money on startups! What are they doing for the city?' Are you kidding me? We've created more jobs than anybody else down here. And it's not one company creating them, but, you know, we've got 100-plus jobs in the last year. Those people want everything to happen overnight; they aren't waiting for companies to mature. It's ridiculous."

For Jeff Shackelford, who got his start as a Kansas City entrepreneur in the mid-nineties as the cofounder of communications provider Birch Communications following a ten-year career at Sprint, the startup resources that he sees in the city today continue to amaze.

"Well, in '96 when we formed Birch Telecom there were not any organizations, or groups of organizations, saying, 'how can we help you?' he says. "Sort of the opposite. You know, it was more like, 'You're starting a company. Come back and see us when you've built something of significant size.'"

The fortunate thing for Shackelford was that the telecom space was incredibly hot at the time, which made up for some of the local hurdles, and allowed Birch to blossom into a profitable business. But he's quick to admit that the deep infrastructure that exists in the region now would have been nice to have back in the day.

"There were no opportunities to reach out and say, 'Can you help me get to this person?,'" he says. "'Can you help me get to this company?' It was more [like] figure it out as you go. Now you look at it and you go, man, anybody trying to do it on their own, totally on their own, in Kansas City is really missing a tremendous opportunity to greatly enhance the chances of their company being successful."

These days he is a major part of that support system as the director of Digital Sandbox, a program of the University of Missouri—Kansas City (UMKC) that works with early-stage startups to help them get from the idea stage to a working prototype. The goal is to get these new companies commercialized, he says, but also to get them in a position to get their first real angel funding and then move on, though Digital Sandbox does offer some early-stage seed funding of its own. The key question for the group is, "What can we help you get done that will significantly help you move forward?" Answering that question is what Shackelford does on a daily basis.

"What we've learned is that at this stage you can really touch a lot of companies for not a lot of money," he says. "I think on average we're probably in the $15,000 to $17,000 range, so they can get some UX or UI coding done on the front end, or some database or back-end coding, maybe even help them get set up with a legal structure or some IP research to figure out if there's a way to protect their intellectual property. You can really help springboard these early-stage people forward, because a lot of them don't have access to these services; they don't have the friends or family connections to make it happen. So it's kind of a gap that we recognized. Take a lot of people with a lot of great ideas that have potential in the marketplace and get them from the back of the napkin, if you will, to the business plan to getting something built that you can show a potential investor. That seems to be a real hurdle that a lot of people still struggle to climb over."

For the city, which provides some funding for the program via the Kansas City Economic Development Corporation and the Missouri Technology Corporation, Digital Sandbox is primarily a long-term economic play, a way to drive job growth in the greater metro area. The key question is how many of the folks who apply for the program can be developed into actual businesses and get to the stage where they are hiring employees and growing.

The Kansas City business community knows that most of the big local employers—Sprint, Cerner, DTS, and so on—were grown and developed in the area; they didn't just uproot their headquarters and move 1,000 jobs to town. "So, you know, we hope to find that next batch," Shackelford says. "It might take ten, twelve, fifteen years, but who's going to be that next batch that one day we look up and they've got a Sprint campus of 10,000 people?"

Maria Meyers, a colleague of Shackelford's at UMKC, is also involved in this effort as the director of the UMKC Innovation Center and the founder of USSourceLink and KCSourceLink. When she started at the university in 2003, Meyers tells me between sessions at a local economic development conference where she is a featured speaker, the primary issue the city faced was connecting entrepreneurs to local resources in an efficient way. Nobody at the time really knew what was available—although there has always been a lot in the area, she says—and communication was a problem. So the school stepped in to act as a central hub.

"We didn't have an angel network in 2003," she says, "so we started KCSourceLink. And I think that what we did that was a little bit different was instead of networking together with the entrepreneurs, we actually went to the support organizations and brought them into a room and said, 'What can we do for you?' So in our network we have incubators, we have small-business development centers, we have our angel networks, we have people that support micro enterprises, we have people that support second stage, and we have mentor programs. Back when we started we had about 140 organizations; we have over 200 now and it's just blossoming."

The organization essentially operates a hotline that entrepreneurs can call on and say, "I need this kind of help with my business," whether it's an established operation or an upstart idea, and KCSourceLink will help them get what they need. Whether it's funding, or business planning, or marketing help, or any of the hundreds of other problems that business owners face. Meyers and company are the central clearinghouse for local information and connections, all at no cost.

As someone who has been involved in the local startup scene for over a decade, Meyers says that it has been a slow boil for the city, as entrepreneurs, local leaders, and support organizations gradually found each other over the years and finally got to work. The process has accelerated in recent years.

"Even back when we started Whiteboard to Boardroom [a Kansas–Missouri partnership program that's dedicated to developing a sustainable technology commercialization process for the local universities that was founded in 2009], entrepreneurship was pretty quiet around here. And certainly back in 2003 you had to go around and look for somebody [who was starting a company]. Nobody knew anybody was here. And then by 2010 in Kansas City, mostly I think because of the recession, people were beginning to recognize entrepreneurship as a market segment, and there was a shift across the country in attitude that entrepreneurs might be what we need to bring this economy back."

Things got interesting locally, she says, in 2011 when the Kansas City Chamber of Commerce decided that entrepreneurship needed to be a focus for the metro area going forward, naming it the Big 5.

"Suddenly, we've got the whole city talking together about the same subject," Meyers says, "which is terrific. And entrepreneurs came out of the woodwork. And interesting new things were developed, like 1 Million Cups, like Digital Sandbox, like Homes for Hackers, and like the Startup Village. For the first time, honestly, we were seeing the entrepreneurs leading what was going on, as opposed to the economic developers or the support organizations. So that's been a really cool new sort of phenomenon."

The city has a lot of young, visible entrepreneurs these days, and that was not necessarily the case six to seven years ago when the area wasn't telling its story very well. New media outlets like *Silicon Prairie News* have changed that, and the increasing publicity is helping to sell Kansas City as a destination for fledgling entrepreneurs.

"It's been interesting lately," she says, "because of Google Fiber, because of the Startup Village, because we're telling the story better of the things that we do here. People are saying, 'Wow.' They call me saying, 'I'm thinking about moving here, because somebody said [I'd] better look at what [you're] doing.' I think it can be a surprise for people."

The positives associated with Kansas City are familiar to anyone who has ever spent time in the Midwest. The cost of living is low, the city has plenty of trees and parks, and the attitude is laid back and relaxed. For entrepreneurs, this can help extend the runway in the startup phase and make it more feasible to work on something on the side while working full-time to pay the bills. I met more than a few young entrepreneurs who were doing time as waiters, retail clerks, and in other jobs to support their startup habit. And, thanks to the low cost of living, they were still able to have the three-bedroom house, the picket fence, and two cars in the garage while all this was happening. Try that in San Jose.

Case in point: Alex Griffin, cofounder of indie music discovery site NewAppetite.com, moved to Kansas City from Chicago to take advantage of three months rent-free via Homes for Hackers, but ended up being surprised by the resources he found in the city itself.

"We saw the awesome startup community," he says. "Google Fiber was one of the main reasons we came here. There's nothing else like it. And the free three months to develop a business? That sealed the deal. We had to come. But we've been blown away; it really is beautiful here."

For many natives, that surprise factor seems to be a point of pride.

"We don't have a beach or mountains, you know," says Meyers, "but we have a very active arts scene here. We have the best performing arts center in the world here. But, you know, we have to learn how to not apologize and tell our story. Kansas City is a little over 2 million people, but it's three hours to Omaha, four hours to St. Louis, three hours to Springfield, three hours to Des Moines, three hours to Wichita. It's not like the coasts where you're driving from [one] big population center to the next. It's isolated."

So, what makes Kansas City a unique place for entrepreneurs? Why is entrepreneurship blooming in the city and what, aside from the temporary Google Fiber advantage (the company announced plans to expand to Austin, Texas, shortly after my visit), makes it a rich vein for founders? To find out, I sat down with Joni Cobb, the CEO of Pipeline, a Kansas City–based networking and mentoring organization for Midwest entrepreneurs, on the patio at Hi Hat Coffee, a tiny, red brick coffeehouse in the midst of an upscale neighborhood a few miles south of the Startup Village on State Line Road.

"There were some investors in from California one day and they said, 'You guys just need to embrace this Fiber thing and just be that,'" she says, rolling her eyes at the memory. "And I looked at [them] and said, 'Well, I was born and raised in Kansas City, and I'm here to tell you that every few years people come in to tell you what you are.' In 2004 all the national people said we needed to embrace our strengths like Marion Labs—'You have some life sciences capabilities and you're a developed center and it's medically related. You really need to leverage this and find your corner in the life science industry.' And that was just in 2004! And then Google does their thing and now they say we have to embrace that. Or somebody says Sprint and Garmin are here, so there's this whole thing."

But the reality, she says, is that entrepreneurs are going to do what they're going to do, no matter what might make the most sense from an economic development standpoint. It's impossible to label these groups as part of any one industry or, in Cobb's view, to define an entire city or an entire region based on the work of just a few people. And she's as upbeat on the area's prospects as anyone.

"With entrepreneurship, I think we've kind of permanently changed the fabric of the Midwest," she says, "and I think that includes Colorado, that includes Illinois and Chicago. I think the Midwest has fundamentally changed. And I hope it's permanent, but it's going take leaders and advocates and success stories to keep it going. Because, you know, things cycle, right? You had years when Wichita was all about entrepreneurship, and you had Pizza Hut and whatever, and before then you had Learjet and all that."

Those cycles have been particularly long in Kansas City, she says, which she calls a city of startups.

"Ewing Kauffman of the Kauffman Center was a startup, and Sprint was a startup, and Cerner was a startup. You can't rest on your laurels because once [those startups] become huge corporations, all of a sudden it's real easy to forget where you came from."

That's not to say startups in Kansas City are having an easy time of it; founders in this city have to deal with all of the same hurdles that entrepreneurs in Silicon Valley, Boston, and everywhere else do, along with the built-in challenges that come with doing business in a city that isn't yet front-and-center on the tech map. This is still the Midwest. But Cobb is optimistic that the tide is turning and that attitudes are changing enough for the next big local success story to emerge. The challenge now is going to be in the follow-through.

"I wrote [an article] in 2012 called 'The Magic Is in the Middle,' I think, and it was on that very thing. I was on my way back from Silicon Valley and I was meeting with a bunch of our advisors and we were having this conversation about money. And I just said, you know the difficulty is in the middle. It's really wonderful and easy and exciting to have startup weekends and startup villages and startup crawls and startup noise. You know what I mean? It's fabulous and it's fun and it's edgy; they all have backpacks and they wear jeans, and it's fun. But then you get to that point where the ugly, nasty, difficult, grimy, not-so-fun work is, and attention spans wander. And I sometimes think helping solving those problems and helping entrepreneurs at that point—whether it's policy, whether it's just funding, whether it's hands-on—whatever it is, is really hard work. And I think we're going to have to embrace the hard work part if we want this to be sustained."

CHAPTER

7

Raleigh-Durham

"What makes Raleigh-Durham a great place for startups? First and foremost, it's an attitude of collaboration. The community—entrepreneurs, service providers, academia, big industry, nonprofits—they really do rally around our startups. It makes it easy for a founder to get integrated into the entrepreneurial ecosystem here. There aren't really social barriers or cliques that I think you may find in certain areas. A young first-time transplant, if they were coming from California, or New York, or wherever, I think they'd find within a few conversations they'd have access to a really broad range of resources, people, talent, and advice, and everyone would be active and eager to help."

—*Adam Smith, former vice president, Square 1 Bank*

THE AREA AROUND THE CENTRAL North Carolina state capital of Raleigh is known locally as the "fall line," in reference to the waterfalls and rapids that are common in nearby waterways. The phenomenon is due to the basic geography of the area, which happens to be where the hilly, upland North America Piedmont and flat Atlantic Coastal Plain meet.

As a result, the region has a rolling quality marked by short, steep hills and winding streams that can be markedly different from the flat lowlands in the state's eastern counties. It isn't mountainous, the average elevation around here is only around 315 feet above sea level, but it is more rugged—a little more interesting, the locals like to say—than the waterfront areas and wetlands that many out-of-state visitors associate with North Carolina. The local tree cover is mostly pine forest, surrounded by a near-permanent fog of humidity.

In the middle of this wooded, rolling countryside, about equidistant from both Raleigh and its sister city of Durham about twenty miles to the west, there is a semi-secret facility tucked back in the woods about half a dozen turns and a few miles off of Interstate 40. There are tall pines in the parking lot, a Hardee's restaurant up the street, and several small startup companies occupying space in the same single-story, brown industrial park. The lobby, as it is, is all but empty when I arrive. Access is granted by knocking on a window.

But the cutting-edge work being done in a few thousand square feet of clean room and lab space beyond that empty lobby belies the bland, suburban exterior. This is the headquarters of Phononic, a five-year-old semiconductor startup that's developing new solid-state cooling technologies in an effort to unseat the thermocompressors that have been at the heart of refrigeration and cooling systems for generations. That's right: They are reengineering the refrigerator. The truth is, the standard fridge that you'll find in just about every kitchen in America has more in common with the appliances our grandparents used than our laptops, smart phones, or even TVs. An update is long overdue.

The company is working to upend this design by taking ultra-thin, solid-state chips of its own design, building them up into circuit boards, and then using those boards to power the next generation of wine chillers, refrigerators, and, eventually, air conditioners more efficiently, more effectively, and at lower cost. Phononic is backed by a pair of blue-chip Silicon Valley venture capital firms, Venrock and Oak Investment Partners, and is, in essence, doing groundbreaking semiconductor work nearly 3,000 miles from the ancestral home of the semiconductor industry.

"For whatever reason, the silicon world laughs at nonsilicon semiconductor devices," explains Dr. Tony Atti, the CEO of Phononic and a former venture capitalist himself who also holds a PhD in organic chemistry. "So as a result, anybody who's not in those established silicon clusters is on the 'outside,' and there's a lot of really deep nonsilicon competency in a couple of core areas." His company's technology is based on nonsilicon semiconductors.

As it turned out, the Raleigh-Durham area is one of those areas (Austin and Phoenix are the other two). Far away from the traditional semiconductor players and with deep experience with the materials science that drives Phononic's chips, the North Carolina Research Triangle region proved to be the perfect breeding ground for the new company. The area is home to three research universities—Duke, the University of North Carolina at Chapel Hill, and North Carolina State—offering access to the tools and equipment Atti needed to secure proof of concept, as well as a steady stream of engineering talent. All the resources of the Research Triangle Park—the largest science- and technology-focused research park in the world—are located just up the road.

"NC State has a really strong materials science pedigree," Atti says, "and I've probably got ten guys out of the NC State PhD program. Duke and UNC aren't as well known for materials science, but they have very strong engineering programs as well. And then you just have to look at success stories like [local semiconductor manufacturer] Cree and [integrated circuit designer] RF Micro Devices as the big anchors that have sort of established that.

"The neat story I love to tell about Phononic is that we now have thirty-seven employees and I have one, just one, classically trained thermoelectric expert. Everybody else, the first day they joined this company had no friggin' clue what this was. So it was neat to bring that kind of talent here."

There's more to locating a materials science–based startup in Raleigh-Durham than just access to talent, though. Phononic's office and manufacturing facility is also located just outside the technical boundary of the world-famous Research Triangle Park, allowing Atti to tap many of the technical resources that are available in the area, including clean room supplies, semiconductor equipment, hard-to-find devices, and other, you-can-only-find-it-here, logistical details.

"Part of the story of the Triangle that doesn't get talked about enough is that, when we moved in, this entire facility was a shell," he says, as we wander between Phononic's various materialization labs, testing spaces, and production facilities. "So there was power and stuff, but we brought all of this from a hollowed-out shell to a highly production-ready facility in three months and under a million bucks. I can count on one hand the number of places in the country where you can get that done, without having any downtime at all. I cannot tell you how important that is [in this industry]. That's huge."

And it is about more than just construction and design basics, he explains. Part of the company's core materials science intellectual property was developed by researchers at Oklahoma State University using specialized semiconductor growth equipment that's very expensive (as in "several million dollars for a machine that only does one thing" kind of expensive) and not very easy to find, even in research university labs. It's production-ready equipment that's used in industry, but not everybody has one, Atti explains. Oklahoma State had one, and, as luck would have it, so does NC State, which the company has been able to use in trade by sponsoring some engineering student research projects.

They even gained testing access to NC State's nuclear reactor—seriously, this is real-deal science going on here—via a similar arrangement.

"Semiconductors have transformed IT," Atti says as we finish up our tour. "They're doing the same for lightbulbs, and yet here we are in this thermal management world and compressors are the incumbent technology for going on 150 years. There's got to be something out there that could displace it."

He's hoping that his North Carolina–based company is the one to finally do it.

The thing about Raleigh-Durham is that it isn't just one city. It isn't even two cities, as the name would imply. In fact, according to the US Census Bureau, the greater Raleigh-Durham-Cary Combined Statistical Area encompasses eight counties with a combined population of more than 1.9 million people. It also covers a large physical area. The metro area consists of more than 4,500 square miles, including everything from Downtown Raleigh, Cary, and Apex to the east, to Durham and Chapel Hill to the west. The formal boundaries of the 7,000-acre Research Triangle Park (RTP) are right between Raleigh and Durham on I-40, about a fifteen-minute drive from either city.

It is bucolic and suburban—traffic seems rare outside of the daily rush hours, and the pace of life is easygoing and generally nine-to-five—but there is serious work being done here in the Park and beyond, courtesy of big-name anchor companies like IBM, BASF, GlaxoSmithKline, and Intel. According to the RTP, nearly 40,000 people come to work every day within the Park's boundaries.

Big, spread out, and with about half a dozen disparate local identities, the area can be hard to wrap your arms around, even for professionals like Derrick Minor, the innovation and entrepreneurship manager for the City of Raleigh. A business development executive by training, he was hired in 2012 and tasked with nurturing the local ecosystem—connecting with local startups, identifying their needs, and finding ways for city government to help them succeed. It's a government-is-here-to-help-you sort of thing, and he is quick to admit that it isn't easy.

"Even just within the City of Raleigh there are all these sub-markets where companies are," he says, as we chat on a balcony overlooking Hillsborough Street, the major east-west artery through Downtown Raleigh and less than a mile from the NC State campus. "There are seven or eight pretty successful sub-markets just within the city that have a lot of different types of companies, a lot of people living there. It's interesting—I can actually get to some parts of Durham faster than I can to some parts of north Raleigh. Logistically, you know, with the way the roads are and all. But you find companies all the time that are just randomly showing up. It's like, 'I've been in North Raleigh for five years.' You just never know."

This makes his job difficult, he says, because if local startups don't choose to be known, and don't choose to participate in the entrepreneurship community that he's trying to build, it limits not only what he can do for them but also their access to talent, mentorship, and investors. There are a lot of founders flying under the radar in Raleigh.

"I probably once a week or so find a company, a new company, and they're decent sized—thirty, forty, fifty people, but still in growth mode—that I had never heard of before. Those are good problems to have, sure, but it's just about uncovering those guys and communicating those successes to everyone else that, hey, there's stuff going on here."

It's a cultural hurdle to some extent, he explains. The region as a whole has been almost humble about what's going on in terms of local startups—"The people here are nice and they don't feel like they need to brag about certain things. But it's not brag-ging, it's just communicating that there is activity here as a way to help recruit talent or companies or capital or whatever it is."

People want to be where there are successful things happening, and southerners are, by their very nature sometimes, too laid back to toot their own horns, even when the local economy is at stake. This problem has been getting better—the Triangle region these days ranks in the top ten municipalities nationwide in terms of venture capital investments, and more than a few homegrown companies are near-household names in the tech space, including open-source software pioneer Red Hat, analytics developer SAS Institute, and Durham-based manufacturer of semiconductor LED materials and devices. In the consumer space, lip balm maker Burt's Bees is another local success story.

The trick to building out the community, Minor says, is translating everything that's going on in Raleigh to the wider region. It's a big place, and big places tend to be very local, each neighborhood and community with its own unique personality and unique flavor. For North Carolinians, that's a major selling point for life in the Triangle. Want to live in a small town? Fine, Apex is for you, and it's only about fifteen minutes south of Raleigh. Prefer a college town? OK, try Chapel Hill. There are options available in the region to suit just about any taste, unless you're looking for true, New York–style urbanism; cars, highways, and open spaces are still very much a part of life in the South.

For startups, rents in the area are fairly reasonable—ranging from anywhere to between $12 and $15 per square foot on the periphery up to $30 per square foot for the downtown high-rises, according to Minor—and talent costs are low, thanks in large part to the area's overall affordable cost of living. Pick a community in the Triangle and you can find a nice, three-bedroom house with a yard and a garage for less than $300,000, sometimes less than $200,000. That keeps salaries on the low side because money just isn't as necessary for day-to-day life in the same way that it is in expensive communities on the coasts, but talent is still available thanks to strong research universities like NC State, UNC, and, to a lesser degree, Duke. (Since so many Duke students come from out of state to attend the private school, multiple entrepreneurs in the area told me that the general trend is for very few of them to stick around after graduation. That typically doesn't happen with graduates from the large, local state schools.)

From a regional perspective, these technology startups have become a legitimate economic driver for both Raleigh and Durham in the last several years. The area has seen a lot of two- and three-person teams spinning out of the universities or the larger companies nearby—like Cisco, Bayer, National Semiconductor, and others—but the local economy is also heavy with midsized companies in the fifty to sixty employee range.

"These are growth companies that have hit certain milestones, have good revenue, have good employment numbers, and have good projections," Minor says of the area's larger startups. "That's a big part of the economy. And these are companies that are growing and have some good results and are building good businesses. We want to bring more attention to them and help them grow."

In Raleigh, at least, Minor and his colleagues are taking the long view.

"One of the things that I try to take as a daily philosophy is from Brad Feld's book on startup communities, and that is to take the long-term time horizon, that twenty-year time horizon. And that's something that certainly I subscribe to, and a lot of the local entrepreneurs and local leadership understand that it is going to take time. Silicon Valley is sixty years in the making, basically, but this is still a very, very young market. Durham had their kind of entrepreneurial focus or initiative probably two years before Raleigh did, but that still makes it only about three years total. That's a fairly short period of time, but we've seen quite a bit of ramp-up just in that time."

From what I can see, it is starting to take root. North Carolina had five IPOs in the first six months of 2013, out of fourteen in the entire Southeast region in that time, and the push for technology actually makes a lot of sense here, playing off the area's history as a center of innovation. But that's not all that Raleigh-Durham is about.

"I think actually a macro benefit to the area is the fact that we're not just one thing," explains Jay Bigelow with the Council for Entrepreneurial Development (CED), a thirty-year-old entrepreneurial support organization based in Durham, in the firm's converted tobacco warehouse office space. "Because four years ago tech was sort of down and life science was way up. Since then, life science has gotten a little quieter and tech has sort of rocketed. So I think having more than one industry has helped the overall economy because one can continue even if it's not in the subject area that's hot."

The Triangle has seen a lot of cycles, he says, and is probably better off for it because the population now knows how to ride the waves of economic change, building when times are flush and pulling back when times are tough. It's all about flexibility, and it has allowed the area to prosper and grow over the decades as industries have come and gone. The one thing they all have in common, though, is a need for the basic resources—talent, research, space, equipment, money, and so on—that the Triangle can provide.

"Whatever is in now is great and we want to see those companies be successful," Bigelow says, "but ten years from now it might be a different area [that's outperforming]. So to have the ecosystem be able to support that and create a bit more momentum, I think, is a good thing for everyone."

Dedication to the growing Triangle ecosystem defines the work being done at HQ Raleigh, one of Downtown Raleigh's largest tech coworking spaces. Cofounded by local entrepreneur Brooks Bell in partnership with her husband, ShareFile Founder Jesse Lipson, as well as Christopher Gergen from Durham's entrepreneurial development agency Bull City Forward, and real estate developer Jason Widen, the space was all but bursting at the seams with some forty-five companies when I visited in the summer of 2013. It has since relocated to a much larger, retrofitted loft space in the downtown Warehouse District that can accommodate more than twice the number of small companies as the original space could as well as dozens of single-user coworking desks.

"It was a year ago this week that I stepped off the plane in Raleigh," co-owner Widen tells me in the office's café, a sleek, wood-and-metal space. "And we were going to develop this space and hire an administrator—I have another company that I run—and, you know, put out a press release, reach out to the community. Maybe we'd have fifteen or twenty companies working out of the space."

It didn't turn out that way. What began as a simple real estate play quickly spiraled in new directions as it became apparent that there was more latent demand for startup space in the city than the founders had anticipated.

"I had 547 communications to me within forty-five days from people interested in being here," Widen deadpans. "So I went back to these guys and said we could go two routes with this. We could do more of kind of a closed platform where we select a group of companies and keep it on a small scale. Or we can participate in what I called at the time a movement, which I still think it is, just this bubbling up of all this interest and people wanting to be a part of this community."

As a result, the program—which runs as a pure coworking space, taking no equity in the companies that work there nor offering any direct investments—outgrew its original space in less than a year. "I don't think we were expecting to move to a new building this year," Widen says with a laugh.

The community is the thing, though, as is the importance of just having a physical space where local entrepreneurs can meet and exchange ideas. The HQ offers up its space for a variety of startup events like programming seminars, career development sessions, and open office hours with local entrepreneurs. The problem with the Triangle, Widen says, is that there have always been so many disparate groups spread out all over the place—meetups happening over here, investor mixers happening over there, networking sessions happening in different cities—and a big part of the problem was that there was no central place for everyone to come and say, OK, this is where entrepreneurs can come and talk about their work. This is where entrepreneurs can come and meet each other.

This is where everything in this community is either happening or where you can find out where it's happening. HQ aims to be that place.

"I come back to this idea of intentionality," Widen says. "I think there were a lot of people that were having the same conversations at the same time and meeting up. You know, back in the day when the Silicon Valley community was being built up, it was the coffee shops, it was the bars, and it was this idea that people were getting out and talking to one another. And if I have to look to anything here, we just have had so many events over the last a year-and-a-half period of time, here and at American Underground [in Durham] and at other places where people were just talking about things. Like-minded people, getting together and talking about what they want to see happen."

Part of the idea behind the HQ, explains cofounder Brooks Bell, who also runs her own enterprise data optimization firm alongside the HQ space, is publicity.

"The thing was we had no buzz happening [before the HQ]," she says. "I've been running my company for ten years, I was president of the Entrepreneurs' Organization (EO), and we could see what was happening with the other twenty or thirty established entrepreneurs in the area, but it was only through EO that we knew what was happening. And we'd see that someone was having this really big release and maybe *Triangle Business Journal* would cover it, but there was never any buzz internally. We had no TechCrunch, no blogs. The whole community was not connected, even within the entrepreneurship scene."

Even successful entrepreneurs have a hard time getting the word out, Widen explains, relaying the story of a founder who had contacted him earlier in the year. He had sold his company, which had been 100 percent homegrown in the Triangle region, for $90 million, but found that there was really no platform available for him to share the news with the community, let alone offer advice or startup capital to up-and-coming founders. As a result, he retired to the beach and took it easy, not able to really do anything to help other Raleigh startups.

"And this was not that long ago," Widen says. "This was just a couple of years ago and this guy sold his company for $90 million. So the entrepreneurs are here, there just hasn't necessarily been a platform for them to speak about their successes and then give back."

As for the seventeen universities that are within a ninety-mile radius of Downtown Raleigh, Bell says they generally do a good job in preparing students for the local job market, but entrepreneurs still face an uphill battle.

"Part of the problem is that none of them have any commitment to the students once they graduate," she explains. "And that's the critical time [for entrepreneurs]. That's the gap that we're trying to fill, that first year. It's easy being an entrepreneur when you're in college, but then you have to graduate and now you have to make money and your parents are kicking you out, you're off the payroll, and they want you to be successful. That first year and keeping people on that entrepreneurial track is our goal. And if we can help by just giving them some time to help figure those things out, get their first client, their first customer, getting them through that first year is our goal."

Up the road in Durham, an altogether different tech startup scene is taking shape in the shadow of that city's century-old tobacco warehouses, its historic Main Street district, and the downtown ballpark of the Triple-A Durham Bulls baseball team. Durham is a smaller city than Raleigh and has a reputation of being more of a blue-collar type of place, with a compact, red brick City Center district that runs for maybe five blocks from end to end and parallels the railroad line. The city is hilly, but crowded and bustling at midday.

"So this was an old department store originally," explains Adam Klein with Capitol Broadcasting, who's the owner of a local TV station, the Durham Bulls, as well as the American Tobacco campus. Klein is responsible for the space we're touring, a tech coworking space that can accommodate about fifty midsized startups, as well as the 26,000 startup-friendly square feet that his group manages in the basement of American Tobacco, a series of former tobacco warehouses that were redeveloped into commercial office space in 2001. "And then it was a bank. When we took over the space, there was this old bank vault, so we took this wall and cut this giant hole in it and just said . . . program it. So we do these beer one-on-one events and other things in here. It's an easy way to get startups together and get them networked."

The two-story space is open and bright, with yellow walls and small office cubicles subdividing the open space upstairs. The small rooms can probably handle three to four employees at a time, and there is space for VC offices here, as well as shared conference rooms, social areas, and a few dozen coworking desks. Klein says the facility, which opened less than a month before I visited, is totally rented out with a waiting list, and he plans to expand into the building's upper floors over the next five years.

"It's been a good run," he says. "The vacancy rate in downtown right now is 4 percent but, if you know the Durham story, five years ago it was 40 percent. I mean it was rough; it was not good. It's just been a total transformation down here."

The Durham story is an interesting one. Although the city is probably best known as the home of Duke University, Downtown Durham has essentially been a wasteland for the better part of a generation, a victim of North Carolina's struggling manufacturing sector and the general economic woes that swept through much of the South in the 1970s and '80s. Shops went out of business, residents moved to the suburbs, and the city's storefronts sat empty year after year. Things started to turn around for Downtown Durham in 1995 when the new Bulls baseball stadium was built in the urban core, and really took off around 2001 when the American Tobacco campus project got under way. That redevelopment converted a group of onetime tobacco warehouses into nearly a million square feet of new commercial space right in the heart of downtown. And we're talking really nice commercial space here, with exposed beams and brick, large brick windows, and a series of local cafés and shops, all situated around a central courtyard complete with a stream and an island. The city never looked back. A boutique hotel is planned for the space across the street from American Underground's Main Street facility, and a twenty-six-story condo town will go in up the block in 2015.

"I think what's happened in Durham is the community has really embraced [startup culture] as part of its identity," Klein says. "So it's gone from kind of a niche, fringe part of the community to something that's really front and center, really part of the identity of Durham. You walk down to the coffee shop and talk to the owners and a large part of their customers are the people who are sitting in [these coworking spaces]. Because coffee drinkers are here all the time working and they walk down to get lunch, and then they come back at night. So it's been a significant part of the overall economic development strategy. It's not the whole thing; we've got to continue to attract companies and help the companies who are already here grow from employing fifty people to one hundred. But for our sake, it's all about entrepreneurship right now."

Jason Massey, the CEO and founder of Sustainable Industrial Solutions, an energy- and efficiency-related software startup that operates out of the American Underground, agrees, citing the importance of having cool, quality, and affordable office space like this in an area where entrepreneurs want to live and work.

"I grew up in a little town called Mebane [in North Carolina]," he says, seated on the covered patio at Saladelia Cafe in the American Tobacco courtyard, "which is just past Chapel Hill. If you would have asked me ten years ago what would have been the startup hub I would have told you Raleigh, just because of NC State and the fact that Red Hat was in that area. But Durham has *far* eclipsed it."

The reason, he says, is that the startup scene in Durham has grown up organically, driven by the entrepreneurs themselves instead of being dreamed up in economic development offices and on university campuses.

"I think they were successful with the campus here just because it's a cool vibe," he says. "It's a cool place. You have some decent restaurants and it's just a cool place to hang out and work."

There are more tangible benefits as well, such as being front-and-center as part of the region's showcase startup campus and a part of a community that other entrepreneurs, not to mention investors and larger corporations, want to be a part of. That kind of visibility can be critical in a small ecosystem like the Triangle, where it can be hard for founders to garner much in the way of national attention. This advantage was demonstrated very clearly in 2012 when the President's Council on Jobs and Competitiveness toured North Carolina and made a stop at American Underground.

"So you had [GE CEO] Jeff Immelt and [Chair of the Council of Economic Advisers] Austan Goolsbee," Massey says of the visit. "You had everybody walk right down the Underground and stop at each one of the companies and sit and talk to the entrepreneurs. And I wouldn't have gotten that somewhere else. I maybe wouldn't have even gotten that if I had office space, cheaper office space, up on Main Street. This isn't the cheapest spot, but the access that we've had by being in the Underground and by being associated with the American Tobacco campus has been really, really good."

The office spaces in the American Underground are separated with glass walls and industrial lighting, likely in an effort to make the onetime basement storage space look somewhat more welcoming and professional. But the rooms are also surprisingly large, designed to accommodate startups with as many as fifty employees. And, although there are no windows down here, it isn't particular dark or gloomy. It's still a basement, but a nice, well-carpeted one.

Nestled among the dozen-plus startup tenants is the office and workspace of the Triangle Startup Factory, probably Durham's best-known technology incubator. The firm has birthed more than twenty companies since its founding in 2012 and has helped put the city on the map as a destination site for software entrepreneurs. Cofounded by longtime entrepreneurs Chris Heivly and Dave Neal, the program offers startup companies $50,000 in seed capital, three months of intensive hands-on mentoring, and another $20,000-plus of add-on funding once they head out on their own. As of my visit, of the sixteen companies that had gone through the program, only two had so far gone out of business after leaving the Startup Factory.

"I live in Chapel Hill and say I probably came to Durham about three times the first three years I lived here, and two of the times it was probably because I made a wrong turn," jokes Heivly, echoing the common theme that Downtown Durham is a *lot* better than it used to be. "There was just no reason to come over here. But I now come over every day and we're thinking about moving over here."

These days, Heivly says his firm likes to think of itself as a major Southeast player in the tech incubator space, claiming pretty much everything in terms of startups from Philadelphia to New Orleans. While there are probably a few VCs in Atlanta, Washington, DC, and elsewhere that might take issue with that, the fact is Triangle Startup Factory is a major part of the Raleigh-Durham ecosystem and has been here since 2012.

"This place was pretty dry [in terms of angel investors] in the mid-2000s," Heivly says. "Some of them got burned in the dot-com crash. But in the last year or two there are some new angel funds that have gone up, so there is definitely lots more activity. All of this you've got to build. The hardest thing is patience. I know we're going to get there, but you can't super-accelerate this stuff. People have to get comfortable. Sometimes we have something of a southern gentlemen mentality around here, so we're maybe a little less risky. It's certainly not bubble-frothy like in California. So it's a little bit more measured, but it's coming along."

The joke about North Carolina investors, at least in the early days, he says, is that the area was once referred to as "two boats and a Cadillac," the idea being that as soon as anyone in the Triangle had some success they went out and bought two boats and a Cadillac. It wasn't particularly common for money to flow back into the ecosystem to support other entrepreneurs. Fortunately, says Heivly, that is changing.

"I think what's happening in this area is there's a new wave," he says. "There are younger guys and they're wired this way. We're already seeing guys starting to put money back in; we just need a lot more of them. So we still have our old guard, fifty-and-up sort of thing, and then you have the new guys coming up. Even some of the guys who are still running early-stage companies are throwing five or ten grand in to be part of some of this. So when they have their exits, hopefully those numbers will go up."

Venture capitalist Mark Easley agrees, but says the area still suffers from a significant "funding gap" beyond the seed stage. It's become such a hurdle, he says, that most of the companies coming out of the Triangle ecosystem today won't be able to find local Series A funding even with a home run of a business idea. The money is just not there.

Still, he's upbeat about the future.

"The way it's working with the accelerators and the financing methods we have, we have all of the elements here just as good as Silicon Valley or Seattle," he says, "just everything's on a smaller scale. We've got the anchor companies we need; we've got Lenovo and Cisco and SAS and a whole bunch of health care [companies]. So to me it kind of looks like [how] Silicon Valley looked twenty-five years ago. A few big core companies—in those days out there it was HP and Intel—a couple big companies that were the motherships of all these people that would come out and create little companies. I followed that path myself way back then, and I see the same thing happening around here."

Easley himself is a Bay Area transplant, having spent twenty-five years as an engineer and marketing executive at a range of Silicon Valley companies, including Intel and Adaptec. He settled in North Carolina in 2000 and soon started advising early-stage companies and doing some angel investing. A large man, he's also something of a character, sporting a black bowling shirt with white piping at our meeting, complete with a medallion on a gold chain. His black ball cap read "Goldhat," the name of his advisory firm, in sparkly gold embroidery.

But as a software investor Easley is all business, and he's realistic about the Triangle's challenges. The fact is, if you're a twenty-three-year-old engineer coming out of one of the local universities, the truth is Silicon Valley is where you need to go if you want to make a name for yourself in this industry. The same is often all too true for Durham-area startups. Easley has seen it happen time and time again.

"This was ten years ago," he says, "but a couple guys from Cisco had a startup idea for a chip that was needed in their routers. And they surveyed the whole industry and they couldn't find anything even close to what they wanted. So they decided to quit Cisco and form a chip company to make this special chip. We worked on it for about a year—I was one of their early investors—and what we found was we just couldn't raise the kind of money they needed in this area. We tried here. There are not enough people who understand this business. So we spread it out into Virginia and other areas and we just couldn't do it. And I finally just had to tell those guys, 'Look, you're going to have to go to Silicon Valley. You're going to have to go to Phoenix.' Somewhere they understand the chip business. So we lost that one."

Oddly enough, there is actually a fair amount of friendly competition between the startup scenes in Durham and Raleigh. It's generally pretty light and not taken too seriously, though more than one person did mention the rivalry to me, prefacing their comments with words like, "It really isn't a big deal, but . . ." that tend to reveal the truth. However, Durham did get a bit of a jump start on the whole startup thing on a citywide level, setting up its own entrepreneurship efforts about a year before Raleigh got on board, and to this day does offer a bit more startup and VC density than the bigger city up the road, where bankers and politicians are still more prevalent on the sidewalks than tech workers or entrepreneurs.

CED's Jay Bigelow, whose offices are located a few doors down from the Triangle Startup Factory in the American Underground, actually calls this separation between the cities—"Balkanization" is what one of the organization's board members calls it, he says— one of the region's more significant challenges, citing it as something that, if left unchecked, could eventually hold the area back.

"The Durham people are Durham," he says, "and the Raleigh people are Raleigh. Cary people are Cary, and Morrisville is Morrisville. And Wake Forest. And Chapel Hill. The rest of the world doesn't know, doesn't care. It's like saying 'the Valley.' The folks in Palo Alto and Mountain View are really in separate towns. The rest of the world doesn't know that and doesn't care."

As a result, Bigelow says CED is working to get the locals to pull back a little bit and think about the region as a whole instead of just town by town. After all, for the Triangle to survive and to thrive as a tech ecosystem it's going to need to be about more than just local loyalties and petty competition. Sure, Chapel Hill is a different place than Downtown Raleigh, which in turn is different than small towns like Apex and Cary, but they're all North Carolina. They will rise and fall together.

"We work in all of those places," Bigelow says of CED; "we love all of those people. It's all good. I get so bent out of shape when I see that [kind of rivalry]. It's the region, dude. You're not fighting each other. Austin? Boston? Sure, I see that. But it's not us versus Durham."

One of the big selling points of the Raleigh-Durham region as a whole, for large companies in particular, is the Research Triangle Park, a 7,000-acre office/research park that straddles the intersection of I-40 and the Durham Expressway. Created in the early 1950s, the nonprofit entity was designed in an effort to keep the many PhDs and other researchers coming out of the local universities in the area after graduation by attracting major research institutions to Raleigh-Durham. (The Park got a boost about a decade later thanks to a deal between then–presidential candidate John F. Kennedy and the North Carolina delegation prior to the 1960 Democratic primary. After Kennedy won the election, he helped former North Carolina governor Terry Stanford, himself an outspoken Kennedy supporter, bring the National Institute of Environmental Health Sciences, a major government installation at the time, to the RTP.)

The Park was, for generations, a smashing success and a model for similar R&D parks nationwide. To this day, the 170-plus tenants of the Park include international players like IBM, Cisco, NetApp, GlaxoSmithKline, Microsoft, and Merck, all working in custom-designed spaces with the latest in scientific equipment and state-of-the-art labs. Cancer research, nanotechnology, semiconductor design . . . it's all still happening here.

"The Park was designed in the 1950s to be the new suburban research park," explains Bob Geolas, the current CEO of Research

Triangle Park, in his office near the Park's southern border. "It was very dynamic thinking at the time. Mom and dad would live in the suburbs. Dad would drive his car to the research park. And that worked great."

The problem, he says, is that while a lot of companies in the Park still operate that way, many of them don't really want to anymore. Driving from home, to work, to lunch, back to work, and then back home is no longer considered an ideal existence, and today's companies want more services. According to Geolas, the Park knows it is time to change to address those needs.

"Take IBM," he says. "They've got the largest number of employees here in the Park, about 10,000 people. Those 10,000 people have to leave every day, or eat at the corporate cafeteria, or work out at the corporate gym. And, frankly, IBM's ready to get out of that business. They don't want to run cafeterias anymore; they don't want to run gyms anymore. And if we can take on some of those obligations then they can get out of that and their employees don't have to drive to [those places] every day. They can walk to where the shops and restaurants are."

So the Park has been undergoing a transformation that, according to Geolas, will completely overhaul the area's image over the next five to ten years. What is now a wide-open, wooded expanse with corporate facilities set back from the two-lane access roads and protected by high gates and hedges will eventually take on more of an urban look and feel. Commercial spaces are in the works, complete with coffee shops, restaurants, hotels, and conference spaces, to be followed by coworking space and office options for startups and smaller companies. Geolas envisions flexible lease terms, customizable spaces, and all of the amenities that modern startups have come to expect.

"How do we secure a place that's not just a place of innovation, but a place of new startup innovation?" he asks. "And we want to do it in a way that's as big and significant as the creation of the Park itself was fifty years ago for America."

It's a tall order for the Research Triangle Park as it is now—and, at 7,000 acres, it's hard to imagine the Park ever becoming the walkable, bikeable ideal that Geolas imagines—but every project has to start somewhere, and if coworking space and meeting rooms make the Park, which does offer truly amazing access to some of the top research firms in the world, a more welcoming place for startups, then it is a victory. The area's small companies may soon be able to tap into the more established players, while offering the large companies a front-row peek into the latest and greatest in emerging software and technology.

But the Park really is a science and research space first and foremost, not focused on software companies. Its pedigree is in the kind of lab-based physics and biology work that's well beyond the expertise of most tech startup founders. But that's exactly the kind of work that the ff Venture Center, located just up the road from the RTP headquarters, has been doing for more than twenty years, supporting the work of biotech, health care, and other entrepreneurs as the premier science-based incubator in the region.

"Our biggest interaction tends to be with senior execs, senior players, with fifteen, twenty, twenty-five years of experience in their industry, who want to leave one of these bigger players because they want to start their own opportunity," explains Andy Schwab, CEO of ff Venture Center. "They've noticed something in the market where they're a subject matter expert and now they want to know, 'How do I start a company around this?' And they find us, because they've been driving by here for years or they've come to some of our events, and they go, 'I have an idea and I'd like to go attack it, and I think I have a very unique way of attacking it. What do you think?'"

The 25,000-square-foot facility includes fourteen wet labs and is currently home to some thirty-seven companies in various stages of development. (Unlike tech startups, where life spans are often measured in months, biotech and science startups are far more involved affairs, as proof of science and intellectual property takes a lot of time and money to develop and commercialize. As a result, Schwab says he generally likes to move companies out of the First Flight facility within three to five years. Yes, years. Most tech incubators aim to graduate self-sustaining companies in a matter of months.)

"For science-based stuff that's normal," Schwab says of the long timeline. "If you're doing a medical device or a new drug compound or any of these things, I mean, even any of the bio-technology plays, less than two years is just not going to happen. Ideally, I think, it would be a few years, but we're pretty kind with folks. We have some levers we can use, financial levers, to encourage folks out so we can make room for more people. But we have a waiting list, and the biggest thing people are waiting for is labs."

As a result, most of the entrepreneurs that Schwab works with are on the older side—in their thirties, forties, and fifties, generally, he says—and come to him with deep market knowledge and industry insights that most twentysomething tech founders can't touch. It makes for a slightly different vibe around the incubator—quiet and serious are two descriptors that come to mind—but also for stronger, more market-ready companies when they leave. The graduates still face the same "crossing the chasm" issues that come with getting customers to adopt new technology, as well as all of the same issues that entrepreneurs face with getting beyond their first product, but the founders here know that they have to be in it for the long haul. Speed is not an advantage in the markets they play in.

"I think they're more accepting of the challenges and they're more realistic that they've got a seven- to fifteen-year plan," Schwab says of the group's entrepreneurs. "And some of them, they've already dedicated a big part of their lives to whatever technology space they're in, so they're OK with it. This is their career. Whereas a younger person could swap ideas five or six times before they settle on a market that they're going to be in, whether it's health care or social or whatever vertical they want. Most of the people here have been pretty stable in something for a while."

Similar boots-on-the-ground work is happening up the road in Raleigh on the campus of North Carolina State University, where a partnership program of sorts has been growing between the university and the local tech community. Situated on what's known as the Centennial Campus, adjacent to the main undergraduate campus, the program has been designed to bring students and professors together directly with industry by offering office space to companies right on campus. It's what university leaders describe as a walkable, let's-go-get-coffee-able, live-learn-work village.

"So if you can crane your neck around over here, that's where we're going to be building the new town center, one of those places with retail and restaurants down below and condos up above," explains Dr. Terri Lomax, the university's vice chancellor for research, innovation, and economic development, from the second floor of the Corporate Research building on the south side of campus. She's in charge of the Centennial Campus that surrounds us, all of NC State's technology transfer efforts (the office that assists professors who are looking to commercialize their research discoveries), and a variety of other research and development–related projects. "And this fall we're opening a 1,200-bed [undergraduate] dorm that's going to be an entrepreneurship living and learning village, so now we're going to have a real 24/7 model here. That's over here, and up above will be the new hotel and conference center."

The whole project is part of a university-wide effort that's baked into its charter as a land grant institution to support the local economy and help the region succeed. In twenty-first-century terms, that means embracing entrepreneurship and supporting local startups by opening up the university and its resources to the business community. (Remember how Phononic CEO Tony

Atti was able to secure free usage of the university's material science equipment to get his company off the ground? That's just one example.) Need a reactor to test your idea or get proof of concept? NC State has one available. Looking for a hardware solution to a problem that's been vexing your R&D department? Sponsor a design competition through the engineering school and let the students and professors hack away at your problem. The possibilities for cooperation between the community and the university are literally limitless, Lomax says, and extend far beyond the traditional work of a university tech transfer office.

"This has evolved into a place where the students can seamlessly go back and forth between doing an internship with industry," she says, "to being in a senior design class that may have advisors from industry in there with them, to working on a research project in a professor's lab that has real practical applications. We decided a few years ago that we already had a great track record of starting companies. We have over 100 startup companies that came out of the university, and some of them are pretty significant like SAS and Cree and things like that, but we could be doing a lot better at it. So what could we do about our ecosystem to make it better? This is what's evolved out of that."

It's a tall order for a part of town that, until the 1980s, was essentially little more than a farm for the state's mental hospital, but it has proven popular with local entrepreneurs. Even during the economic downturn after 2008, Lomax says, office space on Centennial Campus was in high demand, despite high vacancy rates and cheap rents just a few minutes away in the downtown corridor. Part of that has to do with access to cheap talent and potential future employees, via the students, as well as access to the specialized equipment and technology that the university has on hand. But much of its popularity is certainly related to the faculty and the ability for entrepreneurs and their R&D folks to get firsthand knowledge about cutting-edge research and other new work that's happening on campus.

"It's about access," Lomax says. "It's this environment that's really a rich mixing pot. Because what Centennial Campus is really all about are those creative collisions. It's bringing people from different walks of life together and coming up with these great ideas. Whether it be at the food trucks every day or, you know, having your offices and labs adjacent. Or meeting at the coffee shop. That kind of thing."

That general idea of this university-to-industry connection worked for serial entrepreneur Scot Wingo, himself an NC State graduate in computer engineering, when he returned to the area in the early 1990s to start what would be the second of his now three companies, the last two focused on e-commerce and Web applications. His most recent venture, a cloud-based e-commerce service called ChannelAdvisor, allows retailers and manufacturers to quickly and easily scale their online sales efforts by simultaneously tapping channels like Amazon, Google, eBay, and others to find new customers. The company went public in 2013 and has since become one of the Triangle tech community's most notable exits.

"So what's nice about here is the quality of life and the access to talent is huge," he says in ChannelAdvisor's suburban offices. A collectibles nut, his hobby led him to create the first iteration of the company as a scaling tool for eBay Power Sellers. A life-sized statue of *Star Wars* character Anakin Skywalker in the lobby commemorates this little bit of corporate history. "I mean, I'm an NC State grad, so we recruit a lot of folks out of there. Occasionally we'll find a good Tar Heel, and the Dukies are around as well. So you have this ready . . . it's not untapped, but there are a lot of people who go through those schools, who really kind of fall in love with the area, and want to stay here."

He also didn't need to move anywhere in particular to find customers—retailers are generally everywhere, he says—and was lucky enough to find funding from all over. Even as

ChannelAdvisor took off and approached its IPO, there just wasn't any good reason to move.

"We're fortunate to have some good late-stage companies here," says Wingo. "You have Red Hat, obviously. SciQuest has done very well. We've got Cree and some of their innovations. I'm not a hardware guy, but some of what they're doing is pretty amazing. Like reinventing the lightbulb. That seems like a pretty big task, and they seem to be pretty good at it, so that's kind of fascinating to me."

Luke Fishback, the founder of PlotWatt, an energy analytics company that helps residential and commercial end users better understand where their energy dollars are going, agrees that the Triangle has a lot going for it in terms of talent and quality of life.

"So I actually lived out in Silicon Valley before this," he says. "I worked in aerospace, and my wife was a relatively early Googler. I think I got infected a bit with the [entrepreneurial] bug out there, but when it came time to actually start something myself I looked out and said, gosh, the Valley has some really appealing things about it, but when you can kind of step back and look at what a company like PlotWatt needs, particularly in the early stages, what we need is a place where there are lots of smart folks and a good talent pool. Ideally a really good kind of balance of cost of living and quality of living. So, in other words, I want people to be able to work largely for equity in the early days and still not have to live on the streets."

Locating in a smaller ecosystem has also helped PlotWatt stand out from the competition—it ranks on the first page of Google results for "energy startup Durham," which Fishback says certainly isn't hurting them in terms of recruitment.

"I defy you to be able to get on the first page of Google as an energy startup in the Silicon Valley," he says.

What's more, the company hasn't suffered for attention, from customers and others, just because it's headquartered on the East Coast.

"Actually, one of the things that has proven to be appealing from, like, a mind-share or getting people's attention perspective," he says, "is that when you're in an area like the Research Triangle Park you can be *the* cool or *one of* the cool startups in your sector. Right? So an area like this allows you to kind of stand out a bit more when it comes to the mind-share of people that matter. And when you're building a company like we are, the people that really matter are a lot more important than just generic consumer attention."

For Citrix ShareFile founder Jesse Lipson, the choice was even more straightforward. He and his wife knew that the Triangle was a nice place to live, since both had gone to college at Duke, and they noticed that the area kept showing up on those "best places to live" lists. Why should we move, he asks, since everyone is apparently moving here?

"I feel like success is very relative," he tells me over lunch near the RTP. "They've done studies on how as people have gotten richer and richer it's just like this arms race where they have these more extravagant birthday parties for their kids. But it's all relative. Everyone would be just as happy if they all agreed to scale things down. So our feeling is we're probably happier in Raleigh building a successful business than we would be building the same level of business in Silicon Valley, where that's more of the norm."

That attitude fits in with what Lipson calls one of his personal mission statements: to beat the system by avoiding all of the "rat race" types of traps that people often fall into in the course of their careers. "I feel like living in Raleigh is an example of doing that," he says. "Whereas if we were in Silicon Valley we'd be part of that whole machine, which has its advantages and disadvantages. But we wanted to do something a little bit different, and living here is part of that."

It's not all upside, though. Basing a startup in North Carolina comes with its own set of challenges, according to Daniel Chalef, founder and CEO of KnowledgeTree, a B2B sales and marketing software startup located in the hip North Boylan neighborhood just west of Downtown Raleigh. Chalef first moved his company from South Africa to the Bay Area, but eventually relocated to Raleigh in part to help with the time difference between the US and South Africa, where he still maintains an office. Moving to the South has been, he tells me, a bit of a culture shock.

"You know, the Bay Area and South Africa are very similar," he says. "There are strong cultural elements that are similar. And being here in the South was initially very foreign. Very, very foreign. South Africa, particularly Capetown where I lived, is very liberal, very progressive. And I found it challenging being in the South. And this is the liberal part of the South, as well," he says, laughing.

But the real trouble, he says, has been in hiring qualified, experienced support staff. Finding engineers is always a problem, no matter where you are. Everyone can always use more engineers. But Chalef says he's most acutely aware of a shortage of qualified salespeople in the Triangle. Part of it is just due to competition—Citrix is scaling, Netsertive is scaling, and even ChannelAdvisor is scaling still, all of which are essentially going after the same pool of software salespeople and sucking up all of the talent. But there's also another troubling trend that Chalef sees just under the surface.

"In the US, it's very apparent that there's a high degree of structural unemployment," he says. "Where, yeah, there are folks. There are salespeople around and there are engineers around, but they're not the right salespeople and they're not the right engineers. Firstly, it's their skills. Often they're field salespeople who have unfortunately been put out to pasture, and they don't have the energy or the appetite to sit on the phone and make those forty to sixty calls a day as a sales development rep."

As a result, KnowledgeTree and many startups like it can't use them. It's not that Chalef doesn't need the help, but a lot of the employee base in the Triangle region is not well suited to support the area's growing tech sector. And that's a big problem that's affecting more than just KnowledgeTree. Sharefile is hiring hairdressers and bartenders to fill its sales rep openings, Chalef tells me, simply because they can't find enough high-energy people to take those jobs. Software sales is a tough business, he says, and it takes a certain kind of personality to excel at it. What's more, having great schools nearby can be something of a double-edged sword in this industry. Yes, it means there is a steady stream of new talent coming into the ecosystem, but they're often very wet behind the ears, meaning managers will have to spend extra time training them and extra time getting them up to speed. And when you're a startup that doesn't have time or manpower to spare, that's challenging.

"You just have to make peace with the fact that you're in Raleigh-Durham and don't get too caught up in the bullshit," Chalef says. "Because small ecosystems have a lot of bullshit. Large ecosystems have a lot of bullshit, too, but here you just can't get bogged down in it. Just put your head down and focus on what you do."

The truth is, the Raleigh-Durham startup scene is a small ecosystem. And, yes, it does come with its own unique set of challenges. Hiring for particular positions can be more difficult, and raising funds, especially beyond the seed round, is still a major challenge. But entrepreneurs in the Triangle also know that there are special qualities in the area that work in their favor.

"You know, I think one of the things that I find myself trying to encourage in the local startup community is there are things about North Carolina that you can do here that you can't do elsewhere," explains PlotWatt's Fishback. "And I fear that too often startups that are kind of outside of the Valley or are outside of one or two other places are always trying to make their startup community, you know, 'Silicon Valley East.' When, in reality, there are so many things we can do here in North Carolina that you can't do in Silicon Valley because of cost and because of what's available in terms of space."

Take the PlotWatt office, for example. It's located on ten wooded acres outside of town and comes complete with a barn for the company's Ping-Pong table and a gym. It may not be Apple's "spaceship campus" or a penthouse overlooking Central Park in New York City, but it's not a bad place to spend your working hours.

"It's about kind of, you know, embracing the 'North Carolina' of North Carolina," Fishback says. "And I think that when startups do more of that they don't tend to have regrets about being here or bypassing the Silicon Valley path."

The fact is, innovation has been happening in the Triangle region for generations, and the evidence is everywhere for those willing to look. The area is home to some of the finest medical centers in the country, some of the world's leading pharmaceutical companies, and a collection of agriculture technology developers that are leaders in their fields.

"Silicon Valley developed its own unique flavor and capabilities through a wild set of circumstances that's impossible to replicate," says Andy Schwab with the ff Venture Center. "Every region has its own talents."

Entrepreneurs just need to look around at what's already happened, where there are already concentrations in certain industries and certain specialties, and try to leverage that. If a founder suddenly decides that they want to create a new capital of nanotechnology, or whatever field they're interested in, right in the middle of North Carolina, it would require a concerted effort from industry and government, and most likely a lot of money, to make it happen. Whereas, tapping into the resources that already exist in the Triangle, the companies and industries that are already flourishing there and the millions of dollars' worth of infrastructure that they already have in place, is going to be the smarter and easier path.

"We have one group here, Excelerate Health Ventures, which is a physician-based fund targeted toward health-care IT," Schwab says. "I think it's a brilliant strategy, and they've located that here for a reason. They didn't say, well, I think health care might be interesting to focus on. No, we have a very good base to work with already. We don't have to attract people to the area to do this; it's already going on. All we have to do is organize capital around it and figure out how we best support these types of ideas that are already being developed here. I think that's the more interesting strategy."

It is even time, some say, for North Carolina to get over its Silicon Valley complex and embrace what the Bay Area can offer Triangle-region startups, rather than worrying about California snatching away the state's best and brightest.

"I know a lot of investors here who will literally shield people from the Valley," says Jason Massey with Durham's Sustainable Industrial Solutions, "like it's this thing that's shiny and cool. And they're scared that if you send a really solid rails developer out to Silicon Valley they're not going to come back. So you'll see a lot of people really concerned about brain drain around here, rather than embracing it and saying, yeah, we'll lose some people, but we may gain some people back that are smarter, better, and wiser for their time in the Valley."

There needs to be more sharing back and forth, he says. So rather than the startup folks and ecosystem evangelists in North Carolina trying to *be* another Silicon Valley, everyone just needs to accept that Silicon Valley is a special place for a reason and tap into it rather than trying to be it or some variation of it.

"The good entrepreneurs around here have said, I like living here, I can get good core talent here, but I'm still going to get the most out of Silicon Valley and not make it some artificial competition between regions," says Massey. "Just embrace it. A lot of the startups, a lot of the young entrepreneurs that I've worked with as kind of an advisor or mentor, I'd ship them to Silicon Valley and people around here have gotten mad at me for brain drain. And it's sort of like, you gotta let your kids grow up. Some of them will stay, some of them will come back, and hopefully they'll bring the best of what they've learned out in the Valley back to this ecosystem and they'll grow it."

CHAPTER

8

Boulder

"Colorado has developed into a state that every investor should watch. Our startup communities and economy are thriving, and the companies being created here are awesome."

—Brad Feld, serial entrepreneur, TechStars cofounder, and managing director of the Foundry Group

"I VISITED COLORADO back before my junior year of college at DePaul University and I fell in love with the Rocky Mountains," explains Jim Deters, a longtime Colorado technology entrepreneur and the cofounder of Galvanize, a tech-focused coworking space located near Downtown Denver. "Literally ten days within graduating I was on an airplane with one bag of shit, that's all I had back then, a bike, and a snowboard, and I landed in Colorado to start my career."

An economics major, Deters knew he wanted to work in technology but, as a then–newly minted twenty-one-year-old college grad in 1998, didn't really know what was going on in terms of tech, aside from the ever-expanding Silicon Valley scene. The one thing he did know, however, was that he had no interest in moving to California.

"I wanted to play in the mountains. I loved the Rocky Mountains, I was just fascinated. Every fiber of my being wanted to climb up 'em, and ski down 'em, and jump off 'em, and bike down 'em. I just wanted to be in the mountains. And I've been here now for fifteen years."

Deters is making these statements not at his office, not at a tech-friendly coffee shop, but at a multi-industry startup event at the University of Colorado (CU) School of Law in Boulder, Colorado. It's an event that's been organized by university leaders in an effort to bring together local entrepreneurs from the worlds of technology and . . . beer. It isn't as random a pairing as it might seem. Both technology and craft beer have taken off big-time in the Centennial State—according to the Brewer's Association, the state's craft breweries contributed $1.6 billion to the US economy in 2012, with the 139 licensed craft brewers in the state generating $179.2 million in total employment effect in that time. Technology companies currently employ 141,000 people in Colorado and contribute $49.6 billion to the state's economy every year, according to the Colorado Technology Association. In terms of startups, the state-backed 2012 Built in Denver report found that 122 tech startups were launched in the state in 2012, with 70 companies securing funding of $1 million or more and 20 companies being acquired. Colorado-based digital companies raised more than $502 million in total funding in 2012, with $197 million of that going to companies based in Boulder. Of those, about 78 percent of the investment dollars in the state in 2012 went to software and business-to-business digital technology companies.

And popular doesn't even begin to describe these two industries. The startup event in early 2013, which included presentations and Q&As from four founders on either side, was packed when I arrived, filling the CU Law School's main auditorium to capacity with some 250 students, entrepreneurs (the latest TechStars class is here), and even local residents who are just interested in what's happening. Boulder is where local entrepreneurs want to operate, where many young developers want to live, and where many see the future of small-business growth happening in Colorado.

Besides, who doesn't want to gawk at cool new tech while drinking free local beer?

"So I'm a Boulder native but I did spend about ten years in Southern California, [in] San Diego, where I got my start as a developer," explains Ingrid Alongi, the cofounder and CEO of Boulder-based tech services firm Quick Left, which creates custom Web and mobile apps for other businesses. "And I remember thinking, 'Oh gosh, I'm going to have to learn how to golf,' because in Southern California you need to go to La Jolla and drive a nice car and sort of do the networking thing. But when I got recruited to come back here to work at a startup, I was really pleasantly surprised that not only could I do what I love, which is ride bikes, to get the networking done, but also that the culture was really supportive of what we were doing."

The local "Boulder effect" extends beyond networking, Alongi says, although she admits that she did meet some of her first clients, and even her lawyer, on those early bike rides. In this town, the focus is on group support. Entrepreneurs in the area, and there are many, have a reputation for being unflagging cheerleaders for each other and the state as a whole, because, as the thinking goes, when one startup succeeds, the whole region succeeds. This is not an entirely unusual attitude—after all, the raising-all-boats message is essentially what Chambers of Commerce spout from coast to coast—but in Boulder, it has become something of a mantra, a goal for the city's small businesses, tech startups included, to live up to.

"There's also the proximity of being able to walk across the street and see people on a regular basis," Alongi says of doing business in a town of just 100,000 people, where the offices of many of the local tech companies are within a few blocks of each other. "You can just have those one-off conversations that kind of connect you to each other and keep you top of mind. And it's not just, 'OK, this friend of mine is looking for some talent or looking for work,' but it also contributes to that culture of encouragement and support."

Boulder, Colorado, is known for a lot of things—its college-town roots, its laid-back vibe, its epic rock climbing, and its world-famous annual open-air marijuana festival. The city is home to the University of Colorado Boulder and has long been a staple on those irritating annual "best places to live" and "America's healthiest cities" lists (so much so that editors seem to be deliberately excluding it these days). It's an active, outgoing, and winner-take-all type of place, the kind of town where going for a simple morning run can be a humbling, competitive experience.

But Boulder's growing reputation as a hub for technology start-ups? That's a different story, and one that's still in its early stages.

In fact, the high-altitude city is becoming about more than just sun, fun, and powder skiing. Over the last several years Boulder has developed a reputation as a tech development hub and business incubation center, home to some 200 tech startups in industries ranging from software, to energy, to mobile, to health care. And we're not just talking about dorm-room projects. There are well-established companies on this list—like Kerpoof, a kid-focused Web design house that was acquired by the Walt Disney Company in 2009; Socialthing, a social media synchronization tool that is now part of AOL; and Rally Software, a project management developer that went public in 2013 with an $84 million IPO. SparkFun Electronics is a local online retailer/hack studio that sells and develops all sorts of electronic parts for project developers, while Mocavo is creating a free genealogy-focused search engine by tapping into the big data side of family trees.

Google has a Boulder office. Microsoft has a Boulder office, as does Mobius Venture Capital. Major Silicon Valley players like Oracle, IBM, and HP have been in the area for years, tapping into the local engineering and research talent courtesy of CU, and there are no less than fifteen US government laboratories and science institutes in the area, including the National Oceanic and Atmospheric Administration and the National Institute of Standards and Technology.

None of this is an accident, of course. Boulder is one of the most educated cities in the country with the highest concentration of software engineers and PhDs per capita in the US and is second only to Silicon Valley itself in the percentage of workers employed in the tech sector. But Boulder is about more than just smart people, writes Phil Weiser, the senior advisor for technology and innovation to the National Economic Council director. The real key to the city's ecosystem is the open, supportive community that those people have created, and the entrepreneurs it attracts. Weiser should know; prior to his appointment to the Obama administration in 2009, he worked at the University of Colorado Law School for a decade and ran the Silicon Flatirons Center for Law, Technology, and Entrepreneurship. He credits Boulder venture capitalist Brad Feld and his cofounders at local VC firm the Foundry Group for helping build this community, as well for spreading the message of Boulder as a hub for tech startups.

"Many entrepreneurial communities ask how they can be the next Silicon Valley," Weiser wrote in 2011. "As Brad has often explained, that's the wrong question. The right question is how any entrepreneurial community—whether it's Philadelphia, Cleveland, Detroit, Phoenix, or Portland—can be the best it can be. Each community has its own particular attributes and leaders. Working together and supporting each other, as Boulder leaders have done, is a core part of building a more successful ecosystem."

But is that really all there is to it? Is a supportive community really the only thing that's made Boulder's startup culture what it is? Of all the midsized college towns in the country, why this one?

As with just about everything, it all depends on whom you ask.

"You know, the tech scene here really sprung out of TechStars when they got going in 2006 to 2007. I credit Brad Feld with most of it."

"It's just a good place to live and attracts the kind of young people who start companies."

"It's great that CU is here, but they really haven't played a role in the development of the ecosystem. I think that's changing, but they're still catching up."

"CU isn't Stanford, let's say that."

The refrains about the Boulder startup ecosystem all pretty much center on a few key ideas. There is the university, there is the community, there is the talent, there is the money, and there is the quality of life. Boulder, many would have you believe, is just too awesome of a place for this not to have happened. People want to live here, there aren't enough jobs to go around, and so startup-minded folks generally get to work creating their own employment. It just so happens that a number of those entrepreneurs lately have been focusing their efforts on high-growth technology companies.

But the fact is there is more to it than that. In truth, there is no escaping the role that the University of Colorado Boulder and the existing local infrastructure have played in the city's technological development. It may not be as direct a correlation as most people would expect, but it's a connection nonetheless.

Consider the town's beginnings.

Boulder got its start more than 1,000 years ago as a Native American settlement, part of the Southern Arapaho tribe's territory, and was frequented by most of the western tribes of the day, including the Ute, Cheyenne, Comanche, and Sioux. The settlement itself was located northeast of present-day Downtown Boulder, near what is now called Haystack Mountain, a medium-sized rise between the plains and the foothills. In its pre-Columbian heyday, the area is thought to have been home to as many as 20,000 people.

All of this came to a screeching halt in the late 1850s, when nonnative settlers stormed the area in search of gold, which had recently been discovered near the entrance to Boulder Canyon (not far from the Foundry Group's modern-day offices on Walnut Street). The Boulder City Town Company was formed, officers were elected, and the new city was divvied up into 4,044 building lots offered up for $1,000 each, while the town fathers created services like hospitals, fire departments, and downtown infrastructure. Competition to attract residents to what is now one of the most sought-after addresses in the country was steep in the early days, so the town was put on sale, with residential lots going for as little as $500 at one point (the median sale price for a home in the city was $445,000 as of December 2013). Once the city took hold it became a popular supply base for gold and silver miners heading up into the high country—providing the men with gear, transportation, entertainment, and all of the other stereotypes of nineteenth-century western US life. Boulder became part of the United States' Territory of Colorado in 1861.

Further change came soon after, when the new University of Colorado campus was established on what was then called a "barren and wind-swept plain." Funded by $15,000 worth of matching funds raised by Boulder residents and sited on a piece of land donated by a group of prominent local citizens, the university got off to a bare-bones start in 1876, packing all forty-four of its inaugural students and three professors into one building that still stands at the center of campus.

Fast-forward half a century, and the Boulder transformation continued as local academics began to find work in the atmospheric sciences, geology, and engineering labs that were set up nearby after World War II. With twenty-four federal laboratories in the region, Colorado is still home to one of the highest concentrations of government science and research centers in the country, employing nearly 8,000 people locally and generating more than $1.5 billion in annual economic impact. Boulder in particular is home to the National Oceanic and Atmospheric Administration, the National Center of Atmospheric Research, the Cooperative Institute for Research in Environmental Sciences, and an outpost of the National Institute of Standards and Technology. The local community grew in this period to include scientists, businessmen, researchers, and others interested in the promise of technology, forming a group that was at the time very different from the cowboys and miners that had made up most of Colorado's population to date. As a result, Boulder became an island of liberal thought in a sea of open ranchland; this town is known as the "People's Republic of Boulder" for a reason.

But, all of that said, the traditional institutions are just part of the picture. There are good reasons that members of today's Boulder's startup community say that the scene more or less sprang up on its own with little outside help or encouragement. Yes, the city has long been home to an established group of tech thinkers and doers. And yes, the university played a role in bringing all of these people together. And yes, there is a unique cultural element at play in the city. But the fact is, there was really very little in the way of tech startup activity in Boulder prior to the late 1990s. Something big happened in 2006 that really got the Boulder entrepreneurship ball rolling, bringing the right people together at the right time and, most importantly, making sure they had the funds and inspiration needed to get their ideas off the ground: The TechStars accelerator program was founded by David Cohen, Brad Feld, David Brown, and Jared Polis in Boulder.

"When I moved to Boulder in the mid-nineties it had a lot of the roots that you look for, but the startup community itself was still fairly nascent," explains Brad Feld, one of the four cofounders of TechStars, which after getting its start in Boulder has since gone national with programs in Boston, Seattle, San Antonio, Austin, New York City, and London, among others. "But that was common fifteen to twenty years ago."

What the city did have, Feld explains, was a surplus of talented, eager, young go-getters—smart, unemployed folks that were looking for a way to leave their mark on the world. Best of all, they were died-in-the-wool hippies, born thirty years too late. Granola-eating, patchwork-wearing free spirits who weren't tied down to the conventions and expectations of more traditional, coastal-based business ideas. They were tailor-made for the startup lifestyle.

"Richard Florida literally wrote the book on this called *The Rise of the Creative Class*," Feld says, "and one of his great comments was that entrepreneurial companies and creative types of people tend to find themselves in areas that are full of other weird people. And the word 'weird' is deliberate there. If you find yourself in a place where people are more open to weird new things, there's a good chance they'll be open to new ways of doing things and doing business, too.

"The notion of the creative class is a generational one. There's been this huge shift back to cities recently—they're more fun, there's more energy versus a suburban or agrarian life. And when you get back to the city you tend to see people doing interesting and different things."

American society is a long way from the norms of the 1950s and '60s, when the whole notion of the successful working life was a house in the suburbs, a steady job, and a couple of kids. Success these days isn't necessarily about job security and long-time employment, neither of which can be guaranteed anymore, but rather having a good idea and running with it. Finding your own way in the marketplace and your own place in it. This isn't a particularly new idea—US entrepreneurs have been starting businesses for generations—but Feld says the trend has accelerated in recent years thanks to the 2008 recession as the whole idea of American success has "morphed dramatically."

"People are looking for deeper meaning in what they do now," he says. "I think people have realized that they have to take responsibility for their own lives, and that's what entrepreneurs do. They take responsibility for their own life rather than putting it in someone else's hands. That has stimulated a lot of people to start companies, and has also stimulated a lot of people to go work for startups. There was a huge rude awakening in 2008 to 2009 that prosperity wasn't endless, and I think the next generation that's between fifteen and their midthirties right now is coming into a job environment that is very different than anything we've seen before. It's ripe for startups."

TechStars has tapped into this movement, funding and mentoring a select number of promising technology startups through their earliest stages. Mentors associated with the program (not just in Boulder, but program-wide) include Foursquare CEO Dennis Crowley, Birchbox cofounder Hayley Barna, Warby Parker cofounder Neil Blumenthal, and Union Square Ventures partner Fred Wilson. To date, the program has reviewed thousands of potential startups and claims that more than 92 percent of its graduates are still up and running as profitable companies. As of 2013, there were 211 active TechStars alumni companies worldwide—twenty-nine startups had by that point been acquired and twenty-seven had failed—and the average amount raised by each company program-wide was just over $1.5 million. TechStars companies had by then created more than 2,000 jobs nationwide. Among the program's success stories are email marketing firm SendGrid; social discovery network Brightkite, which was acquired by Limbo in 2009; Web-based enterprise software developer Thinkfuse; frequent-flyer rewards management tool GoMiles; and enterprise chat service TimZon. The program's largest exit so far is the 2012 acquisition of location-based mobile ad network ThinkNear by Televan for $22.5 million.

*   *   *

Of course, TechStars is just one part of Feld's involvement with the Boulder startup ecosystem. He is also a partner with local venture capital firm the Foundry Group, a $225 million fund that focuses on early-stage tech startup investments ranging from $225,000 to $500,000. The firm invests in companies both in Boulder and across the country.

"We invest in a series of themes," Feld explains of the fund's objectives. "Computer interaction and rapid transit are happening right now, but it's all about progress. Think about how you used a cell phone a decade ago versus today. How you used a computer then versus a tablet today. All of these things are changing very rapidly, so we have a number of companies in our portfolio trying to hone in on those changes."

Truth is, the Foundry Group's portfolio of companies is really an extension of the firm's partners' personal interests. In addition to the themes mentioned above, the fund also invests in "adhesives," those technologies that combine different services in new ways; digital life solutions; distribution startups; and "glue," or startups that power social content aggregation, human-computer interaction, and protocol startups. All of which tap into the partners' investment interests. It's a roster that has included some fifty companies to date, including household names like video game maker Zynga and Cheezburger, the company behind meme sites like I Can Has Cheezburger? and The Daily What. Among the firm's lesser-known names are StockTwits, a social networking service built around investment information and stock tips; Authentic8, a browser-as-a-service security firm; Gnip, a social media API aggregation company; Jirafe, an e-commerce analytics engine; and Federated Media Publishing, an independent publishing network. Foundry-backed Admeld was acquired by Google in December 2011, while Research in Motion acquired the firm's local contacts-organizing portfolio company Gist in February 2011.

"Unlike many venture capital firms that invest in certain geographic regions or specific technologies and sectors, the Foundry

Group's investing activity is largely driven by a thematic approach," the firm states in its mission statement. "The themes we pursue tend to be horizontal in nature and are often driven by underlying technology protocols and standards or emerging market trends and customer needs. Rather than looking for short-term hits, we focus on themes that have the ability to drive a cycle of innovation (and hence provide multiple investment opportunities) over a period of five to ten years or more."

And, according to Feld, five to ten years is still the "short-term" view for a lot of what happens in a city like Boulder. The city's ecosystem, as self-sustaining and successful as it is at this point, is still in the developmental stages, he says, and still needs thoughtful investment to maintain and grow it over the long haul. The key is having the right tools in place at the right time to allow founders to thrive and their ideas to mature.

"There are four main points," says Feld. "Your startup community has to be led by entrepreneurs, you have to take a long-term view, it needs to be inclusive of anyone at any level, and you need to have a series of activities and events that goes beyond just cocktail parties and business meetings. I think that if you get those things right over a long enough period of time, then you can create a startup community anywhere. I really have a deeply held belief in this. Boulder is the example."

But can the "Boulder model" really be replicated effectively elsewhere? Feld is optimistic but realistic about the challenges in different cities. "It's not the case that today there are effective startup communities everywhere, but I do believe there could be," he says. It's just a matter of local leaders taking the time to nurture their entrepreneurs and develop the sense of community. "You can't be thinking about 2015. You have to think about 2032."

The Foundry Group's office location near the west end of the Pearl Street pedestrian mall, in the heart of Downtown Boulder, makes a lot of sense when you're standing right in the middle of it all. Not only is it close to the CU campus and the research labs on the south end of town, but it sits on the primary north/south artery through town and is also right in the middle of what is essentially Boulder's hottest startup neighborhood. SparkFun's headquarters are in same building at the intersection of Broadway and Walnut Street. Pay-per-click advertising startup Trada is headquartered in the old *Daily Camera* newspaper building across the street, while advertising services firm Lijit is up around the corner. That kind of proximity makes collaboration easy, casual runs-ins common-place, and creative collisions a part of everyday life. It plays into that I'll-help-you-and-you-help-me culture that so many Boulder entrepreneurs rave about. They just run into each other—on the sidewalks, in the cafés, in the parking garages—too often not to.

And, given the entrepreneurial value that Feld and others place on Boulder's social vibe, the Pearl Street district itself is the perfect location for all of this to be happening. Created in 1976 as one of the first pedestrian-only streets in the country, Pearl Street is now a commercial corridor with walkable access to everything from restaurants and bars to high-end boutiques and funky gifts shops, closed off to traffic for four blocks through downtown. It also doles out heaping helpings of countercultural appeal, courtesy of break-dancers, balloon artists, drummers, jugglers, and more.

Between the live-action artists, the living statues, and the bucket drum musicians, the pedestrian mall is like a mini ver-sion of San Francisco circa 1971, complete with the anything-goes sensibility and the "I've seen it all, so I dare you to try and impress me" attitude that the modern tech industry was built on. But the Boulder small-business community extends beyond the realm of the technology industry. This is a town where just about everyone seems to be their own boss, and where supporting your neighbor's up-and-coming business idea is a point of pride. Case in point:

Sitting down at yet another local coffee shop, I find it hard to ignore the fact that the place is packed at 11:00 a.m. on a Tuesday.

It's not uncommon for newcomers to Boulder to walk around in the middle of the day wondering why all these people aren't at work. But the fact is there are so many small businesses here that many locals just don't work regular hours. They go to coffee shops, they meet at the park, they work on the patio. They just don't sit in a cubicle all day.

In fact, according to the US Census Bureau, Boulder has the highest percentage of work-from-home residents in the US, with 10.9 percent of locals working outside of the normal nine-to-five workforce. Nationally, the rate is 4.3 percent.

That means that just about everything I've seen of the Boulder startup scene—the collaborative atmosphere, the focus on local talent, the attitude of friendly competition—applies to the other business niches in town as well. Everyone works on an as-needed basis and there really is a focus on local business in Boulder, on supporting your neighbors and your friends and whatever venture they're working on.

Brad Bernthal, executive director of the University of Colorado's Entrepreneurial Law Clinic and the current director of the Silicon Flatirons Center for Law, Technology, and Entrepreneurship, knows the feeling. In fact, he is so committed to the role that Boulder's hippie vibe plays in the growth of the local startup scene that he wrote an essay on the topic in 2009, dubbing the movement "HipTech."

> HipTech reflects a phenomena to which people ascribe various names. For most Boulder insiders, a defining characteristic of the scene is that, as a regular practice, individuals give away lots of resources for "free." Some call it the karma economy, a coffee-with-anyone place, a mentor-driven culture, a dense and

horizontal network (OK, no one says that one, but I teach it in my classes), the location where potential competitors root for and help each other, and other assorted feel-good monikers. I once considered calling Boulder a tithe-based entrepreneurial community; however, a 10 percent estimate is probably too low. Among big movers in Boulder, I estimate more like 15 to 20 percent of a mover's time veers more toward "volunteer involvement" than "direct professional benefit."

According to Bernthal, part of this attitude really does boil down to the "crunchy culture" that has been present in Boulder since the 1960s (and was common in the Bay Area in those days, too), the open-air jugglers, the community of drifters, the laid-back so-what-if-it's-Tuesday-we're-going-skiing feel that permeates daily life. It can be grating on newcomers—there's that "why aren't these people working?" question again—but there is clearly a live-and-let-live community in Boulder that contributes to the entrepreneurial community by encouraging risk taking, rewarding innovation, and showing potential founders that there can be success outside of the standard nine-to-five job.

"I think one of the big aspects of the scene here is the culture of mentorship and that spirit of helpfulness," he says. "It's sort of a 'go get coffee with anybody' sort of place, whether it's the CEO of a big, established company or your competitor down the block. There's a real culture of intense networking between companies."

And it's all voluntary, he adds. "Very rarely, if ever, does money change hands in all these interactions. Some of it is a generosity of spirit, some of it is this 'pay it forward' attitude."

Back to that 2009 essay:

Boulder's belief in HipTech presents a weird melding of high-tech capitalism meets gift economy. To be clear: few area entrepreneurs and capitalists are into astrology or folk music.

Entrepreneurial mysticism tilts more toward the Singularity and a belief in yet-to-form markets than a trust in crystals. Yet HipTech reflects a homage to the area's hippie commune legacy: take what you need, give what you can. Or, to be fair, a different way to look at it—more transactional in nature (and probably more palatable for my Ayn Rand's Fountainhead-reading friends)—is that Boulder is a high-tech barter economy with exchanges made on a time delayed basis. Take what you need now, your credit is good, and you can pay me back in kind later.

Bernthal, an associate clinical professor at the CU Law School, has also been working over the last several years to bring the university into the local startup scene in more concrete ways, offering entrepreneurial classes to students and serving as a legal resource to local founders. It's a new sort of outreach effort for the school and is a bit outside its mandate as a research university, but it is starting to pay dividends.

"There's generally a conviction that great startup scenes are backed by great research universities," Bernthal told Fox Business TV when the network profiled the local ecosystem in 2013. "But we also believe that great startup scenes help create great universities, in terms of attracting top-tier faculty, attracting top-tier students, and creating job opportunities for our students. There's nothing better that could happen long-term for the University of Colorado than to have this startup scene succeed."

It's true, CU is not Stanford. But, for its part, the university is making a concerted effort to get more involved and support the city's local entrepreneurs. The Silicon Flatirons Center is just one example, offering a range of events for students and locals alike, with a focus on tech law and entrepreneurship. The CU Leeds School of Business has been hosting more startup-themed speakers in recent years, and Bernthal has been getting the law school involved with technology interest trainings and entrepreneurial law seminars. In his view, hosting events and get-togethers like these are a way for CU to contribute to the local scene in a productive and inexpensive way, even if the school's talent output is still catching up to demand.

"As a university, we have access to a wide variety of speakers and thinkers and business leaders that local founders might not be able to reach otherwise," he says. "So that's where we're trying to make our mark—serving as a resource by hosting events and bringing people together, all under the umbrella of the university community."

It's been a long process—more than seven years in the making, according to Bernthal—but many believe it will pay off for CU and Boulder in general in the end. Just having the university in the conversation is a new and important piece of the puzzle, and Bernthal only expects the town-gown relationship to mature from here.

Robert Reich, one of the entrepreneurs behind the Openspace Store, the world's first and only brick-and-mortar app store (formerly located on Pearl Street, now closed), as well as the founder of the Boulder/Denver New Tech Meetup, the largest community-run tech group in the state, agrees that the university is stepping up its involvement, but in his view, it is Boulder's community of entrepreneurs that deserves the real credit for everything that has been happening in the ecosystem.

"We started [the] New Tech [Boulder Meetup] in August 2006 and TechStars hadn't started yet, the Foundry Group didn't exist yet," he says over coffee one snowy morning on Pearl Street. "The town was in a very different state. Brad Bernthal was really just getting going; everybody was starting to build a name for themselves. They were coming out of the [dot-com] bubble, the whole experience, and the community itself was like, 'OK, what's going on here?'"

The meetup, which began as a group of just forty-five people in a walk-up office space near downtown, became a key organizing event for the community, the kind of place where previously disparate entrepreneurs could get together, share ideas, and talk shop for a few hours a month. Although it started out small, the group quickly outgrew its space, moving into a large lecture hall at the CU Law School that, according to Reich, has been sold out every month since for the past five years.

"The event itself was very honest and it became a central gathering for people to catch up with everybody else in town," says Reich, who splits his time as the CEO of app-discovery tool Openspace and as a lecturer at CU. "And the community had a say in it. If you were in Boulder on the first Tuesday of the month, you should go visit [it]. And they became the drivers of it; I was just an organizer."

As a side effect of all this activity, and because New Tech was meeting every month at the CU Law School, Reich himself got involved personally with the school and ended up helping it become a larger player in the local ecosystem. He started lecturing on entrepreneurialism at the business school, worked with university and local leaders to better bridge the town-gown divide, and in 2009 helped lay the groundwork for an advertising technology program called Boulder Digital Works (BDW) that has evolved into a general tech education course under the auspices of the CU engineering school. Reich remains on the BDW faculty and teaches a few classes a year, and he's no longer alone in his involvement with CU. Brad Bernthal and Foundry Group cofounder Jason Mendelson both teach a class on entrepreneurship at the law school; Ryan Martens, the CTO of Rally Software, teaches a class at the engineering school; and a student in the MBA program even recently created a program to connect angel investors with startup-minded students at the university.

"It's been very kind of entrepreneurial and bootstrapped," Reich says of the community's recent growth. "To say, 'We don't know the answers, we're going to fail, let's see what works and approach it that way.' It's been very much like a startup in a way as to how it's actually evolving, which is why I say I don't know that it's that different from most other communities. [This ecosystem] is being led by entrepreneurs who want and need resources, who are willing to kind of put time in over and above, and that's been the approach across the board. It's just been this very scrappy nature of pushing and driving [the community] up."

And it's expanding. According to Reich's research, there were approximately 925 tech startups operating in Colorado, involving some 9,000 people, as of 2013. The majority of these are in Boulder (400-plus) and Denver (200-plus), but Reich has also uncovered startup ecosystems in Colorado towns as far flung as the Western Slope outpost of Durango and the tiny ski town of Aspen. Even Fort Collins, an hour north of Denver and home to Colorado State University, has been developing and emerging a tech identity of its own.

Andrew Hyde is one of Boulder's young tech organizers, and has been involved in the Boulder startup community since the very beginning. He is the founder of Startup Weekend (founded in Boulder in 2007 and which now hosts events in cities all over the world), was the first community manager at TechStars, and is now working on his own startup, Inside Travel Guides, which will soon begin publishing a series of digital travel guides focused on short, international trips. He made his name in Boulder by organizing a variety of events for entrepreneurs—including monthly Ignite panels, at which participants get five minutes onstage to teach the audience about a topic of their choice, and the first local TEDx Talks, a regional version of the popular annual TED conference. Both events, he says, are still the largest in the country for their respective series.

"We [in Boulder] have the combination of a really good tech community and really good organizers," Hyde explains, also over coffee on yet another snowy morning in the late spring of 2013.

"The organizers know how to put on really good events, because it's a zero-sum game around here—if you're going to take 350 people's time you've got to make it worth it. And if you're going to pitch to them or make it a marketing thing, we're going to pull you off the stage and spend the rest of your time making fun of you. So don't even try."

Boulder has done well as a startup community, he says, primarily because it has the lifestyle to match the opportunities that are available. It's not a question of having good jobs or being a good place to live. "This town is 100,000 people, and what other town of 100,000 is performing this well?" he says. "Is it a small-business town? I don't know, but it's an outperforming town."

It's also a surprisingly diverse place, especially given the cost of living, which can be steep near the downtown core. At any given moment on Pearl Street, you're as likely to run into a dirt bag climber as you are a multimillionaire, a small-business owner, or a drifter. And to a lot of people in this ecosystem it really doesn't matter anyway. The professors up the hill at CU have friends in the tech community and show up at Hyde's events on a regular basis, along with just about every other group and subculture in town. They're all there mixing it up, participating in the community, contributing to the startup scene, or just sitting back and watching it all happen.

"The cornerstones to every event I throw is that everyone is welcome, everyone is valued. There are probably a dozen millionaires in this room," he says, glancing around the crowd at the coffee shop, "and there are also probably people who just moved here and are living off of someone's couch. They're both just as important and have just as much to contribute."

It's a Boulder thing, to be sure, and it reflects the kinds of social norms that this community values. Work hard and be happy. If your goals include riding your bike on the weekend, working with interesting people, and doing intellectually stimulating work then, yes, that's an entirely valid approach to life and career. It also happens to be how a lot of other entrepreneurs in this city define success. Take Rally Software, for example. The company, which develops enterprise software systems, went public in mid-2013, becoming the first Boulder-based tech startup to do so.

"They're not successful because they IPO'd," Hyde says, "they're not successful because they have 300 employees. They're successful because they're good people. They're a B-corporation, so they give 1 percent of the company back to Colorado, and they're just good people. That's why we like them. And if they were to fail in three weeks we would still like them, which is where a lot of tech communities are different. Here it's like a 'success-sum game'; it's like, 'just do your best.'

"That's why I like to throw nonacquisition dinners. You fail and you gave it a good shot? Hey, you gave it a shot. Maybe luck wasn't on your side or you messed up or whatever, we'll take you out to a nice dinner. Just like if you had a big exit. Same difference. It doesn't matter to us. We don't give a shit that you failed. But the thing you're going to do, or the next idea that you're going to try, you're going to do it here in Boulder. Not a lot of cities, and especially not a lot of small communities, do that. Here it's swing for the fences. That's the only way you're going to get a hit, even though sometimes you don't."

After all, who really wants to be the CEO of a massive company? Crazy people. Who wants to be president of the United States? Crazy people. The nice thing about working as a tech entrepreneur is that it's possible to reach a well-paying, intellectually stimulating point in your career without having to focus entirely on the big exit. And in Boulder, the quality of life part of the equation is high enough that finding balance between work and fun is a shared goal throughout the ecosystem. Founders in the area are well known for leaving work at 5:00 p.m., going for a run, having dinner with their families, and then coming back online in the evenings. After all, it would be a shame to miss out on all the Colorado foothills have to offer because you're stuck in the office all the time. At the most basic level, that's really why most people live here.

"Boulder has had this decades-long PR campaign," says Hyde. "You had *Mork and Mindy*, you had Stephen King [whose book, *The Shining*, was written in nearby Estes Park], you had Jon Benét. All of these massive things. And when I tell people I'm from Colorado when I travel, people's first guess is generally Boulder, not Denver. They have the sports teams, and all that, but it's still Boulder [that is the draw]. And we've backed it up, thousands of people have backed it up, by being stewards of the game here."

The offices of LinkSmart, a startup that places text-link ads on online content pages, are located in a storefront space near Canyon Boulevard in central Boulder, near the Foundry Group offices, TechStars, and the old Boulder *Daily Camera* newspaper building. Founded in 2009 by Pete Sheinbaum, an online publishing industry veteran whose resume includes stints at Daily Candy, E! Entertainment Television, and others, LinkSmart occupies a unique niche in the online advertising market by allowing publishers to sell ads that live within their own copy, instead of in banners or in the margins of the page.

"There are billions and billions of links on millions of Web pages," Sheinbaum says. "But I was most interested in taking a publisher-centric view of the world, which was if I had the ability to analyze, optimize, and manage text links I could do a lot with that to help my business. So I set out to build LinkSmart to be a platform for people to, with a couple lines of code, understand the engagement that's happening on their pages via the lens of a text link, then to optimize their pages based on the data we're collecting."

Like a lot of Boulder residents, Sheinbaum isn't originally from Colorado. He's from Connecticut, went to school in Los Angeles, and was working in the entertainment industry when he decided to move to Boulder in 2000 simply because it "seemed like there was some tech going on" in the area. Once there, he met his now-wife, had a family, and decided that, as a budding tech entrepreneur by that point, Boulder was a pretty good place to be.

"Over the past five, six, seven years, things have changed a lot in Boulder to make it a lot more conducive to starting businesses," he says. "There's capital now that knows about this place. There's an infrastructure here that helps. There's a community of people that are doing a lot of technology work. There's access to employees. There's reasonable real estate. So there's a lot going for it and it has really started to become one of those cultures where it is OK to take risks and start things. I really thought I could get something going here."

The thing about Boulder, Sheinbaum says, is that its startup scene is about more than just technology. It also extends to other industries, including biotech, natural foods, green energy, and more. You've got Justin's Nut Butter, the maker of various gourmet-flavored peanut butters and other nut spreads; you've got Pangea Organics, the organic skin-care manufacturer; you've got Celestial Seasonings, the $100-million tea manufacturer; and of course there is Crocs, the maker of those ubiquitous foam sandals, which is headquartered nearby. Natural foods retailer Whole Foods has a large presence in Boulder, though it isn't a local company or really even a startup anymore, and well-known advertising and design agency Crispin Porter + Bogusky has a large office in town to tap into the local creative community.

"What I think happens is you get a lot of people who are passionate and smart. They're educated, they're risk takers, they want to be a little bit adventurous, or for whatever reason they're attracted to Colorado. And that's the kind of mind-set that you need to start something and succeed or fail. And so I think what happens here is that there's not a lot of pressure to be safe. Colorado's never been a really safe place. It was the new frontier back in the early days and that mind-set still applies."

So in Boulder, people are encouraged to take risks. And sometimes those risks don't pay off. That's OK, many here say. "In places where it's not OK to fail [people], never really start anything," Sheinbaum says. "People sit around there just punching the clock. That's not what you see here."

But the Wild West side of Colorado life does have its limitation for founders. For starters, the state is far from ethnically diverse, which Sheinbaum says can make it difficult when recruiting engineers and other tech workers from out of state or overseas.

"When you think about LA and San Francisco, a lot of people from Asian communities or Indian communities have landed in those cities and established family networks there. So they're very comfortable knowing that when they get there they will be supported by their communities. We don't have that here. We don't have a large Indian population; we don't have a large Japanese or Chinese population. But if we could attract new people in the same way that other cities attract them, we could have a more diverse culture; we could have more diversity of ideas. It would just be helpful for everybody."

Action on the part of the state of Colorado could make this easier, but the unfortunate thing about life in an up-and-coming tech community is that there are a lot of other businesses competing for government attention, and that's certainly the case for Boulder. In Colorado, oil and gas and other natural resource businesses get most of the attention from the state legislature, along with established local players in industries including telecommunications (Dish Network and Liberty Media are both locally based), hospitality (Vail Resorts has its offices just outside of the Boulder city limits), and financial services (such as Western Union and Janus Capital Group). But, Sheinbaum explains, if the state really wants to attract new money to Colorado, it needs to step up to the plate and make entrepreneurs, tech entrepreneurs in particular, feel welcome here, via tax credits, real estate deals, and other incentives.

* * *

Even with these hurdles, however, there is still plenty of interest in what the state has to offer.

"I came out just over two years ago from Boston, and I had never been to Boulder before," says Ryan Angilly, the founder of Signal Genius, a big data–focused B2B lead-generating startup and an engineer with ROXIMITY, a mobile app that delivers restaurant reviews and menu information based on the user's location. "After two days, I decided I wasn't leaving."

Part of it was the local demand for talent, he says, and the fact that, for a small town, there are a lot of big-city resources available for the taking. It is also just an easy place to do business and a walkable community that's well outside of the big-city, East Coast corridor.

"One of the really interesting things about Boulder, and I don't think this can be overstated, is how big of an impact the small downtown has on the tech community. There's something to be said about having that small downtown where you can literally run into a bunch of CEOs and VCs on the street. It makes it really easy to meet for coffee or go by each other's offices. Sometimes I'll get an email for help and it just makes it really easy to meet with people since everyone is right downtown. I really like that."

Ryan Wanger, an organizer with Boulder Startup Week, has found that particular aspect of Boulder life to be an easy sell to out-of-town entrepreneurs. In fact, so many non-Boulderites are now interested in learning about the local startup scene that his organization has been flying would-be local entrepreneurs to town free of charge for the last several years.

"So the first year it was like, 'Hey, you want to fly out here for free?'" Wanger remembers over lunch in Denver. "Just tell us about yourself and we'll pick some people."

The idea, at least in the early days, was to physically bring new startups to town to show them what Boulder has to offer. Maybe they'd move out, maybe they wouldn't. But either way they would learn more about what the city is all about and hopefully talk about their experiences with other entrepreneurs back home. It was something of a recruitment program for the metro area, backed by the Boulder Startup Week organization. Since then, however, the local scene has grown so much that, rather than looking for new companies to attract to Boulder, Wanger says he is now spending more time flying in potential talent for the city's existing startups.

"We have jobs, but we don't have enough people to fill them. Sure, that's the problem in most cities I guess, but it seems like with programmers in particular we can just never have enough of them here. Boulder has a really high concentration of tech jobs but it's still a really small city in spite of that."

It's been interesting, he says, to watch the local tech job market mature. In the early days, startups in the area were hiring for all sorts of jobs, including marketing, HR, sales, and other general business positions. More recently, though, the openings are limited to almost strictly coding and production. It's a reflection of where the local ecosystem is now—the businesses are up and running, so they no longer need to fill their back office positions. Now they just need engineers to help them build new products and scale their offerings.

Still, Wanger says, Boulder's small business roots still shine through.

"There was a company that was working on ride sharing, taking people to the airport, and another that helps people with legal issues. So yeah, it always surprises me that there are so many companies [in Boulder] that maybe are small and you haven't heard of them, but they're making enough money to survive. But I do sort of wonder how things would change if there was some big sort of success story here like Dropbox or something like that. Would that change things in Boulder? Would it become more of a magnet for people, knowing that there are already a lot of jobs and opportunities here?"

As luck would have it, Rally Software filed for its initial public offering about a month after Wanger and I spoke, becoming the first Boulder tech startup to take that step and become the region's "biggest success story" to date.

But Boulder's evolution into a self-sustaining startup hub has been a slow process, explains David Driskell, the city's executive director of community planning and sustainability, and the effort remains very much focused on the next ten, fifteen, twenty years and beyond.

"I think there's a sense here—and sometimes it's real, sometimes not so much—that we're great at fostering startups," Driskell says. "We have a lot of small startups, and those that are successful grow and reach a point where they have a hard time finding a place to be in Boulder. And then they move on."

The idea at this point, he explains, is to take what's working in and around Downtown Boulder—the high-density office spaces, the walkable neighborhoods, the restaurants and housing options—and extending it out to other areas, including the less-developed areas in east Boulder and the nearby town of Gunbarrel. Downtown has pretty much reached capacity as far as new development is concerned—hence the notoriously high prices in the neighborhood—and the outskirts, Driskell says, are where job growth will likely be happening down the road.

"How do we make those areas more Boulder-like?" he asks. "Because they're really 'Anywhere, USA,' currently in terms of the development patterns. There are some cool things that are happening in those places, but how do we create a richer mix of amenities and greater ability of people to walk, bike, take the bus? That's what people love about Downtown Boulder. The theme is basically how do you make these sort of seventies-style industrial parks into cool and groovy places?"

From the outside it seems like it shouldn't be that difficult. Life in Boulder looks to be pretty sweet—bike paths everywhere, plenty of open space, a compact downtown filled with restaurants and nightlife, and a growing group of interesting high-tech companies to work for. Surely, there are worse places to end up.

"I think we see our role as a city as maintaining this very high quality of life that is attractive to creative people and the talent that we want to attract and retain here," Driskell says. "I think that's our number-one thing; do that and then get out of the way of the creative startups. But at the same time we're listening to what their needs are and factoring some of that into the development decisions that are happening with our planning board and council."

It is time, however, for the local startup community to step up and get involved in city governance, he says. Need more office space? Need better transit options? Need more affordable housing? The city is ready to adapt to this new economic driver, but it needs help navigating this evolving space.

"We hear a lot from our older population, particularly in terms of historic preservation and things, but we tend not to hear much from the entrepreneurial community. So how do we build some bridges there so they're more engaged and their voices are heard when those decisions are happening?"

But Boulder is not the sole driver of the Colorado tech startup ecosystem. Up and down the Front Range, an urban corridor of some 4.5 million people that stretches from Pueblo to Fort Collins, Colorado, and roughly parallels the eastern foothills of the Rocky Mountains, there are entrepreneurs working on all sorts of projects, from software, to hardware, to cloud services, and more.

Denver in particular, thirty miles east of Boulder, is blossoming into a tech startup ecosystem in its own right, with its own Startup Weekend, its own meetup events, and its own business incubators. Most of the local startups so far are based in the Lower Downtown area (a.k.a. LoDo), a neighborhood of converted warehouses and loft spaces that was revitalized in the mid-1990s. It may not have the density of Boulder's Pearl Street, but it is a diverse, interesting, and walkable neighborhood that lends itself to creative collisions and random meetings between entrepreneurs.

"One of the things we really want to do is just help amplify what's going on here," explains Chris Onan, the other cofounder and managing director of coworking space/tech incubator Galvanize at his office near Downtown Denver. "Because if you look at what the TechStars guys got so right in Boulder—and Boulder is a kind of small, pissant little town—what they created is a nexus of activity. It's a place. And when you have that, you can get out-of-state capital, out-of-state investors, who can come through and see five, six, seven deals, have dinner and drinks, and then fly out. It's so brilliant. So what those guys would say is, 'Love Galvanize, because now we have somewhere to send people in Denver.'"

The loftlike Galvanize facility is located in a former print shop building—the onetime home of the Rocky Mountain Bank Note Company, which created and distributed a variety of bank forms and documents in the early half of the twentieth century—and is not in LoDo but on the other side of the Colorado state capitol building off of Broadway and Speer, two of the major arteries through downtown. For startups it offers a variety of coworking options, from individual desks to closed-off suites, along with a community of like-minded entrepreneurs and access to "honorary residents," including successful entrepreneurs like Brad Feld, David Cohen, Andre Durande from Ping, local VC Joe Zell, and others. National car service app Uber's Denver office is at Galvanize. Small-business directory service Manta, which is based in Columbus, Ohio, has its Denver operation at the facility as well, along with music streaming service Pandora, and Closely, the new startup from Perry Evans, who founded MapQuest.

When I visited Galvanize, there were eighty-five tech companies currently working out of the space, with two or three new members joining every week. And the facility offers an education program called gSchool that trains workers from all backgrounds for careers in technology, teaching everything from HTML and

Javascript, to Ruby and SQL. The idea is to provide fresh talent for the community's fast-growing startups.

The idea behind Galvanize isn't to be a coworking space, though. It's really more of an investment model, where companies are brought into the fold, nurtured through their earliest stages, and then set up for funding via the facility's backers. It's like an accelerator program without the immediate seed funding.

"This is a mousetrap for us because we want to make investments," Onan explains. "There's a lot of great karma that comes out of this and it's great for Denver, but selfishly we see a lot of early-stage companies and we want to write checks. People always ask, 'Are you an incubator?' 'Do you take equity?' The answer is 'no.' We make rent cheap and everybody pays it. If we like a company we're going to write 'em a check and buy stock. That's how we operate."

The recent growth in Denver is similar in a lot of ways to the early days of the tech scene in Boulder, explains Bing Chou, managing director of Boulder-based Web development firm Quick Left, and the organizer of the Denver Open Coffee Club, a monthly tech-focused breakfast meetup that meets in the Galvanize space.

"You know it's funny," Chou tells me in the waiting area at Galvanize. "Since stopping in at the Denver Open Coffee Club an hour ago, which was only twenty people, I've been sitting here for maybe ten minutes and I've already run into maybe half a dozen people that I see all the time in Boulder. So I'm really looking forward to the two communities getting more involved and having a lot less friction—because, really, what are we, only twenty-five to thirty minutes apart? And it's really exciting to see Colorado in general feeling like there's more and more activity. It feels like Fort Collins is starting to spin up a bit, and I've been hearing some things about Colorado Springs getting started, so these smaller communities are starting to grow."

That's good news for the state as a whole, he says, because it means the technology economy is becoming more established and likely won't be going anywhere anytime soon. What was (and still largely is) a tourism- and resource-based economy is starting to diversify, developing a reputation for entrepreneurship, business-friendly regulations, and creativity. It's an alternative that appeals to many people.

"For sure, visibility is key," Chou says. "But I think it helps when you see a program like TechStars go from kind of an, 'oh, that's interesting' to what now feels like an international phenomenon. That type of energy and visibility and mentors who might otherwise be totally unknown to the community, I think that starts to have a spillover effect to the rest of the economy. And that's what we're seeing in Colorado."

Truth is, Boulder is still very much a small college town. You can walk across the whole of it in less than an hour, and half the city all but shuts down on CU football weekends. The public high school is well regarded, and everybody's kids go to a handful of local elementary schools where Mandarin Chinese is on the curriculum and hummus is on the lunch menu.

It's America, just a slightly different version of it.

But for entrepreneurs, the Boulder sales pitch is simple: You get all that small-town appeal, all those quality-of-life perks, with many of the amenities that are more often associated with bigger cities. Sure, it doesn't have Menlo Park's Sand Hill Road, but the Foundry Group has ensured that Boulder's own funding network is up and running, and the city has become a regular stop on many VCs' travel itineraries. It may not have Y Combinator, but it has TechStars based right in the middle of Downtown Boulder. And not only do the entrepreneurs that come for TechStars live and work alongside everyone else in the community, they bring a steady stream of new talent and new ideas through town several times a year. The city doesn't have a Stanford, but it has the increasingly involved University of Colorado Boulder, along with a community of software and technology entrepreneurs that's very supportive and welcoming of outsiders. After all, pretty much everyone in Colorado was a transplant at some point.

"The thing that was most appealing to me when I first got here was that, even though it isn't a major metro area, Boulder has a lot of people who are doing really big-time stuff and are really accessible," says Ryan Angilly, the Boston transplant. "Not that New York and San Francisco are not accessible, but within a few months of living in Boulder I was able to sit down and chat with Brad Feld. That's pretty cool."

Epilogue/
Acknowledgments

TO PARAPHRASE author Paul Theroux from his 2002 book, *Dark Star Safari*, travel ends, books get written, and then you look back to see that everything has changed.

This book has been in the works since 2011 and was reported over the course of two years, so it's safe to say that every ecosystem that I visited, every facility that I toured, every company that I met with, and every entrepreneur that I profiled has changed in some way since we met. In some cases, big plans have come up short. In others, expectations have been fulfilled and business continues. A few fortunes have been made, a handful of startups have folded, but the vast majority of the entrepreneurs profiled in this book—as well as many of the mentors, investors, organizers, directors, teachers, and others—are still plugging away on their projects, working to get their companies and ideas off the ground.

That doesn't mean the stories contained in this book are over, however, or even technically incorrect. They are simply incomplete. This book is a snapshot of the US startup ecosystem in cities far away from the Bay Area as it was from 2012 to 2013. No more, no less. Hopefully this book will remain representative of what's happening out there for some time to come (so that people will want to read it), but in all honesty I doubt it will. The world of tech startup companies was evolving fast during my twelve months on the road; it is very likely that the national landscape will be vastly different than it is today by the time this book is published. The ecosystems I profiled here (among many others) were all poised to hit the mainstream in a big way by 2014, and I got a front-row seat to watch that happen. I can't thank enough my publishers at BenBella Books; my agent, Andy Ross; my family; and everyone else who helped make this book happen for allowing me to give this a shot. It's been a fun year.

But the dirty secret about this whole project is that it is nothing if not incomplete. There is simply no way that I could have ever seen it all, no way I could have met with everyone involved in this space. I made a point to take every meeting, talk to as many people as I could, and generally reach out to everyone of consequence in every startup ecosystem that I visited, but I realized early on that cataloging absolutely everything was going to be an impossible goal. There was simply too much going on—still is simply too much going on—for me to be able to take it all in and, most importantly, boil it down to a book-length manuscript. I sincerely apologize to everyone I may have overlooked in my reporting. No hard feelings were intended, and if I overlooked you in the course of my research for this book, please feel free to reach out and correct me.

Of course, the great thing about a book like this is that it's not about one person. It's not even about one city or one company, and it's certainly not something I could have done alone. The list of contributors to this book is long, almost too long to list here, but without the people named below, and the dozens of others I'm surely forgetting, this book would not have been at all possible. What's more, American entrepreneurs are busy, driven, competitive people by nature, and can be hard to pin down for phone calls and meetings. But they are also, across the board, incredibly generous with their time (when they have it), unbelievably welcoming to a stranger like me, and endlessly helpful in ways that go above and beyond the usual reporter-source relationship. I can't thank them all enough. This is an inspirational group, to be sure.

My first out-of-town trip for this project was to balmy Detroit in early spring—home to the greatest rental car fleets in the country—and it wouldn't have gone nearly as well as it did if it wasn't for the help of Alex Southern, who introduced me to just about everyone in the ecosystem and got me on the invite list at Mango Languages. Alex is the founder of Grow Detroit, a local organization dedicated to nurturing the city's startup community, and I can't thank him enough for helping me out. Big thanks are also due to everyone at Mango Languages—there are far too many names to list from that great event—for making a reporter who literally knew no one in town twelve hours earlier feel like an old friend of the ecosystem, at least for a few hours. Also, Midwestern pizza is an underappreciated art form.

Up the road in Ann Arbor, Erick Bzovi and Lance Carlson with HealPay were gracious enough to invite me up to their offices and spend the better part of an hour walking me through the finer points of their online payment systems and the challenges of B2B business development in southeast Michigan. I really appreciate the time, guys. And the same goes for Scott Christopher, then-president of the University of Michigan's student-run entrepreneurship group, MPowered, who is by now probably the deputy head of operations at Facebook, or something.

Big thanks go to Leslie Smith at TechTown, the Wayne State University–based organization that by now should have a statue of Robocop located on its grounds (seriously). To all the entrepreneurs I met in Downtown Detroit—Jeff Epstein at Ambassador, Jay Gierak at Stik, Greg Schwartz at UpTo, Paul Glomski and Dan Ward at Detroit Labs—thanks for taking time out of your legitimately busy schedules (working on far more world-changing projects than just a book) to sit down with me and talk about your companies. And the same goes to everyone at the Madison, including Ted Serbinski and Jared Stasik with Detroit Venture Partners and Ross Sanders with Bizdom. I literally walked into the building that day with only one meeting set up, and walked out with a dozen new stories to explore. Good stuff.

Final thanks go to Eric Randolph with Bedrock Management Services for walking me around the neighborhood and showing me firsthand what Dan Gilbert's vision for the Downtown Detroit core really looks like. That hour was above and beyond the call of duty—really—and was very much appreciated. I hope I did the project justice in my descriptions here. I'm very interested to see how things have changed in that area when I'm back in town.

In North Carolina, thanks have to go to Whitney Rowe, local Kauffman Fellow, investor, and the curator of the local startup digest, for putting me in touch with just about everyone in the local scene (and for putting up with my back-to-back-to-back meetings schedule that meant I didn't actually get to thank her in person). I also can't say enough about Derrick Minor with the City of Raleigh, Daniel Chalef with KnowledgeTree, and everyone at HQ Raleigh, including cofounders Brooks Bell and Jason Widen. Sharefile's Jesse Lipson deserves a shout-out here as well, as an HQ Raleigh cofounder himself and as the CEO of one of the most successful, fastest-growing companies in the region, for taking the time to sit down with me for over an hour to talk about code, management techniques, and his startup days. Thanks again for lunch.

My Durham day would not have happened without the help of Dhruv Patel and his colleagues at CED, including Jay Bigelow (who got all the quotes in the book, but was just one of the CED folks that I talked to). I am humbled by their involvement and assistance. Same goes for Adam Klein with Capitol Broadcasting/ American Underground, Chris Heivly with Triangle Startup Factory, and local venture capitalist Mark Easley for taking the time to sit down with a nobody journalist from Colorado and talk dollars and cents. Thanks also to John Austin with Groundworks Labs for squeezing me in for a quick meeting, and to Jason Massey with

Sustainable Industrial Solutions for spending an hour outside with me in the late-July North Carolina heat.

In the Research Triangle Park, big thanks go to Park CEO Bob Geolas for giving me the lay of the land, as well as to Andy Schwab with ff Venture Center (right next door) for his insights into the world of science- and medicine-based startups. Sounds like a tough business to be in, especially when compared to the typical software startup, but I'm glad someone out there is putting in the time and money to develop world-changing technologies that may someday cure cancer, solve global hunger, or otherwise make this planet a better place for all of us to live. Also in the Park, I have to mention Dr. Tony Atti, CEO of Phononics, for the lengthy, late-in-the-day tour and explanation of just what a semiconductor startup is all about. Fascinating stuff.

Thanks also to Dr. Terri Lomax and Liana Fryer with North Carolina State University for showing me around the Centennial Campus (they even have food trucks), along with Justin Miller of WedPics and Luke Fishback of PlotWatt, another Durham-based company that puts PhDs to work and solves the world's big problems every day. And then there's Scot Wingo, CEO of ChannelAdvisor and one of the Web's early e-commerce pioneers. This didn't come up in our talk, but I really dug the Anakin Skywalker statue in the lobby, and, in particular, the copy of *Prancercise: The Art of Physical and Spiritual Excellence* on the side table. Didn't go unnoticed, I just couldn't find a good way to work those details into the book.

In Kansas City, I can't thank Brittain Kovac with the Kansas City Startup Village (KCSV) enough for helping me sort through the maze of KC-area startups and then for showing me around the Village personally while I was in town. Same goes for KCSV residents Matthew Marcus and Adam Arredondo, the cofounders of Hoopla.io/Local Ruckus, along with Leap2's amazingly smart Mike Farmer and Tyler VanWinkle, who are taking on Google in the search space, no matter how impossible that sounds. Thanks also to Homes for Hackers resident Alex Griffin with Pickle.io—the coffee was free!—and Kayla Riggs with TravelingNuker.com, as well as Ben Barreth, the actual owner of said house. Same goes for Brandon Schatz, the founder of SportsPhoto.com, who works out of a similar house up the street, for welcoming me into his home after work and showing me just what Google Fiber really looks like in action.

Thanks also to Maria Meyers with the University of Missouri–Kansas City (UMKC) Innovation Center for sitting down with me at the Sheraton between conference presentations, Jeff Shackelford with UMKC's Digital Sandbox for tolerating my impossible road schedule (apologies again for missing our meeting), and Cameron Cushman with the Kauffman Foundation for (literally) running between appointments to accommodate my endless questions about the nonprofit side of the Kansas City ecosystem. Same goes for Ryan Weber with KCNext and his amazing office space upstairs in Union Station.

On the money side of things in Kansas City, I have to thank Tyler Prochnow and Blake Miller with Think Big Partners for taking more than an hour to talk with me about arena football, George Foreman, and, oh right, startups in Kansas City. Go Broncos. Same goes for (James Bond villain?) Alex Altomare and his truly amazing BetaBlox underground space, Kevin Fryer at SparkLabKC, and Rodrigo "Rigo" Neri with Startup Weekend Kansas City, who moved to Missouri/Kansas from Brazil nearly a decade ago and hasn't looked back. Mark O'Renick and Mike Wilson with Ingenology on the "other" side of Crossroads—best of luck with the watches and thanks for showing me that tech entrepreneurship is about more than just apps and cloud services. Ditto for DivvyHQ cofounder Brock Stechman, Pipeline CEO Joni Cobb, and media relations rep extraordinaire Jason Grill. I'll see you on the radio.

What can I say about Las Vegas? There really is no place like it, and that goes for the startup community as well as everything else there. Easily the tightest, most personal (if also the smallest) ecosystem that I visited, my trip to Vegas never would have happened without the generous help of Frank Gruber, Jen Consalvo, and everyone at Tech Cocktail for letting me tag along on their monthly showcase and for putting together an amazing "This Is Vegas" program that made my job easy. I even had a roommate on this leg: Rich Winley. Nothing but the best, my friend. His startup is called NoChains, a very cool dining recommendation service built around "the best restaurant you've never heard of." Same goes for all of the other Tech Cocktail participants that I met from all over the world who made me feel so welcome in their community and shared their stories with me.

It's easy to assume that the Vegas scene begins and ends with Zappos CEO Tony Hsieh—and he is near the center of everything that's happening in the ecosystem—but Tony's involvement is just the beginning. Big thanks to Andy White with VegasTechFund for giving me a great look at the money side of the city's tech startups and the Downtown Project, as well as Josh Bowden at Work In Progress, and Gabe Shepard with V2V, the local SXSW outpost.

Rich Duggan from Zappos spent a good hour with me talking about the backstory of the Vegas tech scene—spoiler: It's nothing new—as well as all of the cool stuff that was then going on around his employer's big move to the former City Hall building. Thanks also to Kyle Kelly, also with Zappos, for sharing details about what it is like to be a newcomer to the ecosystem. And how could I forget Jon Sterling, the owner of Vegas' own hacker house (though he has since moved on from the city). Cool project, thanks for taking the time to explain what brings a San Francisco local to up and move to the tech desert, if only for a few months.

So many entrepreneurs to thank in Las Vegas: David and Jennifer Gosse with Tracky, Keller Rinaudo with Romotive (which has since moved to San Francisco), Mike Yoder with WinTech, Chad Ramos with Tabeso, and Geoff Sanders with LaunchKey. All doing cool stuff, all took time out of their busy schedules to talk to an out-of-town reporter, and all of it was much appreciated. Best of luck to everyone. Last but not least, thanks to Richard Ethington at InNEVation, the Switch-owned incubator space outside of town, and all the folks at Switch who made my tour of the SuperNAP data center happen.

In Colorado, I can't forget to thank my old boss at Yahoo, Luke Beatty, currently with AOL and previously with TechStars and Associated Content, for ignoring this project entirely and not giving me a hard time for calling pretty much all of his friends and business partners behind his back. Thanks again, buddy. We'll never speak of this again.

Up in Boulder, I spent a long morning drinking coffee with Andrew Hyde after our interview. Congratulations again on the new house; I hope you didn't get hit by the fires or the 2013 floods. I actually did it all over again a few weeks later with Robert Reich in a completely different café across the street. Fun fact: Both interviews took place in the midst of driving spring snowstorms during a 2013 snow season that never seemed to end. But the conversations were great and the time was much appreciated. Ditto to the City of Boulder's David Driskell, LinkSmart's Pete Sheinbaum, and local developer Ryan Angilly, who holds the distinction of being the very first person I spoke to when I was in the planning stages for this project way back in the day.

Thanks also to Ryan Wanger with Boulder Startup Week and Silicon Flatirons director Brad Bernthal with the University of Colorado Law School for giving me the lay of the land and building out much of the background for the Boulder chapter. Bernthal also helped make my beer-and-tech visit to the Silicon Flatirons event a reality, so big thanks are due to him for keeping me in the loop over the course of a year-plus.

In terms of Denver, it turns out there is way more happening here in my city than I ever realized. Thanks are due to the folks at coworking space/incubator Galvanize, including Chris Onan, for showing me everything that's happening right here in my neighborhood. Ditto for Bing Chou for taking the time to talk with me about all of the new community efforts that are happening between our two cities.

Last but not least, Brad Feld, the godfather of Boulder tech, deserves special thanks. Another of my earliest interviews for this book, Feld provided some great perspective on the statewide scene as well as insights on the national trends—he was involved in the launch of President Obama's big entrepreneurship push in 2011—and his comments helped ground the entire project. (He is also a source of inspiration to founders and investors nationwide, which is a fact that he might not even be aware of. On a number of occasions, in several different time zones, I was asked whether or not I had "talked to Feld yet." And everyone I talked to was curious about him and the work he's been doing in Colorado and elsewhere.) Can't thank him enough for taking time out of his busy schedule to talk to me.

New York City . . . there's almost no way for me to thank everyone in that city that I need to, and as I mentioned in the New York chapter itself, I still feel like I barely scratched the surface of everything that's happening there in tech. That said, I overinterviewed like crazy in that town; so many people deserve my apologies for not making this book. But, I promise, every meeting provided a much-needed look into the city's growing ecosystem, and all of the amazing work being done there filled in the gaps in my story.

First of all, thanks go to Greg Neufeld with ValueStream Labs, Alex Orn with Street of Walls, and Leigh Drogen with Estimize for helping demystify the complex world of financial technology and all of the work that's happening both on the consumer side and behind the scenes. The same applies to Alex Taub with Dwolla and Reddit cofounder Alexis Ohanian, who took time out of his own book tour—*Without Their Permission: How the 21st Century Will Be Made, Not Managed*—to chat with me via phone. Much appreciated.

On the education side of things in New York, I had a number of great conversations with folks including General Assembly cofounder Jake Schwartz, Christina Wallace with the Startup Institute, and Avi Flombaum at the Flatiron School (in their cramped old location closer to Midtown, not their snazzy new downtown digs). Same goes for Dean Dan Huttenlocher and Professor Mor Naaman with Cornell Tech for all of the insights into the education-startup connections in the city, along with Jennifer Ellison with Cornell media relations for making it all happen over several time zones. I also can't thank Andrew Young and Frank Denbow enough for the insights into New York Startup Weekend—or for the tour of the cool downtown WeWork coworking space. Same goes to Graham Lawlor with Ultra Light Startups, Tatiana Bakaeva with Verizon Enterprise Solutions, and Ben Fisher (formerly) of Alchemy. Thank you all so much for your time.

The New York venture community was particularly welcoming to me and very helpful overall, so big thanks go to John Frankel, founding partner of ff Venture Capital, and his communications director, Aishwarya Iyer, for inviting me to their "fitness office" on Sixth Avenue and showing me just what it is they do there. Ditto to Yao-Hui Huang with the Hatchery, Owen Davis with NYC Seed, and Charlie O'Donnell with Brooklyn Bridge Ventures, as well as Nick Chirls with the ever-fascinating Betaworks. I also got to spend an hour with Tarikh Korula, the founder of Seen.co (a startup cofounded by Cornell's Mor Naaman that is being run out of a hedge fund–owned space in SoHo) to discuss how they are working to reinvent social news aggregation with computer science algorithms that I can't even pretend to understand. Much appreciated.

No discussion of the New York tech scene would be complete without talking to officials with the city itself. Thanks are due to Eric Gertler with the New York City Economic Development Corporation for sharing the latest in this department, as well as Maria Gotsch with the Partnership Fund for New York City who gave me a behind-the-scenes look at how private industry is working to develop New York's startup ecosystem for the long term.

And of course my Yahoo colleagues in New York—Aaron Task, Chris Nichols, Rebecca Stropoli, Lisa Scherzer, Siemond Chan, Elizabeth Trotta, Kensey Lamb, Ross Tucker, Caroline Kim, and so many more. You guys weren't part of this project but made me feel welcome in your city and convinced me that this was something that I could actually pull off. Honestly, I can't thank you all enough.

I learned a number of very valuable lessons in Austin. First, Texans are not always the easiest interview subjects; they're pretty quiet by nature. But once you get them going they can talk all day. Second, 8:00 a.m. meetings still exist in Austin, and even that is sometimes considered "late." That being said, however, the city lived up to its billing as the biggest little city in tech and I had a great time there completing what turned out to be my very last trip for this book.

Jacqueline Hughes—the events manager for TechStars Austin, producer of Austin StartupWeek (@AtxStartupWeek), and all-around super connector for the local scene—was hugely helpful to me early on in this project (long before I actually flew to Austin) by giving me an overview of the scene and connecting me with all sorts of interesting folks in the startup community. Can't thank her enough. The same has to be said for Damon Clinkscales with Austin Founder Dating and Austin On Rails. Thank you both for your help with the community side of things in general and for being so generous with your time. Same goes for serial entrepreneur and blogger Erica Douglass as well as everyone at South by Southwest: Hugh Forrest, the director of SXSW Interactive; Christine Auten, the producer of SXSW's Las Vegas entrepreneurship conference, V2V; Chris Valentine, the producer of SXSW Startup Village and Accelerator; Gabe Shepard in Las Vegas; and, of course, Kelly Krause for making it all happen.

Big thanks of course have to go to Josh Baer with Capital Factory for bringing it all together (and eating lunch on the fly while we talked), as well as Kevin Koym with TechRanch Austin, and Isaac Barchas and Kyle Cox with Austin Technology Incubator. Also, while I'm thanking folks in the Austin incubator and accelerator space, I can't forget Jason Seats with TechStars Austin, Kerry Rupp with DreamIt Ventures, and Josh Kerr with Capital Factory/TechStars/everything else in town. I really appreciate it, guys.

Austin was another town where I was well tolerated by the investment community and I greatly appreciate all of the time I was given over my weeklong stay in the city. Thanks go to venture capitalist Rudy Garza with G-51 for literally sitting out in the cold with me for our interview, as well as Jeff Harbach (who was between projects when we met for coffee, but by now has certainly kicked off his VC career and brought new money into the Austin ecosystem) and Brett Hurt, the former CEO of Bazaarvoice and a budding VC himself. Ditto to Brent Elyea with the Central Texas Angel Network for sitting down with me between much-more-interesting-sounding meetings at the golf course to talk about the local angel community.

And of course there are the entrepreneurs: Jason Cohen with WPEngine, Karen Bantuveris with Volunteerspot, John Price with Trilogy and now Vast.com, Joseph Kopser with RideScout, and Josh Alexander with Toopher. Thanks to you all.

In the end, it was the first two chapters of this book—the introduction and overview of the nationwide startup scene—that proved to be the most challenging and most involved parts of the project. As a result, I conducted a lot of interviews and did a lot of background research to bring them both together. Thanks are due to Mitchell Cuevas and Danielle Reyes with UP Global, Jim Franklin with SendGrid, Mark Heesen with the National Venture Capital Association, Holly Magister with Enterprise Transition, Jeff Slobotski with *Silicon Prairie News,* and Marianne Hudson with the Angel Capital Association. Out in Silicon Valley, I'm indebted to Tristan Kromer for sharing his thoughts on the state of the startup ecosystem in the Bay Area, as well as Darius Dunlap with the Silicon Valley Innovation Institute for his insights into the area's history.

Like I said, this book is just the tip of the iceberg, and I expect to see the whole landscape of "other" startup ecosystems really hit the mainstream in the next few years. It's already happening in some places. After I settled on the seven cities that were to be profiled in this book, a long list of other potential candidates began to emerge. In addition to some of the more obvious "why didn't he include city X?" candidates like Boston, Seattle, Chicago, and Portland, there are now ecosystems forming in far-flung locales as varied as Pittsburgh; Washington, DC; San Diego; and even Miami. And that's not to mention the even smaller contenders in places like Burlington, Vermont; Richmond, Virginia; Iowa City, Iowa; and Albuquerque, New Mexico.

Stay tuned—there's certainly more to come.

Bibliography

Angel Resource Institute and Silicon Valley Bank. "The Halo Report: Q2 2013." October 16, 2013. www.angelcapitalassociation.org/data /ACEF/HaloReport1H2013final.pdf.

Avalos, George. "Silicon Valley Job Growth has Reached Dot-Com Boom Levels, Report Says." *San Jose Mercury News*, February 7, 2013. http:// www.mercurynews.com/ci_22524360/silicon-valley-job-growth -prodigious-returned-dot-com-boom-levels.

Barnett, Marissa. "Brain Trust: Restaurateur Revisits Unique Mentorship With Dean Kozmetsky." *McCombs Today*, October 14, 2013. http://www.today.mccombs.utexas.edu/2013/10/john-harkey -mentorship-dean-kozmetsky.

Bay Area Council Economic Institute. "Technology Works: High-Tech Employment and Wages in the United States." December 2012. http://www.bayareaeconomy.org/media/files/pdf/TechReport.pdf.

Brennan, Morgan. "America's Fastest Growing Cities." *Forbes*, January 23, 2013. http://www.forbes.com/sites/morganbrennan/2013/01/23 /americas-fastest-growing-cities/.

Brown, Willie. "Techies Must Nip Growing Scorn in Bud." *San Francisco Chronicle*, November 24, 2013. http://www.sfgate.com/bayarea /williesworld/article/Techies-must-nip-growing-scorn-in-bud -5006404.php.

Cainan, Christopher. "Austin-Area Angel Investing Tops the Nation." *Austin Business Journal*, October 16, 2013. http://www.bizjournals .com/austin/blog/techflash/2013/10/ctan-most-active-2q-angel -group.html.

CBInsights. *The Silicon Valley Tech Venture Capital Almanac*. New York, 2013.

Clifton, Jim. "Wanted: America's Entrepreneurial Freaks of Nature." *LinkedIn*, August 16, 2013. http://www.linkedin.com/influencers

/20130816110819-14634910-wanted-america-s-entrepreneurial
-freaks-of-nature.

Cohan, Peter. "John Price Is Bringing Silicon Valley to Austin." *Forbes*, December 12, 2012. http://www.forbes.com/sites/petercohan/2012 /12/12/john-price-is-bringing-silicon-valley-to-austin/.

CU Leeds School of Business. "Colorado Craft Beer Economic Impact Study Shows Explosive Growth." April 24, 2012. http:// coloradobeer.org/wp-content/uploads/2011/03/CBG-Economic -Impact-Press-Release-04-24-12.pdf.

Dickey, Megan Rose. "How Google's Buses are Ruining San Francisco." *Business Insider*, February 4, 2013. http://www.businessinsider.com /how-googles-buses-are-ruining-san-francisco-2013-2.

Edwards, Jim. "Silicon Valley Is Living Inside a Bubble of Tone-Deaf Arrogance." *Business Insider*, December 15, 2013. http://www .businessinsider.com/silicon-valley-arrogance-bubble-2013-12.

Egan, Timothy. "Dystopia by the Bay." *New York Times*, December 5, 2013. http://www.nytimes.com/2013/12/06/opinion/dystopia-by -the-bay.html.

Ewing Marion Kauffman Foundation. "The Startup Uprising: Eighteen Months of the Startup America Partnership." December 2012. http://www.kauffman.org/~/media/kauffman_org/research%20 reports%20and%20covers/2012/12/suapreport_final2.pdf.

Farr, Christina. "Colorado Entrepreneurs Say They Are Doing 'Awesome,' & Have the Data to Prove It." *Venture Beat*, June 3, 2012. http:// venturebeat.com/2013/06/03/colorado-entrepreneurs-say-they -are-doing-awesome-now-have-the-data-to-prove-it/.

Faulker, Larry. "Address: Memorial Celebration for Dr. George Kozmetsky." The University of Texas at Austin. May 4, 2003. https://www.utexas.edu/president/past/faulkner/speeches/ kozmetsky_050403.html.

Feld, Brad. *Startup Communities: Building an Entrepreneurial Eco-system in Your City*. New York: John Wiley & Sons, 2012.

Florida, Richard. "America's Leading Metros for Venture Capital." *City Lab*, June 17, 2013. http://www.theatlanticcities.com/jobs-and -economy/2013/06/americas-top-metros-venture-capital/3284/.

———. *Rise of the Creative Class*. New York: Basic Books, 2002.

Ginn, Vance. "Texas' Job Growth Rate Outpaces Nation." Texas Public Policy Foundation. September 23, 2013. http://www.texaspolicy.com/ center/fiscal-policy/blog/texas-job-growth-rate-outpaces-nation.

Google. "Google Fiber: Ultra High Speed Broadband Coming to Kansas City, KS." YouTube video, 25:48. March 30, 2011. http://www.youtube.com/watch?v=MQsXVAbcv-M&feature=youtu.be.

Gorski, Eric. "Colorado Craft Brewing Made $1.6 Billion Impact in 2012." *Denver Post*, December 16, 2013. http://www.denverpost.com/news/ci_24736704/colorado-craft-brewing-made-1-6-billion-impact.

Greenwood, Giselle. "IBM, Tivoli—10 Years Later." *Austin Business Journal*, April 23, 2006. http://www.bizjournals.com/austin/stories/2006/04/24/story2.html?page=all.

Hsieh, Tony. *Delivering Happiness: A Path to Profits, Passion, and Purpose*. New York: Business Plus Books, 2010.

Hwang, Victor W., and Greg Horowitt. *The Rainforest: The Secret to Building the Next Silicon Valley*. Los Altos Hills, CA: Regenwald Publishing, 2012.

Korn, Morgan. "Tony Hsieh on Delivering Happiness to Downtown Vegas." *Daily Ticker*, February 26, 2013. http://finance.yahoo.com/blogs/daily-ticker/tony-hsieh-delivering-happiness-downtown-vegas-132719578.html.

Lacy, Sarah. *Brilliant, Crazy, Cocky: How the Top 1% of Entrepreneurs Profit from Global Chaos*. New York: Wiley & Sons, 2011.

———. *Once You're Lucky, Twice You're Good: The Rebirth of Silicon Valley and the Rise of Web 2.0*. New York: Gotham Books, 2008.

LeDuff, Charlie. *Detroit: An American Autopsy*. London: Penguin Press, 2013.

Leonard, Andrew. "Why We Hate The New Tech Boom." *Salon.com*, September 27, 2013. http://www.salon.com/2013/09/27/why_we_hate_the_new_tech_boom/.

Lewis, Michael. *The New New Thing: A Silicon Valley Story*. New York: W.W. Norton & Company, 2000.

Liedtke, Michael. "AOL Founder Looks to Invest Outside Silicon Valley." *Yahoo! Finance*, September 30, 2013. http://finance.yahoo.com/news/aol-founder-looks-invest-outside-181835091.html.

Mandel, Michael. "Building a Digital City: The Growth and Impact of New York City's Tech/Information Sector." Bloomberg Technology Summit. September 30, 2013. http://www.mikebloomberg.com/files/buildingadigitalcity.pdf.

Manjoo, Farhad. "Silicon Valley Has an Arrogance Problem." *Wall Street Journal*, November 3, 2013. http://online.wsj.com/news/articles

/SB10001424052702303661404579175712015473766?KEYWORDS
=silicon+valley.

Mitisek, Eric. "2012 Colorado Startup Report: 'Colorado has developed into a state that every investor should watch.'" June 3, 2013. www .builtincolorado.com/blog/2012-colorado-startup-report.

Obama, Barack. "Presidential Proclamation—National Entrepreneurship Month, 2012." Speech, Washington, DC. November 1, 2012. http://www.whitehouse.gov/the-press-office/2012/11/01/presidential-proclamation-national-entrepreneurship-month-2012.

O'Dell, Jolie. "$4 toast: Why the Tech Industry Is Ruining San Francisco." *Venture Beat*, August 21, 2013. http://venturebeat.com/2013/08/21/4-toast-why-the-tech-industry-is-ruining-san-francisco/.

Ohanian, Alexis. *Without Their Permission: How the 21st Century Will Be Made, Not Managed*. New York: Business Plus, 2013.

Patterson, Scott. "The Minds Behind the Meltdown." *Wall Street Journal*, January 22, 2010. http://online.wsj.com/news/articles/SB10001424052748704509704575019032416477138?mod=WSJ_hps_MIDDLEForthNews.

———. *The Quants: How a New Breed of Math Whizzes Conquered Wall Street and Nearly Destroyed It*. New York: Crown Business, 2010.

Priceonomics. "The San Francisco Rent Explosion." July 18, 2013. http://priceonomics.com/the-san-francisco-rent-explosion/.

Rich, Laura. "Why You Should Start a Company In . . . Raleigh-Durham." *Fast Company*, November 1, 2010. http://www.fastcompany.com/1699323/why-you-should-start-company-raleigh-durham.

Roose, Kevin. "The Government Shutdown Has Revealed Silicon Valley's Dysfunction Fetish." *New York Magazine*, October 16, 2013. http://nymag.com/daily/intelligencer/2013/10/silicon-valleys-dysfunction-fetish.html.

Sager, Ryan. "Tyler Cowen's 10 Reasons Texas Is Our Future." *Time Magazine*, October 17, 2013. http://ideas.time.com/2013/10/17/10-reasons-texas-is-our-future/.

Senor, Dan, and Saul Singer. *Start-Up Nation: The Story of Israel's Economic Miracle*. New York: Twelve Books, 2009.

Shontell, Alyson. "10 Creative Startup Promotions At SXSW." *Business Insider*, March 11, 2012. http://www.businessinsider.com/10-creative-startup-promotions-at-sxsw-2012-3.

Smith, Robert L. "Cleveland's Startup Community Is Growing into Something Big, Study Says." *Cleveland.com*, July 16, 2013. http://www .cleveland.com/business/index.ssf/2013/07/clevelands_startup _community_i.html.

Srinivasan, Balaji. "Silicon Valley's Ultimate Exit." October 28, 2013. http://nydwracu.wordpress.com/2013/10/28/transcript-balaji -srinivasan-on-silicon-valleys-ultimate-exit/.

Tsotsis, Alexia. "Fear And Loathing OF Silicon Valley." *TechCrunch*, June 18, 2013. http://techcrunch.com/2013/06/18 /no-sympathy-for-the-devil/.

Vance, Ashlee. *Silicon Valley: Insider's Guide*. Guilford, CT: The Globe Pequot Press, 2007.

Weiser, Phil. "Boulder Is for Startups." May 11, 2011. http://www .whitehouse.gov/blog/2011/05/11/boulder-startups.

Winley, Rich. "How to Shine Outside Silicon Valley." August 12, 2013. http://richwinley.com/how-to-shine-outside-silicon-valley/.

Ydstie, John. "A Walking Zip-Code Look-Up." *NPR*, August 21, 2005. http://www.npr.org/templates/story/story.php?storyId=4809365.

Interviews

Alexander, Josh, CEO and cofounder, Toopher; November 2013

Altomare, Alex, CEO and cofounder, BetaBlox; September 2013

Angilly, Ryan, owner, Trenta Fueled; September 2012

Arredondo, Adam, cofounder, Hoopla.io; September 2013

Atti, Anthony, cofounder and CEO, Phononic; August 2013

Austin, John, director, Groundwork Labs; August 2013

Auten, Christine, producer, South by Southwest V2V; November 2013

Baer, Joshua, executive director, Capital Factory; January 2013 and November 2013

Bantuveris, Karen, founder and CEO, VolunteerSpot; November 2013

Barchas, Isaac, director, The Austin Technology Incubator; November 2013

Bell, Brooks, cofounder, HQ Raleigh; August 2013

Bernthal, Brad, associate professor of law, University of Colorado Law School; September 2012

Bigelow, Jay, director of entrepreneurship, Council for Entrepreneurial Development (CED); August 2013

Bowden, Josh, COO, Work In Progress; May 2013

Bzovi, Erick, cofounder, HealPay; March 2013

Carlson, Lancelot, cofounder, HealPay; March 2013

Chalef, Daniel, CEO, KnowledgeTree; August 2013

Chirls, Nicholas, seed investments, Betaworks; October 2013

Chou, Bing, managing director, Quick Left; April 2013

Christopher, Scott, president, MPowered; March 2013

Clauson, Taylor, analyst, OpenAir Equity Partners; September 2013

Clinkscales, Damon, organizer, Austin On Rails; November 2013

Cobb, Joni, president and CEO, Pipeline Entrepreneur Fellowship Program; September 2013

Cox, Kyle, director, IT/Wireless & University Development Portfolios, The Austin Technology Incubator; November 2013

Cuevas, Mitchell, marketing director, UP Global; July 2013

Cushman, Cameron, senior advisor, Kauffman Foundation; September 2013

Davis, Owen, managing director, NYCSeed; October 2013

Denbow, Frank, New York Startup Weekend; July 2013

Douglass, Erica, founder MarketVibe and Simpli Hosting; November 2013

Driskell, David, executive director of community planning & sustainability, City of Boulder; June 2013

Drogen, Leigh, founder, Estimize; September 2013

Duggan, Rick, director of technical development, Zappos; May 2013

Dunlap, Darius, board of advisors, Silicon Valley Innovation Institute; founder, Syncopat; July 2013

Easley, Mark, president, GoldHat Ventures; August 2013

Ellison, Jennifer, Cornell Tech; October 2013

Elyea, Brent, executive director, Central Texas Angel Network; November 2013

Epstein, Jeff, founder, Ambassador; March 2013

Ethington, Richard, general manager, InNEVation; May 2013

Farmer, Mike, cofounder, Leap2; September 2013

Feld, Brad; cofounder, TechStars; managing director, Foundry Group; September 2012

Fishback, Luke, founder and CEO, PlotWatt; August 2013

Fisher, Ben, cofounder, Lean Startup Machine and Alchemy; October 2013

Flombaum, Avi, founder, Flatiron School; July 2013

Ford, Scott, managing director, OpenAir Equity Partners; September 2013

Forrest, Hugh, director, South by Southwest Interactive; November 2013

Frankel, John, founding partner, ff Venture Capital; October 2013

Franklin, Jim, CEO, SendGrid; May 2013

Fryer, Kevin, founder and managing director, SparkLabKC; September 2013

Fryer, Liana, director of planning and communications, Office of Research, Innovation & Economic Development, North Carolina State University; August 2013

Garza, Rudy, founder and managing general partner, G-51 Capital; November 2013

Geolas, Robert, CEO, Research Triangle Park; August 2013

Gertler, Eric, executive vice president and managing director for the Center for Economic Transformation, New York City Economic Development Corporation; August 2013

Gierak, Jay, cofounder, Stik; December 2012

Glomski, Paul, cofounder, Detroit Labs; March 2013

Gosse, David, founder and CEO, Tracky; May 2013

Gosse, Jennifer, CMO, Tracky; May 2013

Gotsch, Maria, president and CEO, Partnership Fund for New York City; October 2013

Goulas, Mike, COO and cofounder, Mango Languages; March 2013

Grill, Jason, owner, JGrill Media & Consulting; September 2013

Harbach, Jeff, venture capitalist, Central Texas Angel Network; November 2013

Heesen, Mark, president, National Venture Capital Association; August 2012

Heivly, Chris, managing partner, Triangle Startup Factory; August 2013

Huls, Julie, president, Austin Technology Council; November 2013

Hurt, Brett, cofounder and vice chairman of the board of directors, Bazaarvoice; November 2013

Huang, Yao, founder and CEO, The Hatchery; September 2013

Hudson, Marianne, executive director, Angel Capital Association; October 2013

Huttenlocher, Dan, dean, Cornell Tech; November 2013

Hyde, Andrew, founder, Inside.co; and organizer, Ignite Boulder; May 2013

Iyer, Aishwarya, director of communications, ff Venture Capital; October 2013

Kelly, Kyle, manager of business development and analysis, Zappos; May 2013

Kerr, Josh, CEO, Written.com; November 2013

Klein, Adam, operations manager, American Tobacco; August 2013

Kopser, Joseph, CEO and founder, RideScout; November 2013

Kovac, Brittain, coleader, Kansas City Startup Village; September 2013

Koym, Kevin, cofounder, Tech Ranch Austin; November 2013

Kromer, Tristan, startup advisor, Lean Startup Circle; July 2013

Lawlor, Graham, founder, Ultra Light Startups; July 2013

LeMay, Lance, managing director, OpenAir Equity Partners; September 2013

Lipson, Jesse, vice president and general manager of data sharing, Citrix ShareFile; August 2013

Lomax, Terri, vice chancellor of the Office of Research, Innovation & Economic Development, North Carolina State University; August 2013

Magister, Holly, founder, Enterprise Transitions; January 2013

Marcus, Matthew, cofounder, Hoopla.io; September 2013

Marker, Brandon, analyst, TechStars Austin; November 2013

Massey, Jason, cofounder and CEO, Sustainable Industrial Solutions; August 2013

Meyers, Maria, CEO, USSourceLink and KCSourceLink; September 2013

Miller, Blake, partner, Think Big Equity Partners; September 2013

Miller, Justin, CEO, WedPics; August 2013

Minor, Derrick, innovation and entrepreneurship manager, City of Raleigh; August 2013

Morris, George, organizer, TEDxBoulder; August 2012.

Naaman, Mor, associate professor, Cornell Tech; cofounder and chief scientist, Seen.com; October 2013

Neri, Rodrigo, cofounder, Instin; September 2013

Neufeld, Greg, founder and managing partner, ValueStream Labs; July 2013

Ohanian, Alexis, cofounder, Reddit; November 2013

Onan, Chris, founder and managing director, Galvanize; April 2013

O'Donnell, Charlie, partner, Brooklyn Bridge Ventures; October 2013

O'Renick, Mark, founder and CEO, Ingenology; September 2013

Patel, Dhruv, program director, Council for Entrepreneurial Development; August 2013

Prochnow, Tyler, senior partner and cofounder, Think Big Equity Partners; September 2013

Ramos, Chad, cofounder and CMO, Tabeso; March 2013 and May 2013

Randolph, Eric, leasing manager, Bedrock Management Services; March 2013

Reich, Robert, cofounder, Medium; and founder, Boulder Denver New Tech Meetup; April 2013

Rinaudo, Keller, cofounder and CEO, Romotive; May 2013

Ruhe, Thom, vice president of entrepreneurship, Kauffman Foundation; August 2012

Rupp, Kerry, managing partner, DreamIt Ventures; November 2013

Sanders, Geoff, cofounder and CEO, LaunchKey; May 2013

Sanders, Ross, executive director, Bizdom; March 2013

Schatz, Brandon, founder, SportsPhotos.com; September 2013

Schwab, Andy, president, First Flight Venture Center; August 2013

Schwartz, Greg, cofounder and CEO, UpTo; March 2013

Schwartz, Jake, cofounder and CEO, General Assembly; August 2013

Seats, Jason, managing director, TechStars Austin; November 2013

Serbinski, Ted, partner, Detroit Venture Partners; March 2013

Shackelford, Jeff, director, Digital Sandbox at UMKC Innovation Center; September 2013

Sheinbaum, Pete, founder and CEO, LinkSmart; February 2013

Shepherd, Gabriel, business development, Tech Cocktail; community liaison, South by Southwest; May 2013

Slobotski, Jeff, cofounder, *Silicon Prairie News*; February 2013

Smith, Leslie, president and CEO, TechTown; March 2013

Stasik, Jared, vice president, Detroit Venture Partners; March 2013

Stechman, Brock, cofounder, DivvyHQ; September 2013

Sterling, Jon, founder, Vegas Tech House; May 2013

Taub, Alex, business development, Dwolla; September 2013

Teshuba, Jason, founder and CEO, Mango Languages; March 2013

Teshuba, Mike, cofounder and CTO, Mango Languages; March 2013

Valentine, Chris, producer of South by Southwest Startup Village and Accelerator; November 2013

VanWinkle, Tyler, director of product, Leap2; September 2013

Walker, Kathy, managing director, OpenAir Equity Partners; September 2013

Wallace, Christina, director, Startup Institute; October 2013

Wanger, Ryan, organizer, Boulder Startup Week; April 2013

Ward, Dan, cofounder, Detroit Labs; March 2013

Weber, Ryan, president, KCNext; September 2013

White, Andy, partner, VegasTechFund; January 2013

Widen, Jason, cofounder and executive director, HQ Raleigh; August 2013

Wilson, Mike, president, Ingenology; September 2013

Wingo, Scot, CEO, ChannelAdvisor; August 2013

Winley, Rich, founder, No Chains; May 2013

Yang, Andrew, founder and CEO, Venture for America; January 2013

Yoder, Mike, cofounder and CTO, WinTech; May 2013

Young, Andrew, cofounder and CTO, Swill; October 2013

Index

About the Author

B ASED IN DENVER, COLORADO, Tim Sprinkle has more than fifteen years of writing and editing experience, including stints with Yahoo Finance, Seeking Alpha, and a range of niche business publishers. In addition, his work has appeared in a wide variety of print and online publications—including *Wired*, *Entrepreneur*, *Outside*, and many more.